# The Coming Battle
## for the Media

# The Coming Battle for the Media

## Curbing the Power of the Media Elite

### WILLIAM A. RUSHER

**William Morrow and Company, Inc.**
**New York**

Library of Congress Cataloging-in-Publication Data

Rusher, William A., 1923–
    The coming battle for the media / by William A. Rusher.
        p.    cm.
    Includes index.
    ISBN 0-688-06433-7
    1. Mass media—United States—Objectivity.   2. Mass media—
Political aspects—United States.   I. Title.
P96.0242U664   1988
302.2'340973—dc19          87-33778
                            CIP

Printed in the United States of America

First Edition

1  2  3  4  5  6  7  8  9  10

BOOK DESIGN BY MARK STEIN

For
Dr. William K. Runyeon,
friend and adviser

# *Contents*

# Introduction

Politics in a modern democracy would be inconceivable without the media. It is the media that tell us what's happening, and what's being said and done about it. Only by relying on that information can a free citizenry hope to play an intelligent part in the political process.

It follows that what is and isn't reported as "news," by that segment of the media which specializes in reporting it, is of absolutely central importance to our politics. We ought not to be surprised, therefore, that the performance of the media in this regard is an intensely controversial issue.

It is the thesis of this book that in recent decades the principal media in the United States, responding to liberal intellectual trends once dominant but now much less so, have allied themselves with those political forces promoting liberal policies (meaning primarily the Democratic party), and have placed news reportage at the service of those policies.

As long as the Democratic party remained dominant in our national politics, this fact was to some extent obscured, and in any case probably didn't matter quite so much. But beginning two decades or more ago American politics began shifting perceptibly to the right, and media behavior that might previously have been excused as simply robust journalism began to be perceived as politically biased and tendentious.

At about the same time, journalistic practices underwent sharp modification in the direction of more aggressive, conclusion-oriented reportage. And, coincidentally, technology chose that moment to place in the hands of both print and electronic media techniques that multiplied the impact of their activities many times.

Small wonder, then, that many conservatives have come to regard the dominant media as their enemy, and have cast about for various means of either limiting the media's direct involvement in politics or moderating its impact. The media have responded by claiming for themselves a special, protected role in our society and its political processes. They have also frequently denied the charges of political bias, or at least insisted that their own political opinions do not affect their reportage of the news.

That, then, is the controversy with which this book is concerned. We shall look first at a few examples of what the conservatives are complaining about, and next examine with statistical rigor the evidence that the media elite are in fact overwhelmingly liberal, and that their bias saturates their work-product. We shall inquire who is responsible for this state of affairs, and how it came about. We shall examine the claims made, on behalf of the media, for a special status in American society, and take note of the efforts that have been made to moderate or counter media behavior that many consider offensive.

Finally, after a look ahead at just one of the crises that may soon confront us if the role of the media in our politics is not reconsidered and modified, we shall discuss ways and means of coping with the problem.

I owe it to my readers to caution them that, although I have been a magazine publisher for more than thirty years and might thus be presumed to look at the world from the standpoint of a journalist, I was a practicing lawyer for nine years before I changed careers. This dual background enables me to view the media from a wider perspective than is ordinarily available to one individual, and has undoubtedly influenced my thinking on many aspects of the subject.

I take this opportunity to acknowledge the invaluable help of my assistant, Claire Wirth. The errors herein, however, not to mention the opinions, are traceable strictly to me.

—WILLIAM A. RUSHER

*New York City*
*September 15, 1987*

I charge that the major media in the United States are a bunch of slanted liberals who have deliberately, systematically, over a long period of time delivered the liberal line.
—William A. Rusher

This is the most nonsensical thing I've ever heard in my life. The idea that the press of this country, whether at the national or at the state or at the local level, is dominated by liberals is, by any liberal standard, an absurdity.
—Hodding Carter III, TV commentator and columnist.

On ABC's *Viewpoint*, April 17, 1985

# CHAPTER 1

# *The Trouble with the Media*

THERE ARE SEVENTEEN hundred daily newspapers and thousands of weeklies, plus thousands more weekly, fortnightly, monthly, and quarterly magazines, as well as thirteen hundred television stations and ten thousand radio stations in the United States, all of which are entitled to be included in that broad category called "the media."*

Fortunately it won't be necessary to deal with all of them in this book. Our attention will be confined to those which regularly deal with national and international events and the issues arising from these. That excludes, at the outset, many local newspapers, many "specialty" magazines, and even a good many radio and television stations (for example, those of an exclusively religious nature). It also excludes, for all practical purposes, the many newspapers and radio and television stations whose reportage of national and international events is essentially derivative—i.e., consists of reprinting or broadcasting stories distributed by the major wire services or other primary news sources, or broadcasting "news programs" prepared and produced elsewhere (e.g., by the television networks).

We will also exclude from our discussion those media (the classic example being the relatively small magazines called "journals of opinion") which specialize in commenting editorially on national and international events from a specific political viewpoint. Of course many newspapers and magazines, as well as a good many radio and television stations, reserve specific segments of space or time for editorial comments by management, but we are speaking here of those media, such as the aforesaid journals of opinion (*The*

---

* A plural noun, by the way (the singular form is *medium*), which will herein be scrupulously so treated.

*Nation, The New Republic, National Review,* etc.), that exist, openly and primarily, to press the case for a particular political viewpoint.

These exclusions reduce the media on which we shall focus our attention to a much more manageable number. A good many newspapers around the country, especially in the larger cities, maintain news bureaus of their own in Washington and even in certain important foreign capitals, and there are a number of "independent" radio and television stations (i.e., not affiliated with a network) which also conduct reportage on national and international events. But with a few important exceptions these individual newspapers and stations do not, either individually or collectively, shape to any great extent the character of the news coverage available today to the average American.

For all practical purposes the typical sentient American receives his or her information on what is happening in the world from a relatively small number of sources, which are often referred to as "the media elite." By fairly common agreement, these include:

- the two major wire services: the Associated Press and United Press International
- the three major commercial television networks: ABC, NBC, and CBS
- the two principal newsmagazines: *Time* and *Newsweek*
- three newspapers, each of which is nationally important for a different reason: the *New York Times,* the *Washington Post,* and the *Wall Street Journal*

In addition, most observers would probably be willing to add to the above select circle a few other contenders:

- the "educational," or at any rate noncommercial, radio and television networks of the Public Broadcasting System
- a third newsmagazine: *U.S. News and World Report*
- A relatively new "all-news" network available on cable television: Cable News Network

These do not, of course, by any means exhaust the sources of information on public events available to Americans today. The *Reader's Digest,* for example, if only by virtue of its huge circulation, cannot be disregarded when it ventures into news reportage. But it is perfectly fair to say that *most* people receive *most* of their information from the above sources. Furthermore, these particular sources are the ones which happen to have, broadly speaking, the highest prestige *as* sources—and also, partly because of that fact, the most influential readers and viewers.

The bewildering variety of the American media becomes still less overwhelming when we reflect that the television networks have contrived, for our comfort and convenience, to have their important share of the day's information served up to us by a remarkably small number of familiar faces. Probably only the more careful newspaper readers bother to notice the by-line over a story from Washington or London in the *New York Times,* or would recognize the author's name if they did. The wire services (usually) and the newsmagazines (sometimes) transmit their news stories anonymously. But an astonishingly large proportion of America's daily supply of national and international "news" is received from a tiny handful of familiar television personalities—most notably the anchormen of the three major commercial networks' evening news programs: currently Dan Rather (CBS), Tom Brokaw (NBC), and Peter Jennings (ABC).

The universe of television personalities, dealing with "news," whose faces are familiar to most Americans is, of course, somewhat larger than these three, but not overwhelmingly so. It would include a few network "news desk" types such as NBC's John Palmer and ABC's Jed Duvall, the more prominent White House correspondents like ABC's Sam Donaldson, NBC's Andrea Mitchell, and (formerly) CBS's Lesley Stahl, and those few interviewers and talk-show impresarios (Barbara Walters, Roger Mudd, and Ted Koppel come to mind) who retain enough superficial objectivity, and deal directly enough with news stories, to retain some claim to the title of "reporter."

Just outside this inner circle of "news reporters" is a somewhat larger but still relatively small group of television personalities whom the networks present to their viewers for the purpose of "analyzing" the news. These are often recruited from the ranks of Washington reporters—journalists who have retired from the arduous work of gathering the news to the pleasanter and far more lucrative task of commenting on it from the vantage point of their accumulated wisdom. These commentators may be presented individually if their prestige and apparent objectivity warrant it (John Chancellor and Walter Cronkite, for instance), or in groups that purport to represent a spectrum of opinion (Robert Novak, Jack Germond, Carl Rowan, etc.). The ranks may also be fleshed out with former reporters who have established themselves as commentators ("columnists") in the print media (Tom Wicker), or who became columnists without benefit of a reportorial background (William F. Buckley, George Will).

To the extent that such individuals speak frankly from a given viewpoint, or to the extent that groups of such people do in fact represent a reasonably wide spectrum of opinion, the networks, and those print media that follow their example, are of course not open to criticism. But straight news reporters and their editors, in both the print and electronic media, purport to be dealing with news events in a fairly objective or at least a reasonably balanced way.

And it is precisely here—in the presentation of news and news analysis by America's media elite, both print and electronic—that we come upon the quarrel with which this book is concerned. It is the conviction of a great many people, not all of them conservative by any means, that news presentation by the media elite is heavily biased in favor of liberal views and attitudes.

It is important, right at the outset, to specify precisely what is being objected to. This is a free country, and journalists are every bit as entitled to their private political opinions as the rest of us. But the average newspaper or television news program, and certainly those we have categorized as the "media elite," purport to be offering us something more than the personal opinions of the reporter, or the chief editor, or even the collective opinions of the journalistic staff. In one way or another, to one extent or another, they all profess to be offering us the "news"—which is to say, an account of as many relevant events and developments, in the period in question, as can be given in the space or time available. Moreover, in offering this account, the media we are discussing implicitly claim to be acting with a reasonable degree of objectivity. Their critics sharply challenge that claim.

But just how much objectivity is it reasonable to expect? The question is more complicated than it may at first appear. There is a school of thought—popular, perhaps naturally, among a certain subcategory of journalists themselves—that a journalist is, or at least ought to be, a sort of vestal virgin: a chalice of total and incorruptible objectivity. But this, of course, is nonsense, and is certainly not expected by any reasonable person.

Journalists too are, after all, sons and daughters of Adam. Their conception was far from immaculate; they share our taint of Original Sin. They were born into our common society, received the same general education we all received, and had roughly the same formative experiences. How likely is it that, simply by choosing to pursue a career in journalism, they underwent some sort of miraculous transformation, to emerge shriven and pure, purged of all bias and dedicated henceforth solely to the pursuit of the unvarnished Truth?

To be sure, a certain amount of detachment is always welcome in a journalist, and sensible reporters are careful to cultivate a reputation for it. Probably the average man or woman in the street would even agree, if questioned, that a reporter ought to be "fair" or "unprejudiced" or something of the sort. Certainly, at a low level, we expect—or anyway hope—that he will at least get the basic facts right: The defendant's name was Jonas, not Jones; he pleaded nolo contendere, not "guilty"; he was sentenced to two years in jail, not twenty; and so on. Questioned further, the average person would probably also agree that a reporter ought not to simply ride his personal hobbyhorses: e.g., "expose" only individuals or organizations that he happens to dislike. But anyone who probes the average American much more deeply than this will start running into very pronounced doubts about exactly how fair or unbiased most journalists are—and also about how unbiased it is reasonable to expect them to be.

Consider, after all, the reporter's dilemma. More often than not he will find, upon investigating a possible story, far more factual material than he can possibly report. His duty, then, becomes to choose among these facts—decide which are important and must be reported, and which are irrelevant or repetitious and can be ignored. By this act of choosing, however, the reporter progresses from being the mere conduit of facts to being the determiner of their relevance. And that inevitably raises the question: relevance to what?

Against his will, if necessary, the reporter will be forced to answer this question by developing a *theory* of what the story is all about. In so doing, he moves into a brand-new role: Far from merely "reporting the facts," he becomes to some degree the creator of the story.

To take an example, let's suppose that a teenager holds up a delicatessen owner at gunpoint and escapes with eighty-nine dollars from the cash register. What facts might a reporter investigating the story and writing an account of it deem relevant?

Almost certainly, nowadays, if the teenager was black, the reporter will omit that fact, even if he himself privately thinks that the high unemployment rate among teenage blacks is the proximate cause of most crimes committed by individuals in that age category. Beginning about a quarter of a century ago, most of the American media made a conscious decision not to mention, in news stories, the race of accused criminals— the more or less official conclusion of American society being that this was, save in very special circumstances, irrelevant.

Would it be relevant that the store owner was Jewish? Here again, the reporter may feel that the background tensions in the neighborhood in question, between idle black youths and Jewish store owners, very definitely contributed to the choice of the victim in this case. But whether he will raise the point may well depend upon what additional facts he can cite in support of this concept of the story: e.g., other recent attacks by black youngsters on Jewish-owned stores in the neighborhood.

What if it transpires that the robber in this particular case is a drug addict, who committed the crime (and has committed others) to support an expensive habit? Alternatively, what if the youth has hitherto been a model student, and committed the robbery only to obtain money for food or medicine for his widowed mother?

There is, in short, often no way a conscientious reporter can avoid developing, and including in his report by implication or otherwise, some underlying theory regarding a story he is investigating. Certainly the bare bones of the one we have discussed (Youth Robs Delicatessen Owner) are far from the whole story, and any reporter who thought they were enough would be open to legitimate criticism. But if the reporter chooses (as we have argued he usually must) among a wide selection of facts, stressing some and omitting others in obedience to his theory or concept of the story, he cannot then legitimately argue that he is merely "the Fates' lieutenant," passively reporting what is there to be reported. The story he writes is necessarily an act of creation, and therefore an act of will.

Very well, then: *Choice* is inevitable. But is *bias* inevitable? According to the College Edition of *Webster's New World Dictionary of the American Language*, a "bias" in this meaning of the word signifies "a mental leaning or inclination; partiality; prejudice." If we can imagine a reporter making a choice among alternative concepts of a story (and therefore among the available facts) *without* consulting some a priori "mental leaning or inclination" or indulging in "partiality" or personal "prejudice," then bias is, at least theoretically, not inevitable.

But realism forces us to admit that it is also very widespread in journalistic practice, especially if we focus our attention not on such local events as a delicatessen robbery but on the brightly lit and hotly contentious stage of national and international affairs. It is asking a lot of a Washington political reporter, say, to insist that he rigorously exclude his own political biases when formulating the theory upon which a particular news story is to be based and selecting the facts to support it. And if he achieves such godlike objectivity in a particular story, it is asking far more to insist that he achieve it routinely, in story after story. The reporter, being human, will ordinarily be unconscious, or only subliminally aware, of the workings of his own political prejudices. If a story of his casts conservative Senator X as a villain—well, Senator X is a villain, that's all, and in suggesting as much the reporter is merely doing his duty by the facts, which are spelled out in the story. The fact that conservatives regard X fondly, and consider liberal Senator Y a villain, may be noted, but without supporting evidence of any actual villainy on the part of Y and largely as indicative of the conservatives' mind-set. In seeking to keep the biases of individual reporters under control, therefore, any reasonably conscientious editor will edit their stories if necessary.

But the chief editor of one of our elite print or electronic media has yet another and far more effective technique for correcting for bias, and that is the concept of *balance*. This concept is perhaps most familiar to us in the coverage of political campaigns. Even the most biased newspaper or television station will assign reporters to cover the major speeches of rival candidates. And those that cover ongoing controversies, in or out of Washington, will usually make at least some effort to interview people on both sides of the issue. It is not, let us repeat, a matter of achieving, or perhaps even pursuing, some ideal of absolute objectivity. All that can be asked or expected is a reasonable effort to avoid the worst excesses of journalistic ax-grinding in particular stories, coupled with a *balanced* coverage that permits both (or all) sides of controversial issues to be aired.

But that is exactly what the American people are *not* getting, and have not gotten for decades, from their media. On the contrary, the version of events served up by our media elite is, with a relatively few exceptions that merely prove the rule, a steady diet of tendentious "news" stories carefully designed to serve the political purposes of American liberalism. The stories themselves, far from being edited to eliminate the worst consequences of the reporters' own biases, are often timed to maximize their political effect. And the editors, far from trying to moderate the consequences of individual bias in particular stories by providing a balanced selection, frequently seem to be trying to enhance those consequences by cumulating their impact.

It is, therefore, among editors too that we must search for the explanation of the phenomenon of bias, as we see it on display in our major media. They too, of course, are human; they too have their opinions, and their personal biases. But they don't have the reporter's excuse that he is virtually compelled to adopt some theory of the story. Why do they so often turn their backs on the concept of balance?

It seems likely that the mental processes of the editor resemble rather closely those of the reporter because, in most cases, the editor was once a reporter himself. An editor today not only tends to adopt the reporter's theory of a given news story and combine it with others having a similar bias; he will often try to fit the story into a larger conceptual framework of his own: a sort of "supertheory" representing his own personal overview of current history.

Of course, there are wide areas of news reportage to which the above description doesn't apply. Just as there are individual news stories—about fires, auto accidents, the birth of quadruplets—that don't have self-evident political implications, so there are entire areas of news coverage—sports and art, to name only two—where political consider-ations are comparatively rare. Much of the "news" we read and see, therefore, is relatively free from the sort of political bias we have been discussing. But the rest is simply grist for the mills of the dominant editors in the higher ranks of the media, and these do not hesitate to construct, from the stories fed to them by their reporters, a conspectus of events that conforms to their own private view of the world.

This analysis was expounded brilliantly by Joseph Sobran in an article in the March 27, 1987, issue of *National Review*. His immediate subject was the "Howard Beach incident," in which a black youth was killed by a car on a highway while trying to escape, with two friends, from a gang of white youths who were allegedly attacking them with baseball bats. But Sobran uses this episode to illustrate what he contends are underlying habits of mind on the part of the media. I shall take the liberty of quoting his article extensively, because I have never read a more incisive analysis of the psychological process that results in the media's manifest liberal bias:

> Why did Howard Beach get so much media coverage? An indirect answer comes from Thomas Friedman, Jerusalem bureau chief of the *New York Times*, grappling with the question why Israel, a faraway country the size of New Jersey, gets so much media attention. The answer is *not* the number of Jews in the American media, he argues, since the European press gives Israel just about the same amount of coverage. The answer is that Israel has mythic resonance for all Westerners.
>
> "Men have never taken the world just as it comes," [Friedman] observes. "We need to explain the world to ourselves, and, to do so, we have used stories—myths and fables—to record our experiences and shape our values. In most cultures, these narratives are tied together in what has been called a 'super story.' Religions are a super story. Ideologies can be a super story."

Sobran then proceeds to apply the concept of the "superstory" to the Howard Beach incident:

All news is "biased," in that it's the selection of information in accordance with tacit standards of relevance. We notice the bias when the news is chosen to fit a "super story" the audience doesn't necessarily subscribe to. All earthquake stories are biased against earthquakes, but the bias is unanimous, and nobody complains. But the super story behind the Howard Beach story was Racist America. . . .

"News" consists not only of high-impact events, but of local events of low impact that can be assimilated to pet myths. But most journalists are unaware of their commitment to myths, and think of themselves as, in Dan Rather's words, "honest brokers of information." You don't shoot the messenger for bringing bad news! Except that the messenger exercises a lot of discretion as to which news to deliver. If the mailman did that, he'd lose his job. . . .

The media are so saturated with myth that it's fair to see "news" as an early stage on the assembly line whose final product is a *New York Times* editorial. The Howard Beach incident, of no national importance in itself, offered an occasion to attitudinize. It had less to do with raw "fact" than with *l'art pour l'art*. It achieved the maximum ratio, this side of Janet Cooke, of opinion to datum. . . .

Finally, Sobran generalizes his point:

The super story is Progress, the long view. "Value judgments" of good and evil represent unseemly impulses or old prejudices; they are "simplistic." . . .

In the progressive myth, there is no Good or Evil, as traditionally understood: The ultimate categories are Past and Future. The world is broadly divided into the forces of the Past versus those of the Future, reactionary and progressive, politely termed "conservative" and "liberal" when necessary. Most political conflicts can be typed in these terms and treated journalistically as so many little segments of the super story. . . .

The progressives' own value judgments don't have to be stated. They're built into the form of the stories themselves. The forces of the Past come equipped with a discernible set of traits: bigotry, greed, hate, selfishness, ignorance, zealotry, extremism—terms that by now all have a "right-wing" whiff about them. Ever heard of a liberal or left-wing bigot or hate-group?

By the same token, the forces of the Future can be discerned by their compassion, idealism, hope, intelligence, openness to new ideas. (Who ever heard of being open to *old* ideas?) . . .

The mythology determines the tone of just about any specific story on South Africa, "social" spending, the Pentagon, "civil rights," disarmament talks, Chile, abortion, and various other perennial topics. . . .

Consciously or unconsciously, most editors go through the process Sobran describes, assembling the news stories that cross their desks into a far larger, more enduring, and more meaningful edifice: the superstory (or supertheory, as we earlier described it) that constitutes their notion of the world. Unlike their reporters, they are not compelled to do so; the impulse is derived from their own reportorial experience, fortified by self-indulgence. It lies within their power to present a more balanced picture of the "news"; but they don't, because they prefer to paint the world in the primary colors of the liberal superstory.

But why do the editors of our elite media display such an overwhelming preference for the *liberal* superstory? In a monograph published by the Media Institute of Washington, John Corry, the nonfiction television critic of the *New York Times*, concedes that "of course" television reflects "a liberal bias." But he argues that this is not so much deliberate as because it necessarily reflects "the dominant culture," which in turn is the product of the opinions and preferences of the country's artists and intellectuals. "This culture," Corry contends, "is rooted firmly in the political left, where it finds its own closed frame of reference. Little dissent is tolerated and little is found."

Corry's proposition that the media elite are heavily influenced by the "dominant" culture is undoubtedly correct (see Chapter 7). It can, in fact, be argued that the liberal superstory described by Sobran simply reflects the world view of that culture. But that scarcely constitutes, in 1987, much of an excuse for the behavior of the media elite. The day is long gone when one could say, as Lionel Trilling correctly said in 1950, that "in the United States at this time liberalism is not only the dominant but even the sole intellectual tradition." Liberalism may still be, in a narrow sense, America's "dominant culture"—the overwhelmingly popular viewpoint of intellectuals, especially in the academy. But no profession as closely in contact with its environment as journalism claims to be can seriously contend that conservatism simply doesn't deserve, today, better-balanced coverage than it is receiving.

After all, conservatives took control of the Republican party nearly a quarter of a century ago, since which time the party has won every presidential election except 1976. Even in the purely intellectual realm, William F. Buckley has presided over a discussion program on PBS (its sole concession to conservatism) for more than twenty years. The influence of the "dominant culture"—liberalism—on the media is indisputable; the justification for it, however, is no longer valid.

But there is, in addition, no lack of evidence that at least a great many members of the media elite are far more than merely other-directed fellow travelers of the dominant culture. When we learn from a 1983 *Mother*

*Jones* interview that NBC's Tom Brokaw says Ronald Reagan's values are "simplistic and old-fashioned," that he lives in a "fantasy land," that his supply-side economics policy "was just a disaster," and that human rights in El Salvador are "a sham," or are told by David Blum in a 1986 *New York* profile of the same network's Bryant Gumbel that "the veins in his forehead seem ready to pop as he attacks the [Reagan] administration's policies toward the poor and hungry," we are entitled to assume that these people participate enthusiastically in, rather than merely go along with, the liberal bias that characterizes NBC News.

In the case of Richard M. Cohen, however, we don't have to assume anything. In an article on the Op-Ed page of the *New York Times* on August 31, 1987, Cohen, who is senior producer of foreign news for the *CBS Evening News,* described the thought processes and news-manipulating techniques of a powerful member of the media elite as clearly as it has ever been done, or is ever likely to be done.

What loosened Cohen's tongue, presumably, was the fact that his immediate subject was South Africa, concerning which American public opinion is comfortably monolithic and which therefore exposed him and his network to no danger of a bruising collision with American conservatives on the merits of the particular issue. But Cohen seems not to have realized how much he was revealing, concerning his own attitudes and techniques, that was applicable to a whole spectrum of far more controversial subjects.

Cohen's article was a call for Western news organizations to pull out of South Africa altogether, rather than try to soldier on under the severe restrictions currently being imposed by the white regime. Under the state-of-emergency regulations now in force, both publications and broadcasts concerning events in the black townships and homelands are heavily censored to exclude what the government considers inflammatory or likely to incite violence. With specific regard to television, Cohen complained: "We cannot broadcast or even shoot pictures of any unrest, which is defined by South African authorities. We cannot show police or security forces acting in their official capacity trying to 'keep the peace.' Our cameras are not supposed to be within telescopic range of such events."

Worse yet, though Cohen doesn't mention it, there is evidence that these regulations have had considerable effect. In late 1985 and early 1986 there were riots, fire bombings, and "necklace" killings of suspected black "collaborators" in many of the black townships of South Africa. A year later Allister Sparks, a liberal South African correspondent, reported in a dispatch to the *Washington Post* that "a mood of battle weariness has settled over [black revolutionaries]. . . . [It] is recognized that a popular insurrection leading to a seizure of power is unlikely." Without the stimulus of intensive press coverage, and especially television coverage, a very substantial measure of calm had returned to the townships.

It was not, however, the impact of the emergency regulations on developments in South Africa but their effect on the formation of American public opinion that chiefly concerned Cohen:

> The American consciousness about South Africa, I believe, was formed and maintained by the constant television images of brutal repression in many forms: the image of the padded, faceless policeman, club raised; the image of a black youth with fear covering every inch of his face as he throws a rock. These were constant and common images, and now they are missing.
>
> One day in October 1985, an innocuous truck, driven by whites, moved ostentatiously through the streets of Cape Town. It was out of place and provocative, and when black kids began throwing rocks, the truck stopped and armed police jumped out of boxes on the back of the truck.
>
> At CBS we always referred to that day as the "Trojan Horse" incident. The surprise attack, the beatings and arrests were captured in frightening detail on videotape by a CBS cameraman who risked great injury to keep his camera rolling. Such were the risks our South African colleagues took daily. Those pictures were broadcast that night on the CBS Evening News and were seen by millions of Americans. By the next morning, they were all over European television.
>
> They are called tight shots. The camera moves in close enough to see the expression on a face, even the look in an eye. In South Africa, they are the narrow, harrowing images of oppression. If a picture is worth a thousand words, television can do what column inch after column inch of newspaper copy cannot. Television can raise the consciousness of a nation.

It is important not to let one's perception of the significance of the above quotation be distorted by a natural sympathy for Cohen's indignation at the situation he found in South Africa. One may wonder, in passing, why Cohen and the *CBS Evening News* so rarely manage to find and photograph equally compelling evidences of state despotism in the Soviet Union, or Communist China, or Cuba, or Nicaragua—or why, if they are forbidden to photograph such scenes in such places, Cohen doesn't recommend that Western news organizations withdraw from those countries too. But that, also, is beside the point.

The point is that Cohen clearly arrogates to himself, as a passionate and well-positioned liberal, the right—indeed, as he probably conceives it, the obligation—to "form and maintain" the "American conscious-ness" on foreign political topics about which he cares deeply. To this end, he has no compunction about subjecting viewers of the *CBS Evening News* to "constant television images," including "tight shots" and similar emotive devices, designed to produce the desired impression. He is acutely aware that these confections will be "seen by millions of Americans," and that within twenty-four hours they will also be spread "all over European television." In this way, he boasts, "television can raise the consciousness of a nation."

There is, of course, nothing in the least new or surprising about this. Every American who has seen a "news" broadcast on one of the TV networks can testify that the technique is used ad nauseam. All that is surprising is to see such a candid and vivid description of it displayed on the Op-Ed page of the *New York Times*. Verily, the boys are getting careless.

For of course Mr. Cohen and the *CBS Evening News*—and their opposite numbers at ABC and NBC and PBS—don't limit their consciousness-raising efforts to such relatively unobjectionable targets as the white government of South Africa. They hew wood and carry water for every imaginable liberal propaganda ploy, from denigrating the Nicaraguan resistance to pooh-poohing the Reagan administration's Strategic Defense Initiative, and from denouncing Ronald Reagan's economic policies to caricaturing the American Right.

Was it, do you suppose, Richard Cohen who treated us to those "tight shots" of perspiring fat ladies with straw boaters and palmetto fans at Goldwater rallies back in 1963, and took all those dramatic pictures of Alabama police dogs lunging at conveniently invisible targets during the race riots of the 1960s, or was all that before his time? Was it the *CBS Evening News*—I rather think it was—that regaled us with shot after shot of "burning bonzes" in Saigon during the Vietnam War, so that America might at last understand how unwanted out help was in that unhappy country? Was it NBC or ABC, or CBS again, or all three, that deluged us with tendentious stories about soup kitchens and block-long unem-ployment lines in 1982, and have dwelt ever since, with loving care, on so-called pockets of poverty that still, after five years of the longest economic boom in our postwar history, allegedly testify to the existence of "hunger" and "homelessness" as ineradicable stigmata of the Reagan administration?

But even such examples are not necessarily persuasive. After all,

Richard Cohen may be right about all these things, and his critics may be wrong. The real point is: Who is this Richard M. Cohen, and how does he find himself in a position of such power that he can decide, all alone (or more likely with the enthusiastic concurrence of a few similarly minded colleagues), the political issues on which "the American consciousness" is to be "formed and maintained"?

For make no mistake: Cohen is no fluke. He is a stellar example of what is wrong with the American media elite. There are many hundreds and probably thousands of others like him, in positions high and low, visible and not so visible, diligently taking in the laundry of the liberal Left. They are strongly opinionated, highly politicized individuals. They know very well what they are doing, and they are under no illusion that their views represent, or are even close to, the American mainstream. They are merely convinced that they are right, and they are positively delighted that they occupy positions from which they can "form and maintain" the "American consciousness." They have, in addition to jobs that are well paid by almost any standard, the satisfaction of wielding genuine power on behalf of causes in which they deeply believe. Not surprisingly, their typical attitude toward their critics is one of silent arrogance.

But just how inevitable is this state of affairs? Is it right, is it even tolerable, that news organizations pledged to a reasonably balanced presentation of the "news," and claiming all sorts of special constitutional powers and privileges to assist them in achieving that high objective, should be able to use the First Amendment or their federal licenses to shove such loads of biased bushwah down the throats of the American people without contradiction night after night? That is what this book is about.

But now let us look at a few more examples of the bias we are talking about.

# CHAPTER 2

# *Some Examples*

DEMONSTRATING STATISTICALLY THE liberal bias of the media elite, and its powerful and indisputable effect on their presentation of the news, is the work of later chapters of this book. But let us consider a few examples of such bias, simply to get the flavor of what we are discussing. The following instances were chosen, not because they are in any way particularly horrendous, but precisely because they are so typical.

• John Corry, one of the few television critics who regularly blow the whistle on liberal or leftist bias in that medium (and does it, moreover, in the *New York Times*), described a thirty-minute documentary on Channel 13, New York's educational TV station, as follows in the *Times* for March 22, 1986:

> Speak no ill of the dead, we are told, but that does not mean we have to make things up. "Witness to Revolution: The Story of Anna Louise Strong" does not just apologize for Miss Strong; it presents her as something she never was. In real life, she was a press agent for some of this century's least attractive people. In the 30-minute documentary, on Channel 13 at 3:30 this afternoon, she was "a woman ahead of her time." History is turned upside down.
>
> Miss Strong, who died in China in 1970, was an American radical who settled in the Soviet Union in 1921 and promptly fell in love with totalitarianism. Other radicals did, too, although many grew disenchanted. . . . Miss Strong never wavered. In articles and books, she pleaded Stalin's case. . . .
>
> [Yet] the narrator . . . tells us that Miss Strong was "deported by the Russians as an American spy" while she was "hounded by the F.B.I. as a Communist courier." We are meant to think that, as a disinterested truth-seeker, she was getting it from both sides.
>
> In fact, Stalin expelled Miss Strong in 1949, the same year he began one of his last great purges. Many were killed; even the wife of Foreign Minister Vyacheslav Molotov was imprisoned for "conspiracies." It was the beginning of Stalin's final descent into paranoia, and Miss Strong was lucky to escape with her life.

As always, however, she remained loyal; when she arrived in New York, she blamed the American press, not the dictator, for her deportation.

It is fatuous to equate this with a hounding by the Federal Bureau of Investigation. How much could the F.B.I. have hounded Miss Strong, anyway? She lived most of her life outside the United States.

How does nonsense like this get promulgated?

• Contrast that affectionate and highly deceptive account of the life of a world-renowned Communist sympathizer with the long refusal of New York's Channel 13 to broadcast "Harvest of Despair," a fifty-five-minute Canadian documentary on the Ukrainian famine of 1932–1934, which Stalin deliberately precipitated and which resulted in the deaths of at least seven million people, three million of them children under the age of seven. This ghastly case of genocide, which the Soviet Union and its Western apologists have labored for more than fifty years to conceal, is so brilliantly described in "Harvest of Despair" that the film won the gold medal in the documentary category at the Twenty-eighth International Film and Television Festival of New York in November 1985—and then went on to receive the Gold Award Trophy Bowl as the "most outstanding entry" among 837 competitors in all ten categories comprising the Television Entertainment and Specials Group. Yet Peter Paluch, in *National Review*'s issue for April 11, 1986, stated, "At this writing 'Harvest of Despair' has been shown only on two small U.S. television stations."

• The Op-Ed page of the *New York Times,* so called because it appears every day opposite the *Times*'s own editorial page, is allegedly intended to afford space for the expression of a large variety of views on public questions, including views at variance with the opinions of the *Times* itself. In practice, especially in recent years, it has tended to become increasingly a sort of Hyde Park Corner for various leftish and liberal opinions for which the *Times* doesn't care to take responsibility. One of its regular columnists, William Safire, who worked in the Nixon White House as a speechwriter and appears on the Op-Ed page twice a week, is supposed to assure the representation of conservative views and does this reasonably well—when he appears. On the other days, it is often hard to find any viewpoint being expressed that is arguably right of center. On Tuesday, June 18, 1985, for example, the four offerings on the page were: "Reagan's Untruths About Managua," in which Abraham Brumberg compared the President's "contempt for truth" in the matter of the Sandinistas with the "pernicious innuendos and outright fabrications" of the late Senator Joseph McCarthy; "Twenty Downhill Years," in which passionately liberal columnist Tom Wicker anguished over recent Democratic defeats in presidential elections; "Musings Inspired By an Amtrak Ride," in which Charles Peters declared that he wanted to "summon liberals to a counterattack" against "David A. Stockman's campaign to abolish Amtrak"; and "The Crooks Are in Charge," an attack by another liberal columnist, Sidney Schanberg, on "the corrupt construction industry in New York."

• One of the key liberal-versus-conservative battles of 1986 was the conservative drive to defeat the bid of Rose Bird for reelection to the position of chief justice of the Supreme Court of California, to which she had originally been appointed by Governor Jerry Brown. Bird, an extreme liberal even by California standards, was especially unpopular with conservatives for her apparent determination to block any execution in the state, despite the fact that the legislature had provided for the death penalty in certain cases and law-enforcement officials, up to and including the new governor, were prepared to enforce it. On January 14, 1986, NBC news reporter Heidi Schulman interviewed Chief Justice Bird on the network's *Today* show. The "interview" was totally friendly, amounting to little more than a five-minute speech by Bird in her own defense. No tough questions were asked, and no critic of Bird's was interviewed or even allowed to state briefly the case against her. It was, even by the standards of America's media elite, a "sweetheart" performance.

• In the spring of 1985, President Reagan unveiled his own proposals for tax reform, and proclaimed such reform the top priority of his second administration. On May 31, on the *Today* show, Mike Jensen, NBC's "chief financial correspondent," undertook to explain why one group would, in Jensen's introductory words, "make out extremely well in all this." Here, uncut, is Jensen's presentation, in which I have inserted, after each major point, the comments of the senior partner of a major New York firm of tax accountants to whom I submitted the transcript:

JENSEN: President Reagan likes people who have made it. He admires them, and he takes care of them. In the President's new tax proposal, people with incomes of over $200,000 would actually see the total share of tax money they pay into the Federal Treasury decline from 14.8 percent to 14.3 percent, whereas people earning between $30,000 and $200,000 would see their share increase. In the President's tax plan, there are five different ways the richest people would benefit.

The first is something called tax-exempt bonds, sold by government bodies to finance public projects. The interest paid on these bonds to investors is not taxed. One type of tax-exempt bond, used by private companies, would be eliminated in the President's plan. But the public-purpose bonds would remain as a device for the rich to avoid taxes.

[COMMENT:   It is rank demagogy to describe tax-exempt public-purpose bonds as "a device for the rich to avoid taxes." They are in fact the principal way all sorts of municipal improvements are financed—sewers, bridges, etc. Without the tax-exempt feature it would be impossible for America's states and municipalities to finance their activities.]

Item number two. Charitable contributions, a favorite way for rich people to get tax deductions by donating art works, for example, to a charity. There was a move to limit charitable contributions, but it lost out. The President would deny charitable contributions to people who do not itemize their returns, but for the wealthier third who do itemize there are no limitations.

[COMMENT:   Once again Jensen attacks a provision that was invented to aid a good cause—in this case, charitable institutions— and not as an ingenious and unfair "way for rich people to get tax deductions." Without the deductible feature, people obviously couldn't afford to contribute as much to charitable causes. Besides, Mr. Reagan's plan makes no major changes in this part of the law, so he has done nothing to improve the situation of the rich in this respect. As a matter of fact, by proposing lower overall tax rates Mr. Reagan diminishes the value of a contribution's deductibility. (Incidentally, anybody who wants to can itemize his tax return. But people with small incomes are not required to do so, being given the option of claiming a 10 percent overall deduction instead, without having to prove it.)]

Item number three. Tax shelters. One popular form of tax shelter is called the limited partnership. Wealthy people often buy shares of big real estate or oil deals. And the tax advantages of these deals filter through to the investor. There was a move to close down such shelters, but under the President's plan they would still be permitted to operate.

[COMMENT:    Tax shelters long antedate the Reagan administration, and
            in fact have prospered in plenty of years when the
            Democrats controlled both the White House and both
            houses of Congress. The Reagan administration has been,
            if anything, more zealous than most in restricting these
            shelters administratively. But the big point is that Mr.
            Reagan's proposed tax reform would limit the utility of
            these tax shelters severely, for the same reason that it
            would limit the usefulness of charitable contributions: By
            reducing overall tax rates it diminishes the value of such
            shelters.]

Item number four. Deduction of interest paid on borrowed money. The
President would set a ceiling of $5,000 on such deductions. But there's a
loophole for rich people with lots of investments. It's complicated but
important. They can deduct that $5,000, plus an amount equal to any
income they have in interest and dividends from investments. Say, for
example, someone has investment income of $50,000. He can deduct
$55,000 in interest if he wants to.

[COMMENT:    Here Jensen is distorting the purpose of a thoroughly
            sound proposal. The reason for allowing the deduction of
            income from interest and dividends is to prevent an old
            abuse whereby a highly salaried taxpayer could create an
            artificially large interest income and deduct the entire
            amount, rather than being taxed on the part that was
            actually salary. The purpose of the Reagan proposal, in
            short, is not to favor "rich people with lots of invest-
            ments," but to make the law more equitable.]

Item number five. Capital gains taxes. Most people never have to bother
with this, but for rich people it's very important. It's the tax you pay on the
profit you earn when you cash in or sell an investment in property or stocks
or bonds, for example. If you've owned that property for six months, you
pay a capital gains tax which is currently 20 percent maximum. Under the
President's plan, it would actually be lowered to 17½ percent. That means,
in effect, that people who have money to work for them would be paying
a lower tax rate (17½ percent) than people who are out there working for
themselves and paying 25 percent or 35 percent.

[COMMENT:    The proposed reduction in the capital gains tax will not be
            a bonanza for the rich. As a matter of fact, the reduction of
            the maximum income tax from 50 percent to 35 percent
            will make capital gains relatively *less* attractive under the
            new law (where they will be taxed at 17½ percent) than
            they were when they were being taxed at 20 percent under
            the old law. Because, for taxpayers in the top bracket (i.e.,

Jensen's "rich people"), the effective tax on capital gains will now be 50 percent of the tax on straight income, rather than 40 percent (as before).]

There is, of course, one final way rich people will benefit from the President's plan, and it's the biggest of all. Their marginal tax rate will be reduced from 50 percent to 35 percent.

[COMMENT:

But this advantage must be balanced against the diminished utility of the various provisions Jensen has just been itemizing (charitable contributions, tax shelters, capital gains, etc.) to determine what the real net benefit will be. In many cases, these "rich people" will just about break even, in terms of tax consequences.]

It is impossible to read Jensen's analysis of Reagan's tax reform proposals without recognizing the clear intent to rouse envy against "rich people" and portray Mr. Reagan as their special friend and protector. Mike Jensen has every right to feel that way if he wants to, but NBC, in broadcasting his views without any rebuttal whatever, is abandoning any pretense of balance and simply reinforcing its well-earned reputation as a megaphone for liberalism.

• The use of slanted terminology is one of the media's oldest tricks. One recent and particularly glaring example is the dogged use of Teddy Kennedy's felicitous invention, "Star Wars," to describe what the Reagan administration calls its important (and, of course, highly controversial) new strategic concept: the Strategic Defense Initiative, or simply SDI.

The name of a policy or program often plays, rightly or wrongly, an important part in determining its popularity. It certainly seems likely that the conservative success in naming the Right to Work laws contributed substantially to their appeal in many states. Similarly, and quite aside from the merits of the abortion issue, there is little doubt that Right to Life, simply as a slogan, resonates more effectively than Freedom of Choice.

On the liberal side, one spectacular early success with a slanted phrase involved the Bricker Amendment—Senator John Bricker's 1952 effort to prevent President Truman from circumventing Congress by writing desired legislation into executive agreements with foreign countries. (Under the Constitution such agreements then miraculously became, in their capacity as treaties, a part of "the supreme Law of the Land.")

The liberal opponents of the amendment centered their objections on a subordinate clause that they dubbed "the 'which' clause," insisting that it was pregnant with all sorts of potential evils. Not one American in a thousand could have described "the 'which' clause" accurately, let alone explained its allegedly deleterious effects, but the massed bands of liberalism played the tune tirelessly anyway until the Bricker Amendment was safely defeated. More recent liberal crusades are brought to mind simply by such phrases as "acid rain" and "nuclear winter."

Terminological skirmishes, then, are a normal aspect of political warfare. What makes them relevant here is the extent to which the media serve the liberal cause in this regard.

No doubt Mr. Reagan devoutly wishes he had introduced a short, snappy term for his Strategic Defense Initiative when he first broached the concept in a television address to the American people on March 23, 1983. Senator Kennedy (or someone on his staff) is entitled to considerable credit for coming up, next day, with the catchy and faintly derisive term "Star Wars." It was so far superior to the unwieldy "Strategic Defense Initiative," or even "SDI," that there was considerable excuse—certainly among headline writers—for preferring the liberals' negative formulation.

But this was a battle that supporters of the concept could ill afford to lose, and in due course various short phrases were hit upon (e.g., "Space Shield") that served to describe the idea both briefly and favorably. On the theory that a parent is entitled to name his own child, the media were implicitly invited to drop "Star Wars."

The media, however, were determined to continue using the negative term. Some still do, without surcease or apology. Slightly less impassioned members of the fourth estate have compromised, and now refer to the proposal as "President Reagan's Strategic Defense Initiative (popularly known as 'Star Wars')." The only difficulty with this solution, of course, is that it utterly fails to achieve the brevity that everyone was supposedly groping for in the first place.

Another familiar example of slanted terminology involves the description of the head of a foreign government. One can often calibrate the liberal position on such a figure with exquisite precision simply by noting how *Time* or *Newsweek* or the *New York Times* characterizes him.

As a rule, for example, a right-wing authoritarian head of government (Augusto Pinochet of Chile is the best current example) will be referred to as a "dictator"—the term used, during World War II, for Hitler and Mussolini. Mikhail Gorbachev and his predecessors, however, are never thus described; they are grouped with their Politburo colleagues and referred to collectively as "the Soviet leaders" or "the Soviet leadership." The same applies to Deng Xiao-ping, and even to such second-string Communist tyrants as Poland's Wojciech Jaruzelski. Fidel Castro was, early on, always respectfully described by the *New York Times* as "Dr. Castro," in remembrance of a long-disused law degree. He too, however, has now become "the Cuban leader." The term "dictator" is simply not applied to contemporary Communist figures, even though most of them clearly have far more arbitrary power than Pinochet.

It was almost amusing, in the light of these rules, to watch the swift deterioration in the status of Ferdinand Marcos when he finally swam into the gunsights of our liberal media late in 1985 as a candidate for early destruction, politically speaking. Marcos, who had been president of the Philippines since 1965, had grown increasingly autocratic and corrupt and was known to be in poor health, but retained considerable personal popularity despite a growing Communist insurgency and the mysterious assassination of a political foe, Benigno Aquino, in 1983. He was simply "President Marcos" to all but the extreme left fringe of the American media until the latter half of 1985, when a series of events led to the final crisis of his regime. Within a matter of weeks this feeble and corrupt old autocrat was transformed by the American media into a fire-breathing "dictator." And so he remained, until he fled into exile in February 1986.

• In the *Wall Street Journal* for October 11, 1984, Irving Kristol discussed a UPI story, carried by the *New York Times* on page 5 of its issue dated October 6, which illustrates the almost limitless receptivity of the media to "news" congenial to their liberal opinions:

> The headline reads: "Study Says Blacks Have Lost Ground." The subhead reads: "Find Reagan's Policies Have Hurt the Poor and Imperil Emerging Middle Classes." The story itself then goes on for half a column providing the statistics to "prove" the case.
>
> Now, anyone who is familiar with the scholarly literature on the topic will immediately realize that he is reading propaganda based on twisted statistics. But that is not really the point. The point is: What is the source of this "study"? The Times tells us that it was done by the "nonpartisan, nonprofit Center on Budget and Public Priorities." That immediately identifies it as a liberal organization, since only liberal organizations are ever clearly designated as "nonpartisan, nonprofit." But one would like to know more. Just what is this organization? What scholars are associated with it? Who wrote that report? Why should anyone pay attention to it?

There are no answers to these not unimportant questions. The reporter, in fact, was summarizing a press release—but since it was a press release issued by liberal critics of the administration, it could be uncritically transmitted. It was "news."

• One of the most vicious tactics used by the media on public figures they dislike (and these are, of course, mostly conservatives) is to dust off and bring up, year after year, totally unproven or even thoroughly discredited charges against them, as if they were an essential part of the victims' curriculum vitae.

For example, Roberto d'Aubuisson, perhaps the leading conservative figure in the politics of El Salvador, is routinely referred to in the American media as "Roberto d'Aubuisson, whose name has been linked to right-wing death squads"—although he has not only never been convicted of any such misdeed but has never even been specifically accused of a deniable crime in any nonprivileged arena from which he could take an accuser to court for libel.*

Similarly Bert Lance, the "good ol' boy" from Georgia who was Jimmy Carter's budget director, is often casually described as "Lance, who resigned as Carter's budget director in the wake of allegations involving bank loans"—although he was duly tried by a jury of his peers and never convicted of anything.

Another favorite punching bag of this type is—or was—Richard Allen, who lost his job as President Reagan's national security adviser in 1982 in a White House power play. About the same time, somebody discovered that he had told an aide to turn over $1,000, paid by a Japanese magazine for an interview with Nancy Reagan, to the proper authorities and had then forgotten about it. (The money subsequently turned up in a White House office safe.)

Allen and his wife had also accepted three $135 wristwatches from personal Japanese friends.

Investigations of these sinister actions, by the Justice Department and the Office of White House Counsel, resulted in published findings that no crime was involved in either case, and the matter was dropped.

Except, that is, by the media. In April 1983, *USA Today* casually asserted that Allen "resigned as National Security Adviser for President

---

* In November 1987, Salvadoran President Duarte at last officially charged his old rival with complicity in the 1980 assassination of Archbishop Romero. *New York Times* correspondent James Le Moyne remarked that "the government has a long way to go to prove its case."

36 THE COMING BATTLE FOR THE MEDIA

Reagan following allegations that he accepted bribes from Japanese journalists.''

Then, in the spring of 1984, when the media was zeroing in on the President's nomination of Edwin Meese to be attorney general, it became fashionable to classify the burning issue of certain cuff links presented to Meese by the government of China as merely the latest in a series of "scandals" that had supposedly plagued the Reagan administration.

Thus it was that the *Wall Street Journal'*s notably liberal news staff came up with this beauty: "Mr. Allen, then President Reagan's national security adviser, received $1,000 from Japanese journalists for helping arrange an interview with Nancy Reagan.''

The late Joseph Kraft, in his column, recalled that President Reagan once "had a national security adviser who took watches from Japanese businessmen.''

Anthony Lewis of the *New York Times* was more specific: "Allen," he said, "had resigned when found to have accepted $1,000 and three watches from representatives of a Japanese magazine for whom he had arranged an interview with Nancy Reagan.''

Finally, according to an ABC network news report, Allen "set up an interview with Mrs. Reagan for a Japanese magazine but resigned when it turned out he'd accepted $1,000 payment for his trouble.''

Appalled, Allen took his problem to Arnold and Porter, one of Washington's most formidable law firms. As a result of stern letters from them, every one of the above-mentioned organizations and individuals retracted and apologized for their misstatements.

Arnold and Porter then wrote letters to every major news organization in the country—newspapers, wire services, magazines, television and radio networks and stations, syndicated columnists, and others—advising them that future misrepresentations of the same type would be "actionable at law.''

Is that going to have to be the recourse of all other or future victims of this particular journalistic technique?

• On April 15, 1985, appropriately enough, Channel 5 in New York (the Metromedia station) featured on its evening news program a story about taxes. Dave Browde, one of the station's staff reporters, told viewers that certain "hugely profitable" corporations "pay no taxes" for "years on end." This shocking datum was accompanied by a film of an unidentified corporate executive being sworn in, like a courtroom defendant, before a grim-faced congressional committee. As nearly as could be told from anything Browde said, the corporations' failure to pay any taxes was either a sly abuse of unspecified but apparently enormous "loopholes" or the result of a simple and cynical flouting of the applicable laws. The segment was quickly followed by another, in which a different Channel 5 reporter described the efforts of Harlem residents to compute their taxes—while their "benefits," he declared, were scheduled to diminish.

Actually, there are (or rather were, under the tax laws then applicable—this was before the 1986 tax reform law) at least three perfectly legitimate reasons why a profitable corporation might pay no taxes. In the first place, a multinational corporation often makes large profits in a foreign country. Such profits are taxed here, but the government sensibly allows the corporation to deduct first any taxes it was obliged to pay to the government of the country where the profits were actually made.

Second, a corporation engaged in a long-term contract (typically, for the construction of large defense items such as aircraft carriers, which may take a good many years to complete) might be entitled, under the contract, to partial payment year by year—obviously, to finance the project. But the IRS allowed the corporation to defer taxes on its hypothetical "profit" until the contract was completed and the tax actually due could be computed precisely.

Finally, a corporation was usually allowed to deduct from its taxable income profits that were not distributed but plowed directly back into the business, thereby generating new jobs (and new tax revenues).

But all of these perfectly defensible instances in which taxes could be deferred or avoided were lost on Browde, his editors at Metromedia Channel 5, and (perforce) its viewers. The latter were implicitly invited to grind their teeth over the outrageous sight of corporate fat cats paying no taxes at all while Harlem residents struggled to compute theirs.

• Presidential campaigns are admittedly not occasions when anyone interested in politics is likely to be scrupulously objective, but an article that appeared in the *New York Times* on October 9, 1984, as the Reagan-Mondale race thundered toward its close, surely exceeded any bounds that might be assumed to apply to a publication with the *Times'*s pretensions.

In his first debate with Mondale on October 7, President Reagan had asked the American people whether they believed the country was better off economically than it had been four years before (when he first took office). The pro-Mondale *Times* two days later offered an article by reporter Peter T. Kilborn in implicit response to Mr. Reagan's question. The article was accompanied by a chart, entitled "The Carter and Reagan Terms: How the Economy Fared," and if a Museum of Journalistic Dishonesty is ever opened, that chart deserves a glass case all to itself.

The chart purportedly set forth comparative figures for the Carter and Reagan administrations, in seven categories of economic measurement. The first was "economic growth," as reflected by "increases in the GNP, adjusted for inflation." The figure for the Carter administration was given as 13.6 percent; that for the Reagan administration as 10.3 percent— reflecting the negative impact of the 1982 recession. So far, so good.

The next category was interest rates. One might suppose that the proper comparison, in view of Mr. Reagan's question, was between the prime rate when Mr. Carter left office (an astronomical 20.16 percent) and the prime rate in October 1984 (12.75 percent). But instead the *Times* ignored the prime rate altogether, and chose to concentrate instead solely on "home mortgage rates (25-year fixed rate)"—a notoriously sluggish indicator. And instead of accepting Mr. Reagan's invitation to compare 1980 and 1984, even on this basis, the *Times* offered two other measurements: an "administration average" (10.60 percent for Carter, 13.86 percent for Reagan) and an "administration peak" (Carter 14.15 percent, Reagan 16.38). Both of these figures, of course, conveniently obscured the supremely important point, which is that interest rates in general rose steadily under Carter and fell just as steadily under Reagan.

The third category was "inflation," which the *Times* defined as the "rise in the Consumer Price Index during the administration." Here the *Times* simply threw in the sponge: Carter 45.7 percent, Reagan 26.1 percent. Once again, however, by averaging the figures over the entire respective periods of the two administrations, the *Times* managed to conceal the all-important *trend,* which of course was strenuously *upward* under Carter and dramatically *downward* under Reagan.

The fourth category was the "unemployment rate." Mr. Reagan's question invited a response comparing the rate when he assumed office (7.5 percent) with the rate in October 1984 (7.4 percent)—this despite the fact that 5.5 million more people had joined the work force between those two dates. But the *Times* was not about to let him off so easily. Instead, it offered a rather strained comparison between the "average administration rates" (6.4 percent under Carter, 8.6 percent under Reagan—thus taking into account the large but temporary rise in unemployment caused by the 1982 recession) and a comparison between the raw numbers of unemployed at the end of the Carter administration (7.6 million) and in

October 1984 (8.5 million)—*without, however, mentioning the large increase in the size of the work force.* The decrease in the *percentage* of the work force unemployed was thereby finessed altogether.

On the basis of its performance thus far, one might suspect the *Times* of having some inherent preference for comparing administration averages rather than final results; but not so. The fifth category was the "national debt," and here the *Times* skipped the fancy footwork and used (since it was highly unfavorable to him) the comparison Mr. Reagan had invited: Carter $914.3 billion in fiscal 1980, Reagan $1,575.6 billion in fiscal 1984.

In the sixth category, "poverty," the *Times* resorted to the old liberal dodge of counting only cash support and disregarding noncash benefits (which can rise to as high as 70 percent of total income). On that basis, it found 13 percent of the population to be below the poverty line at the end of the Carter administration, versus 15.2 percent in October 1984.

Finally, comparing "disposable personal income in 1972 dollars," the *Times* conceded that there had been an increase of only 7.9 percent under Carter, versus 9.8 percent under Reagan.

Thus did the *New York Times,* in October 1984, seek to demonstrate— and not on its editorial page but in its news columns—that America had been better off economically under Carter than under Reagan by five out of seven measurements.


• Finally, as an example of tendentious reportage at its worst, let us examine an article by Karen de Young that appeared in the *Washington Post* in June 1985. At that moment, President Reagan was debating whether to disregard the weapons limitations in the (unratified) SALT II treaty, as he would do by permitting the launching of the first Trident submarine unless he ordered the dismantling of a Poseidon sub at the same time. Liberal sentiment was strongly in favor of continuing to observe the SALT II limits.

Ms. de Young's article appeared, with exquisite timing, just days before Mr. Reagan made his decision, and its lead paragraph nicely summarized her basic point: "The Western European allies believe that any decision by the United States to no longer observe the limits set by the 1979 (SALT) treaty would be a setback for arms control, a number of allied government officials said in recent interviews."

Note the sweep of Ms. de Young's opening assertion: "The Western European allies believe . . ." Not some of them, or most of them, or individuals in any of them, but (apparently) everybody in all of them. In support of this proposition we are to hear from "a number of allied government officials." Well, let's see.

The second paragraph of the article states, "Several [NATO] governments, as well as Lord Carrington of Britain, have let the Reagan administration know that a refusal by the United States to respect the limits of the unratified treaty with the Soviet Union could generate a hostile public backlash."

Now, the word "several" means "three or more," but Ms. de Young leaves the governments in question carefully unspecified, even though she could presumably have identified them without, by that simple act, compromising some confidential source. So we have no way of knowing whether the alleged warning came from half a dozen major NATO powers or (as seems more likely, in view of Ms. de Young's reluctance to identify them) merely from a few of the smaller and notoriously more timorous ones such as Holland, Belgium, and Denmark.

Note, moreover, that only one individual is named as endorsing the warning: Lord Carrington. But he, far from being a "government official," was by 1985 merely a NATO bureaucrat, having been forced to resign as British foreign minister after bungling the Falklands crisis.

Ms. de Young continues: "A European political leader said that doing away with the treaty would make it more difficult in general for allied governments to defend the idea that the Reagan administration is sincere about arms control." Observe, however, that De Young doesn't even claim to have obtained this gem of argumentation from a "government official." Her cautious formulation—"a European political leader"—suggests that she is actually quoting some opposition figure: e.g., a British Laborite or a German Social Democrat.

Finally we are vouchsafed one authentic Western European government official: Foreign Minister Hans van den Broek of the Netherlands—one of NATO's smallest and shakiest props. And what does Ms. de Young quote Van den Broek as saying? Well, he "is said to have told Mr. Shultz that ignoring the treaty's limits would make it even more difficult for his government to win public support for the deployment of 48 cruise missiles this fall."

Interestingly, Ms. de Young doesn't say that she herself even spoke to Van den Broek. On the contrary, her formulation (he "is said to have told Mr. Shultz") implies that the statement is sheer hearsay. And its author, to make matters worse, is anonymous.

The article goes on to quote or paraphrase various unnamed "officials in Britain and in West Germany,'' but (significantly) mostly to the effect that our allies are reluctant to express any views on SALT II at all, since it is purely a United States–Soviet affair. Ms. de Young does claim that one ''British official'' disagreed with a peripheral remark by Assistant Defense Secretary Richard Perle; but even this ''official'' is veiled in anonymity.

In fact, the only other named individual in Ms. de Young's entire article is ''David Owen, leader of Britain's Social Democratic Party,'' who she asserts gave President Reagan ''a hint of likely European opinion'' when he ''strongly urged U.S. compliance with the treaty limits.'' But Owen, of course, far from being a British ''official,'' is an outspoken foe of the British government.

That is the sort of thing that was passing for ''journalism'' in one of America's most influential and most staunchly liberal newspapers in the Year of our Lord 1985: a flat assertion as to what our ''Western European allies believe,'' according to ''a number of allied government officials,'' substantiated by supporting quotations from one NATO bureaucrat, one opposition politician from an unspecified country, and a hearsay report on what the foreign minister of the Netherlands told Mr. Shultz.

It is not, however, the quality of Ms. de Young's journalism but her (and the *Post*'s) transparent intention to use it to influence administration policy toward SALT II that warrants its inclusion here. What makes our media elite think that the sort of tendentious nonsense cited in the foregoing pages goes unnoticed, or unresented, or that they can go on forever, peddling it as a reasonably balanced presentation of the ''news''?

Thus far, however, we have confined ourselves to citing a few flagrant examples of liberal bias in the media. But such examples can always be defended individually on one theory or another or, if necessary, dismissed as unrepresentative. We shall now turn, therefore, to *statistical* evidence of the media's bias, and then to its influence on their work-product. This may be, as Seymour Hersh once complained when I used the same technique in a debate, ''banal,'' but it has the surpassing virtue of being extremely difficult to refute.

# CHAPTER 3
# *Some Statistics*

IF WE ARE to address this question of bias seriously, we had first better define "liberal" and "conservative."

Although politicians often try to obscure their meaning, the better to flummox voters as to exactly what they're doing, there need be no serious confusion over the definitions of "liberal" and "conservative" in the modern American political context. In other times and places, both terms have meant many other and different things; but in the United States, in the four decades since the end of World War II, their meaning has been stable and reasonably clear.

The word *liberal* is the term applied to that series of political and social impulses which elsewhere has more commonly been called "democratic socialism" or "social democracy." Without necessarily subscribing to the historical analysis of Marxist socialism, and while maintaining a sincere commitment to democracy that many avowed Marxists regard as outmoded, democratic socialists in the world at large, and liberals in the United States, have consistently favored the expansion of government's role in the management of the national economy and a correspondingly severe and comprehensive regulation and limitation of private economic activity. In foreign affairs, liberals have usually managed to oppose direct Communist aggression, recognizing it as implacably hostile to the democratic principles they espouse. But the economic goals they tend to share, to a greater or lesser extent, with Communist systems of government make total opposition to communism ("in theory") psychologically difficult for them. And when Communist aggression is masked as, for example, a Third World country's rebellion against "capitalist exploitation" and in favor of some ambiguous form of socialism, liberal resistance often collapses or even, temporarily, turns into support.

*Conservatism,* in the United States since the end of World War II, has meant far more than simply opposition to liberalism's programmatic goals—though it certainly means that too. But conservatism, especially since 1950, has made major strides in explaining *why* it opposes liberal goals, and has gone far toward spelling out affirmative alternatives. To the liberal concept of constantly expanding government control of, or intervention in, the economy, conservatism has juxtaposed the virtues of the "market": that net product of myriad private economic decisions which sensitively detects and responds to the demands of the economy while simultaneously encouraging maximum economic growth and prosperity. To liberalism's compassion for the poor and its expression in the form of transfer payments, conservatism has responded that such policies have demonstrably destroyed much that they were designed to save, creating instead a vast permanently dependent underclass, and that only general prosperity, brought about by the application of conservative principles, can truly benefit America's poor.

In the field of foreign affairs, having (unlike the liberals) no innate sympathy for the professed economic aims of the Communist powers, conservatives have been able to oppose these regimes unreservedly, condemning them as based on a flawed and inadequate analysis of history and, indeed, of human nature itself. And conservatives have been equally resistant to those tendencies, especially in the Third World, which have combined socialist economics and indigenous political authoritarianism in ways that, in the name of combating exploitation and corruption, have all too often ended by serving communism's international purposes.

Few Americans will have any trouble identifying the Democratic party as the chief political vector of the above-described liberal policies in the United States during the past forty years, or in recognizing the Republican party as the political home of most of the conservative tendencies that have developed over the same period.*

But an important word of caution is necessary at this point. Ambiguity is the mother's milk of politics, and neither major party, let alone the average individual politician in either, ever feels happy for long in a position that is unmistakably clear and explicit. Thanks in part to the accident of history that kept the concept of democratic socialism in America masked behind the term *liberalism*, Democratic politicians and the party itself have been able to avoid any taint of socialist dogma, while on the other hand individual Republican politicians have been able to ingest substantial doses of liberalism without being convicted of demon-

---

* Their home, but not always their source. The important bloc known as the "social conservatives" originally consisted largely of Democrats, independents, and nonvoters. They have voted Republican only since the mid-1960s, or even later.

strable heresy. Even a political figure as closely and firmly identified with liberalism as Senator Edward Kennedy can rack up an impressive record as an exponent of the conservative principle of "deregulation" and in the process simply enhance his reputation for nonideological broadmindedness.

Still, when all due allowances have been made for the shifting courses of ambitious politicians, and for the inevitable tendency of both major parties to cast their nets over as wide a spectrum of American political opinion as possible, and when respectful acknowledgment has been made of all that fate and circumstances can do to impede or even contradict the rational application of principles to politics, the fact remains: American politics since the end of World War II has consisted largely of a contest between liberalism and conservatism. In the first part of that period liberalism was comfortably dominant; in the middle years the battle grew more even; recently conservatism has clearly been ascendant.

Let us have done, then, with the pretense that the word *liberal*, as we have used it, is somehow fundamentally unintelligible. But what concrete, statistical evidence is there of a liberal bias among our media elite? Bear in mind that we are speaking here, not merely of political reporters, but of the whole infrastructure of the media: the newspaper and television editors, the publishers and producers, the anchormen and anchorwomen, and the rest of the creative community, both visible and invisible to the public. For it is all of these who have contributed to the key ingredients of *bias* and *imbalance* in news coverage.

In a way it is odd, and to a conservative rather annoying, to be called upon to demonstrate the liberal bias of the media elite. To conservatives, that bias is as obvious as the faces on Mount Rushmore. But these clever and influential people have every right to put us to our proof. There is no reason why a conservative's *ipse dixit* ought to be regarded as an adequate substitute for evidence.

Besides, the media's systematic denial of bias may persuade them, however little it persuades others. The sheer near-universality of liberal attitudes on the Washington journalistic scene probably helps to reassure them that their inherent bias, to whatever extent it actually exists, is comfortably mainstream and therefore does little violence to acceptable reportage and presentation of the news.

But if we conservatives must take seriously the media elite's denial of a liberal bias, at least until we have established it beyond the possibility of effective contradiction, the media in turn would be well advised to acknowledge the criticism and respond to it if they can. For the issue is an important one, involving the distribution, use, and abuse of power in the American society, and it is not going to go away. Involved are important political and social processes, some of them constitutionally protected (and others claiming constitutional protections which they in fact have never enjoyed). In one way or another, the media elite are going to be called to account for grave abuses of power, and on the outcome of the controversy may well depend the future direction, and future leadership, of the American society.

Just how does one go about demonstrating that the media elite are, in the matter of their private opinions, overwhelmingly partial to liberal policies and liberal political personalities? A general impression, based on familiarity with their work-product as on display in the *New York Times* or the *Washington Post,* in *Time* or *Newsweek,* or on the evening news programs of one or another of the major networks, is absolutely worthless. You will be told that your perception is distorted by your own partiality to conservative policies and personalities. You will be assured that the liberals complain just as loudly as conservatives about maltreatment by the media (though on inspection it turns out to be the harder left—e.g., Alexander Cockburn—that complains; liberals typically, and understandably, complain very little about distortion by the media elite). You will be referred to news stories in which there was no liberal bias, and to news presentations well and truly balanced—shining exceptions that merely emphasize the rule.

There is, in fact, only one way to ascertain with precision anyone's political leaning, inclination, or prejudice, and that is to interview him or her in depth. Moreover, if the intention is to evaluate the opinions of an entire group, the sample interviewed must be large enough to be dependably representative. Fortunately there have recently been several conscientious surveys of the political views of America's media elite, and the results are thoroughly unambiguous.

In 1976 the media were one of eight "leadership groups" whose opinions were sought in a study conducted by the *Washington Post* and Harvard University. According to a report that appeared in the *Post* on September 29 of that year:

> More than 300 members of the news media were interviewed through lengthy mail questionnaires. Sixty percent of them work for newspapers, the rest for radio or television. About half work out of Washington and were selected at random from lists of those who hold passes to the House and Senate press galleries. The other half are newspaper managing editors

or radio and television news directors, people who generally run the day-to-day operations of their organizations.

It would thus appear that about 150 of those interviewed were Washington reporters, at least if a press pass to the House or Senate galleries qualifies a person as such. It is unclear whether the "other half" of the sample—i.e., the managerial types—included any Washingtonians, and if so how many. But the political sympathies of the Washington reporters were unmistakable:

> [T]hose in the Washington-based group are younger than the bosses, and, according to their own descriptions, much more liberal in ideology. . . . Among the reporters, 20 per cent see themselves as moderate, 59 per cent as liberal, and 18 per cent as conservative. . . . [Moreover] 61 per cent say they voted for McGovern [in 1972] and 22 per cent for Nixon.

Of those reporters *who voted,* 70 percent chose McGovern; only 25 percent voted for Nixon. (Nationwide, of course, Nixon won by 61 to 38 percent.)

It may be objected, however, that the study just cited was skewed because, in the case of the Washington sample, it concentrated on reporters as distinguished from managers. Reporters being, on the whole, a younger group, their views might be unrepresentative of the media— even the Washington media elite—as a whole. Moreover, the sampling was conducted by means of a mailed questionnaire rather than by in-depth interviews, and the *Post*'s article does not indicate how many of those polled completed and returned their questionnaires.

A study conducted in 1978 by Stephen Hess for the Brookings Institution was also vulnerable, at least in part, to several of these objections.* Hess mailed a written questionnaire to a comprehensive list of 1,250 reporters whose names were obtained from "all news operations listed in Hudson's Washington News Media Contacts Directory and the Congressional Directory." Anonymity was promised, and 292 "usable responses" were received.

Hess then administered a second questionnaire by phone. He explained his methodology as follows:

> Reporters were called at random, but because respondents to the mail questionnaire had indicated their type of employer (wire service, television

---

* See Stephen Hess, *The Washington Reporters* (Washington: The Brookings Institution, 1981).

network, and so forth), it was possible to adjust the telephone sample so
that telephone-plus-mail-questionnaires would accurately reflect the relative sizes of the various components that make up the Washington press
corps. The telephone survey yielded 194 usable responses. . . . [Whereas
the mail questionnaire had concentrated on] very specific questions relating
to the work of the day, in the telephone survey the reporters were also
asked to explain their views on matters that could best be handled as
open-ended questions, such as political bias in the press corps. . . . It was
possible to devise codes that translated the answers to some of the
open-ended questions into numbers and percentages; otherwise, the information was used in narrative form. Since by far the largest group of
Washington reporters—nearly 40 percent—works for newspapers, this
group becomes the focus of this part of the study.

At any rate, Hess reports that 178 "Washington reporters" were asked
(apparently by telephone), "Some reporters feel that there is a political bias
in the Washington news corps. Do you agree?" Forty-nine percent disagreed; but 51 percent did agree that they had noticed signs of political bias.

Bias in which direction? "*Liberal* said 96 percent, *conservative* said 1
percent."

When asked about their own political views, however, Hess's telephone respondents were somewhat less unanimous: "Forty-two percent
consider themselves liberal, 39 percent say they are middle-of-the-road,
and 19 percent identify themselves as conservative."

Valuable as these two studies were in illuminating the political biases
of Washington reporters, they both suffered from their aforementioned
defects: an unjustified concentration on reporters, to the exclusion of
managerial personnel (newspaper and television editors, etc.) who are at
least as important in shaping the presentation of the "news," and a
failure to conduct face-to-face interviews. These objections were both
finally overcome in a remarkable survey whose results were published in
1981.

It is a fair guess that, if they had it to do over again, many of the
representatives of the media elite who consented to be interviewed would
decline the honor. The results of the survey were devastating, and (as we
shall see) triggered some grim attempts to find out who had blabbed.
Probably the incontestably academic sponsorship of the survey assuaged
many doubts: Liberals are so accustomed to support from academic
quarters that the possibility of embarrassing revelations from that direction was in all likelihood not even considered.

The study was conducted in 1979 and 1980 by two professors of
political science—S. Robert Lichter of George Washington University

and Stanley Rothman of Smith College—as part of a larger inquiry into the attitudes of various elites, under the auspices of the Research Institute on International Change at Columbia University. The survey itself was supervised by Response Analysis, a survey research organization.

Lichter and Rothman began by defining the following organizations as America's "most influential media outlets": three daily newspapers—the *New York Times*, the *Washington Post*, and the *Wall Street Journal;* three weekly newsmagazines—*Time, Newsweek*, and *U.S. News and World Report;* the news departments of four networks—CBS, NBC, ABC, and PBS; and the news departments of certain major independent broadcasting stations.

Within these organizations they then selected at random, from among those responsible for news content, individuals to be approached for interviews. In the print media, these included "reporters, columnists, department heads, bureau chiefs, editors and executives responsible for news content." In the electronic media, those selected included "correspondents, anchormen, producers, film editors and news executives." A remarkably high proportion of those contacted—76 percent, or 240 individuals—completed the hour-long interview. Such a response rate makes it certain that the results of the survey are valid as a representation of the views of the media elite.

Lichter and Rothman reported their findings on the media elite in the October/November 1981 issue of *Public Opinion*, a publication of the American Enterprise Institute for Public Policy Research. (Reports on other sections of the survey, concerning business elites and others, appeared in subsequent issues of *Public Opinion*.)

Their report begins with some suggestive demographic statistics:

The media elite is composed mainly of white males in their 30s and 40s. Only one in 20 is nonwhite; one in five is female. They are highly educated, well-paid professionals. Ninety-three per cent have college degrees, and a majority (55 per cent) attended graduate school as well. These figures reveal them as one of the best-educated groups in America. They are also one of the better-paid groups, despite journalism's reputation as a low-paying profession. In 1978, 78 per cent earned at least $30,000, and one in three had salaries that exceeded $50,000. Moreover, nearly half (46 per cent) reported family incomes above $50,000.

Geographically, they are drawn primarily from northern industrial states, especially from the northeast corridor. Two-fifths come from three states: New York, New Jersey, and Pennsylvania. Another 10 per cent hail from New England, and almost one in five was raised in the big industrial states just to the west—Illinois, Indiana, Michigan and Ohio. Thus, over two-thirds of the media elite come from these three clusters of states. By contrast, only 3 per cent are drawn from the entire Pacific coast, including California, the nation's most populous state.

Most were raised in upper-middle-class homes. Almost half their fathers were college graduates, and one in four held a graduate degree. Two in five are the children of professionals—doctors, lawyers, teachers and so on. In fact, one in 12 is following in his father's footsteps as a second-generation journalist.

Another 40 percent describe their fathers as businessmen. That leaves only one in five whose father was employed in a low-status blue or white collar job. Given these upper-status positions, it is not surprising that their families were relatively well off. Forty-five per cent rate their family's income while they were growing up as above average, compared to 26 per cent who view their early economic status as below average.

In sum, substantial numbers of the media elite grew up at some distance from the social and cultural traditions of small-town "middle America." Instead, they were drawn from big cities in the northeast and north central states. Their parents tended to be well off, highly educated members of the upper-middle class, especially the educated professions.

How do these people describe *themselves,* in political terms? The interviewers do not seem to have encountered any overwhelming impulse to claim that the individual being questioned was ideologically "neutral," as a matter of personal inclination. On the contrary, 54 percent described themselves as left of center, and 19 percent considered themselves right of center. What's more, when asked to evaluate their fellow workers 56 percent said the people they worked with were mostly on the left, while only 8 percent (or one seventh as many) described them as mostly on the right.

Certainly the voting records of those questioned bear out their own assessment. The survey was conducted before the 1980 presidential election took place, but included a question as to how the individual who was being interviewed had voted in the previous four elections: 1964 (Johnson versus Goldwater), 1968 (Nixon versus Humphrey and Wallace), 1972 (Nixon versus McGovern), and 1976 (Carter versus Ford).

It transpires that, of those who voted in these elections at all (and this was 82 percent in 1976, when all but the youngest among those interviewed in 1979–80 would have qualified), *never less than 80 percent of the media elite voted for the Democratic candidate.**

---

* The percentages that follow express the proportion of votes received by the two major-party candidates. Third-party candidates never received more than 2 percent of the media elite's votes, even in 1968 when Wallace nationally garnered 13.4 percent.

This is a truly striking divergence from the national averages. Goldwater, to be sure, lost heavily to Johnson in 1964, receiving only 38 percent of the votes to Johnson's 61 percent. But among the media elite who participated in the 1980 survey, 94 percent voted for Johnson and only 6 percent for Goldwater.

In 1968, Nixon narrowly defeated Humphrey nationwide—43.5 percent to 42.8 percent, with Wallace receiving 13.4 percent. But among the media elite Wallace was almost totally blanked out, and Humphrey was their overwhelming favorite (87 percent) vis-à-vis Nixon (13 percent).

In 1972, Nixon ran for reelection and carried every state but Massachusetts, winning 61.8 percent of the popular vote to McGovern's 38.2 percent. But McGovern swept the media elite: 81 percent to Nixon's 19 percent.

And in the election of 1976, which Carter won over Ford by the narrow margin of 51 percent to 49 percent, Ford could do no better among the media elite than Nixon had done in 1972, receiving 19 percent of their votes to Carter's 81 percent.

In-depth questioning by the interviewers revealed that the media elite's social and political attitudes in general were as liberal, and in most cases as far from the national norm, as their votes in presidential elections would suggest.

For example, a full 50 percent of the media elite have no religious affiliation whatever. Only 8 percent go to church or synagogue weekly; 86 percent "seldom or never" attend religious services.

Like many American liberals, the media elite accept the essential free-enterprise basis of the United States economy, but they are devoted to welfarism. Over two thirds (68 percent) believe "the government should substantially reduce the income gap between the rich and the poor," and nearly half (48 percent) think the government should guarantee a job to anyone who wants one.

On sociocultural issues, the media elite's support for liberal positions is overwhelming. Ninety percent believe it is a woman's right to decide whether or not to have an abortion. A solid majority (53 percent) can't even bring itself to affirm that adultery is wrong.

There is far more to the Lichter-Rothman survey than the above brief sample of its findings, but the basic thrust of the study is unmistakable: America's media elite are far to the left of American public opinion in general on the great majority of topics.

As already noted, the results of the Lichter-Rothman survey, so far as concerned the attitudes of the media, were reported in the October/November 1981 issue of *Public Opinion*. One might suppose that a study so carefully conducted, and producing results so emphatic, would immediately have attracted considerable attention and elicited, from the media's defenders, a good deal of criticism. On the contrary however, the response of the vast majority of the media was . . . silence. The study was not widely reported, not contradicted, not greatly criticized; it was simply ignored, no doubt in the hope that it would sooner or later go away.

But America's conservatives would not let the subject die quite so easily. *Human Events,* the conservative Washington tabloid, reprinted the survey's principal findings regarding the media in its issue dated January 16, 1982. *National Review* summarized the survey's results in its January 22 issue. I myself wrote a column on the subject for release February 5. The Fall 1982 issue of the neoconservative quarterly *The Public Interest* contained an article reworking and augmenting the original material.

From that point forward, the Lichter-Rothman findings were a staple in the armory of conservative critics of the media; but still the media's liberal defenders preserved a stubborn silence. It was not until mid-1983—roughly a year and a half after the original publication of the survey—that the *Columbia Journalism Review* deemed it worthy of editorial comment. In an editorial sniffily entitled "The Return of the Nattering Nabobs" (an allusion, of course, to Spiro Agnew's description of the media in his 1969 speech in Des Moines), *CJR* wasted little time disputing the survey's main point concerning the political views of the media elite, but threw up the usual barricade at the traditional fallback position (see the discussion of this on page 64): "[T]here is little beyond wishful evidence in the study, or elsewhere, that journalists carry their personal opinions over into their work."

Then the curtain of silence descended again, pierced only by occasional references to the study in conservative publications. It was July 23, 1985—not far short of four years after the report's initial publication—when Albert R. Hunt, the liberal chief of the Washington bureau of the *Wall Street Journal,* finally lumbered into action with a counterattack.

Professor Lichter had informed Hunt that, although Response Analysis (the organization that conducted the confidential interviews) never told either him or Rothman the names of those interviewed, he had been advised that sixteen worked for the *Wall Street Journal.* Hunt thereupon questioned his staff, and declared triumphantly that no one in the Washington bureau recalled being contacted by Response Analysis.

Hunt added that, while Response Analysis told the *Washington Post* that at least thirty *Post* staffers had been included in the survey, "Ben Bradlee, the paper's editor, can find only three." On the basis of Bradlee's researches and his own, Hunt concluded that the Lichter-Rothman survey was "full of flaws" because the pool of interviewees "seems elusive."

There is something faintly comical about these two ranking journalists ransacking their own staffs in search of the culprits. But, of course, at least five years had elapsed since the interviews, and everyone questioned would have had ample opportunity to note—and in most cases regret—the use the media's conservative critics were now diligently making of the results. Those questioned can hardly have been eager, in most cases, to acknowledge their participation in the study—least of all to a superior trying strenuously to discredit it.

Another attack on the survey appeared in the November/December 1985 issue of the *Columbia Journalism Review*—a spectacular example of letting an issue ripen (in this case for over four years) before deigning to address it at length. The author was Herbert J. Gans, a professor of sociology at Columbia, and his article was entitled "Are U.S. Journalists Dangerously Liberal?" (The title ought to have warned readers to expect a polemic, because Professor Gans was a member of the board of directors of Americans for Democratic Action from 1969 to 1975 and can hardly be suspected of considering any degree of journalistic liberalism "dangerous.")

Gans skated past the central point of the whole Lichter-Rothman survey in a single dismissive sentence on the second page of his article: "In some respects the study is a conventional survey, and many of the findings—for example, that many journalists call themselves liberal and that most vote Democratic in presidential elections—are neither new nor especially noteworthy."

No doubt noteworthiness, like beauty, is in the eye of the beholder. As to novelty, however, it is a little hard to understand why, if Professor Gans is so familiar with (and persuaded by) other evidence of liberal and/or Democratic preferences among journalists that the subject rather bores him, he went to the trouble to write an entire article for the *Columbia Journalism Review* attacking various methodological aspects of the Lichter-Rothman study, which merely confirms what he says he already knew.

That is, however, what he did, and here for the record are his objections:

1. Lichter and Rothman "hide a political argument behind a seemingly objective study." Gans concedes that "researchers may advance political arguments, of course," but contends that Lichter and Rothman "are less than scientific in their failure to announce their political agenda in advance"—not that he bothers to establish they had any such agenda (or denies that he has one himself).

2. They "report findings about journalists which do not accurately reflect the answers they gave to the survey questions they were asked"— a sweeping and unsupported generalization from the survey's paraphrase of the interviewers' response to a single question (on the income gap between rich and poor).

3. They "violate basic survey methodology by first inferring people's answers to single questions and then treating their answers as strongly felt opinions in a way that makes the journalists appear militant and radical"— one (of four) examples being that " 'many leading journalists' are said [by Lichter and Rothman] to 'voice a general discontent with the social system.' "

4. They "violate scientific norms by forgetting an explicit promise to their respondents"—namely, to take into account, when analyzing the results of the survey, "all of the possible nuances or qualifications that might occur to a sophisticated person."

5. "The fifth, and perhaps most serious, unscientific practice of the researchers is their presentation of a mass of data on the personal backgrounds and alleged political opinions and values of the journalists without any evidence that these are relevant to how the journalists report the news."

To repeat, it is unclear just why these supposed defects of the Lichter-Rothman study required airing more than four years after its first publication, in a five-page article in the *Columbia Journalism Review* under the title "Are U.S. Journalists Dangerously Liberal?", since Professor Gans is prepared to characterize the propositions "that many journalists call themselves liberal and that most vote Democratic in presidential elections" as "neither new nor especially noteworthy." New or not, and noteworthy or not, a solid confirmation of those propositions is the chief finding of the Lichter-Rothman study.

It is not surprising therefore that Professor Gans, in his fifth criticism above, goes altogether beyond the stated scope of the Lichter-Rothman study and condemns it for failing to demonstrate that the overwhelmingly liberal predilections of the media elite "are relevant to how the journalists report the news." That is indeed an important question, and we shall be addressing it shortly; but it is a different question, and it most certainly is no valid criticism of Professors Lichter and Rothman that they did not seek to answer it in some sort of appendix to their careful study of the opinions of the media elite. What that study demonstrated, beyond serious cavil, is that *America's media elite personally hold opinions that are, on most subjects, far to the left of the American norm.* Whether, and how much, that influences their treatment of the "news" remains to be seen.

Since the Lichter-Rothman report on the media was published late in 1981, there have been very few other important studies of the views personally held by journalists (as distinguished from the degree, if any, to which their actual coverage of the news is biased). This is regrettable, but not surprising: The issue of the preponderance of liberals in the media is highly visible these days, and it can be assumed that liberals, especially among the media elite, are going to be reluctant to add fuel to the fire.

One survey that deserves mention was conducted in the autumn of 1982 by *Business Forum* and published in its Spring 1984 issue. The specific purpose of this study was to determine to what extent, if any, business managers and the media differed on matters of policy. To this end the magazine conducted what it called "a comprehensive survey of business and the media." So far as the media were concerned, "Questionnaires were mailed to journalists at the fifty largest daily and Sunday newspapers, [plus] a stratified random sample of journalists at weekly newspapers." Journalists in the electronic media were apparently not included. From the mailing, a "usable sample" of 162 responses was received.

In terms of self-description, these 162 journalists rather closely resembled the Washington reporters questioned in the Washington Post–Harvard University survey of 1976. Fifty percent called themselves liberal, 29 percent moderate, and 21 percent conservative. When it came to voting, however, the self-described "moderates" turned out to be liberals in sheep's clothing: 77 percent of the sample had voted for McGovern in 1972, and only 21 percent for Nixon. In party terms, 61 percent were quite content to call themselves Democrats, and another 19 percent "independent"; only 20 percent admitted to being Republican.

The *Business Forum* survey also included a question on the 1980 election, which the Lichter-Rothman study had been too early to cover. It indicated that 51 percent of those responding had voted for Carter in 1980, and another 24 percent for the liberal-Republican independent, John Anderson, who had run that year as the alternative for voters dissatisfied with both Carter and Reagan. Only 25 percent had voted for Reagan. (Americans as a whole reacted very differently, of course: 51 percent voted for Reagan, 41 percent for Carter, and less than 7 percent for Anderson.) These figures are particularly useful in evaluating the media's claim (which we will discuss later) that their often-critical treatment of Carter in 1980 amounts to a refutation of charges of liberal bias.

A much larger and more comprehensive study was conducted by the *Los Angeles Times* between February 23 and August 2, 1985, and took the form of half-hour telephone interviews, consisting of 106 questions, with 2,703 news and editorial staff members on 621 newspapers of all sizes in all parts of the country. These papers, in turn, were chosen because they had been specified by 2,993 randomly selected members of the general public as the papers they read. As far as possible, the number of journalists interviewed at a given paper was proportional to the number of times that paper was specified by members of the public, thus ensuring that the larger papers would be proportionately represented in the sample. However, in the case of four newspapers (the *New York Times, Washington Post, Los Angeles Times,* and *Chicago Tribune*), an attempt was made to interview virtually every member of their staffs; and it corroborates our assumption about liberal reticence on this delicate subject that only 215 of 451 people on the *Times,* and a bare 60 of 286 contacted at the *Post,* would consent to be interviewed. (The staffs of the *Los Angeles Times* and the *Chicago Tribune* were considerably more forthcoming: 224 of 263 at the former, and 164 of 189 at the latter, agreed to participate.)

It should be noted that the *Los Angeles Times*'s study was conducted among a sharply different journalistic group than the Lichter-Rothman survey. The latter focused on the media elite, notably in New York and Washington; the former covered the entire nation. The latter included journalists working in the electronic press (radio and television), on newsmagazines, and for the wire services; the former confined itself to those employed by newspapers. The latter included a somewhat broader spectrum of staff members even on newspapers; the former concentrated rigorously on reporters and editors. In addition, the Lichter-Rothman survey addressed itself solely to the problem of ascertaining the personal views of the media elite, without seeking answers to such related questions as whether these views influence their work-product. The *Los Angeles Times* survey, on the other hand, asked some three thousand members of the general public their own opinion on this matter.

Given the very different pools of individuals interviewed, it is striking how thoroughly the *Los Angeles Times* survey confirms the basic findings of the Lichter-Rothman study concerning the personal opinions of journalists.

Here are the major results of the *Los Angeles Times* poll, as summarized by David Shaw, a staff writer for that newspaper:

> In the poll, 55% of the newspaper journalists say they're liberal, 26% say they're middle-of-the-road and 17% say they're conservative. Only 24% of their readers describe themselves as liberal, 33% say they're middle-of-the-road and 29% say they're conservative.
>
> Even other college-educated professionals, who generally share many demographic characteristics with the press, do not consider themselves as liberal as newspaper journalists consider themselves: 37% of the college-educated professionals say they're liberal, 27% say they're middle-of-the-road and 30% say they're conservative.
>
> Newspaper reporters and editors are not only much more liberal than their readers, but the reporters and editors also tend to be Anglo (96%), male (73%) and college-educated (88%) in proportions far greater than their readers and with average incomes far in excess of their readers'.
>
> The poll also shows that newspaper journalists are only about half as likely as their readers to be strongly religious—and that newspaper journalists are about twice as likely as their readers to practice no religion at all.
>
> Moreover, journalists are much less likely than their readers to consider such personal/social issues as crime, drugs, inflation or unemployment as "the biggest problem facing the country today." In contrast, reporters and editors are much more likely than their readers to consider the federal budget deficit or the control of nuclear arms as "the biggest problem facing the country today."
>
> The results of the Times Poll clearly lend substantial credence to the claim of many conservatives that there is a "liberal media elite" in this country.

Note that 55 percent of the journalists interviewed *identified themselves* as "liberal"; only 17 percent called themselves "conservative." Another 26 percent apparently answered "middle-of-the-road" when asked the question; 2 percent refused to answer it at all. It is interesting, however, that the journalists who call themselves "conservative" (17 percent) are very close to the proportion (never more than 20 percent) who, according to the Lichter-Rothman study, voted Republican at least once in the four presidential elections commencing with 1964. This suggests that the *Los Angeles Times* poll can be reconciled even more closely with the Lichter-Rothman study by assuming that the 26 percent who considered themselves "middle-of-the-road" in the former are in fact principally liberals who, by 1985, had decided to be a bit more cautious about proclaiming their personal political preferences. Adding this 26 percent to the self-admittedly liberal 55 percent, we arrive at 81 percent—almost exactly the proportion of the media elite who, according to Lichter-Rothman, never voted for a Republican for president from 1964 to 1976 inclusive.

Asked specifically whether they favor or oppose Ronald Reagan, the journalists interviewed by the *Los Angeles Times* were slightly less monolithic. Answering that question between February and August 1985, considerably less than a year after Reagan had been reelected by a historic landslide, carrying every state but Minnesota, 30 percent of the journalists interviewed claimed to "favor" him; only (!) 60 percent identified themselves as opposed. This time, just 10 percent asserted neutrality or declined to answer.

Small wonder, then, that William Schneider and I. A. Lewis, who had supervised the *Los Angeles Times* survey, began their report on the poll in the August/September 1985 issue of *Public Opinion* as follows:

> Whether journalists are or are not a liberal elite, and what difference that makes, has been a hot debate in the United States for the past twenty years. A recent *Los Angeles Times* survey addressed the subject, and it offers some convincing evidence. Newspaper journalists are, indeed, a liberal elite—far more liberal than the general public on a wide range of issues.

The first report on the results of the aforesaid Times Mirror survey appeared in the *Los Angeles Times* on August 11, 1985. That may help to explain the not essentially dissimilar but spectacularly more cautious response of 1,333 journalists from fifty-one daily newspapers to a detailed questionnaire circulated that August by Minnesota Opinion Research, Inc. on behalf of the Associated Press managing editors and the Associated Press itself.

The AP poll concentrated on other issues (e.g., journalists' perceptions of their own accuracy, the differing attitudes of younger, "transient" journalists and older, more settled ones), but when asked to identify themselves as liberal or conservative a full 60 percent of those questioned declined to answer. Even so, 30 percent still insisted they were liberal, and just 10 percent stated that they were conservative.

It would seem pointless to cumulate more data on this question, even if a great deal more was available (which it is not).* If the surveys cited

---

* By now, moreover, any new study is legitimately suspect as having its own hidden political agenda, and those questioned are of course well aware that the media are widely accused of a liberal bias. Professors David H. Weaver and G. Cleveland Wilhoit of the University of Indiana published in March 1986, under a grant from the Gannett

don't establish that most American journalists are far more liberal than the public at large, surveys are utterly useless.

Before turning away from the question, however, let us pause to reflect for a moment on certain evidences of liberal opinion among journalists in general and the media elite in particular that may lack the scientific character of the Lichter-Rothman studies but appeal mightily to ordinary common sense.

Consider, for example, the one-sentence news item that turned up in a paragraph of "Minor Memos" on page 1 of the *Wall Street Journal* for August 16, 1985: "Dotty Lynch, Gary Hart's pollster, will become political editor at CBS." Actually, the item does far less than justice to Ms. Lynch's dual careers as a media maven and a liberal apparatchik. In the early 1970s she was a researcher at NBC News. She left that post to work as a deputy pollster for George McGovern's 1972 presidential campaign. Then in 1973 she formed Lynch Associates, becoming in 1980 a pollster for Ted Kennedy's presidential bid. After that there were polling assignments for the Democratic National Committee, and in 1984 she signed on as chief pollster for Gary Hart's drive for the presidential nomination. When that failed, the Mondale-Ferraro campaign became one of her clients. In August 1985, Ms. Lynch, tiring perhaps of partisan politics (or then again perhaps not), was appointed political editor of CBS News.

Or how about this account of a game of musical chairs, which appeared on the page of Washington chitchat in the *New York Times* early in January 1986: "Brian Lunde, executive director of the Democratic National Committee since last February, plans to leave that job and enter private business, committee sources say. They say his replacement will probably be Wally Chalmers, a political researcher for CBS News until last fall and a former member of Senator Edward M. Kennedy's staff."

Not to be outdone, NBC announced in September 1986 that Timothy J. Russert, whom NBC News president Lawrence Grossman had hired in 1984 as his vice president for public affairs, would henceforth assume responsibility for "coordinating editorial content" of the *Today* show,

---

Foundation, a study of American journalists which, by using a nationwide sample and including small-town newspapers (but excluding network news programs), managed to come up with a profile of a "typical" journalist almost indistinguishable from the average American. Even this paragon was cautiously pulling in his ideological horns, however: In a similar 1971 study which the professors used as their baseline, almost 40 percent of those questioned had described themselves as "a little to the left of center" or "pretty far to the left," whereas in the Gannett study only 22 percent did so. Self-described "middle-of-the-roaders" had soared from 38.5 percent to 57.5 percent.

the *NBC Nightly News,* and *Meet the Press.* Before joining NBC, Russert had served as a top political adviser first to Senator Daniel Patrick Moynihan and then to Governor Mario Cuomo of New York.

In March 1987 the Media Research Center released a study identifying no less than "48 people with connections to liberal or Democratic groups" who had gone on to become TV network or major print media employees. By contrast, only fourteen individuals who could be identified as having conservative or Republican ties did so. Moreover: "While most of those associated with non-liberal political causes get public relations or commentary positions in politics and/or the media, a large number of those who worked for liberals, like NBC's Tim Russert, moved from political policy jobs to positions responsible for news content."

Herewith, as set forth in the issue of *Newswatch\** dated February 1987, are the political activities and subsequent major media assignments of some of the forty-eight individuals discussed in the MRC's report:

Sidney Blumenthal, a writer for the far-left *Progressive* and *The Nation* and the socialist weekly *In These Times,* became a political reporter for the *Washington Post* in 1986.

Ken Bode, who was an aide to Morris Udall in the latter's 1976 presidential campaign and then politics editor of *The New Republic* from 1975 to 1979, is chief political correspondent of NBC News.

David Burke, who served as chief of staff to Senator Ted Kennedy from 1965 to 1971 and as chief of staff to Governor Hugh Carey of New York from 1975 to 1987, became vice president of ABC News in 1977 and executive vice president in 1986.

Kathryn Bushkin, who was press secretary for Gary Hart's 1984 presidential campaign, signed on as director of editorial administration for *U.S. News and World Report* in 1985.

The aforementioned Wally Chalmers had been northeastern coordinator of Udall for President in 1976, and midwestern and southern coordinator of Kennedy for President in 1980, as well as executive director of the Nuclear Freeze Foundation and the Fund for a Democratic Majority and assistant secretary of health, education and welfare in the Carter administration, before serving as director of broadcast research for CBS News from 1984 to 1986—the position he left to become executive director and chief of staff of the Democratic National Committee.

---

\* For a description of the origin and activities of *Newswatch*, perhaps the liveliest conservative publication now regularly commenting on the lopsided liberalism of our major media, see page 178 et seq.

Richard Dougherty was press secretary for the 1972 McGovern presidential campaign before becoming NBC News manager in New York in 1973.

Mary Fifield was press secretary to Governor Michael Dukakis in 1974–75 and a press officer on the Carter campaign plane in 1976 before becoming an assistant producer of ABC's *20/20*, associate producer of CBS's *Nightwatch* (1984), and producer of CBS's *Face the Nation* (1985–86).

Leslie Gelb, who had served as deputy secretary of state for political affairs in the Carter administration, became national security correspondent for the *New York Times* thereafter—and deputy editor of its editorial page in 1986.

Jeff Gralnick, who was Senator George McGovern's press secretary in 1971, went on to become a vice president of ABC News and executive producer of *World News Tonight* from 1979 to 1983. He then became ABC's executive producer for political broadcasts from 1983 to 1985, and its executive producer for specials in the latter year.

Rex Granum, who had been deputy press secretary to Jimmy Carter, was named southern bureau chief of ABC News in Atlanta in 1986.

Seymour Hersh, who served as press secretary in Eugene McCarthy's 1968 presidential campaign, was of course a Washington correspondent for the *New York Times* from 1973 to 1979.

Deborah Johnson, one of the founders of the far-left publication *Mother Jones* in 1975, was serving as executive producer of *NBC News Overnight* in 1983, and had become executive producer of CBS's *Nightwatch* by 1986.

Stephen Kinzer worked for the gubernatorial campaign of Michael Dukakis in Massachusetts in 1974 before landing a job with the *New York Times* and becoming one of its Central American reporters in 1979—just in time to cover the Sandinista revolution.

Bill Moyers was press secretary to Lyndon Johnson, of course, before going on to glory as a CBS commentator and documentary reporter in the decade 1976–1986.

But how many viewers of the *Today* show are aware that Jane Pauley, its co-host since 1976, was an administrative assistant in the offices of the Democratic State Committee of Indiana back in 1972?

Jack Rosenthal was a spokesman for the Department of Justice in the Kennedy and Johnson administrations from 1961 to 1966, and executive assistant to Johnson's secretary of state, Dean Rusk, in 1966 and 1967. He then joined the Washington bureau of the *New York Times,* became deputy editor of the editorial page in 1977, and rose to be its editor in 1986.

Thomas Ross, an assistant secretary in the Carter Defense Department, became senior vice president of NBC News in 1986.

Getting tired? Bear with me. You wouldn't want to overlook Pierre Salinger, press secretary to John Kennedy and later United States senator from California (Democrat, naturally), who since 1983 has been the chief foreign correspondent of ABC News, based in Paris.

Or Maria Shriver, co-host of the *CBS Morning News* in 1985 and 1986 and more recently a reporter for NBC News, who worked for Ted Kennedy's presidential campaign back in 1980.

Or Amanda Spake, an editor of *Mother Jones* from 1977 to 1982, who is now a senior editor of the *Washington Post Magazine*.

Or Lesley Stahl, the CBS News correspondent of *Face the Nation* fame, who used to work for New York mayor John Lindsay.

Or . . . but surely you get the point. These are the credentials and backgrounds of just a few of the journalists who, on the TV networks and in the most influential print media, tell the American people the "news" about Vietnam and Watergate and Ronald Reagan and the Space Shield and the Iran/contra affair and the federal deficit, etc., etc.

Of course, there's an exception or two, just to prove the rule. The most notable is Diane Sawyer, who somehow managed to live down her service as a press assistant in the Nixon White House from 1970 to 1974 and go on to fame and fortune as co-host of the *CBS Morning News* and, more recently, as a correspondent for *60 Minutes*. Then there's Joanna Bistany, special assistant to President Reagan for communications from 1981 to 1983, who was director of news information for ABC from 1983 to 1985 and is now a vice president of ABC News.

But, looking over the Media Research Center's pathetic list of fourteen media-affiliated individuals with conservative or Republican connections, one notices an interesting thing. Unlike the liberals listed above, who almost invariably went *from* liberal political activities *to* the media, no less than seven of the fourteen (Richard Burt, Ed Dale, Sid Davis, Bernard Kalb, John Koehler, Peggy Noonan, and Burton Yale Pines) went *from* jobs in the media *to* positions in the Reagan administration (or, in the case of Pines, to the Heritage Foundation)—thus doing nothing whatever to damage the media's reputation as a fur-trimmed rest home for liberal activists.

That reputation has received some additional polishing even since the MRC published its survey. One month later, in its March issue,

*Newswatch* disclosed that Rich Inderfurth, who became deputy staff director of the (Democrat-controlled) Senate Foreign Relations Committee in 1979, left when Republicans took over the Senate in 1981 to become the Pentagon reporter for ABC News. (Since 1985 he has been its correspondent for national security affairs.)

And in May 1987, *Newswatch* reported that Jodie Allen, who served in the Carter administration as deputy assistant secretary of labor for policy evaluation and research, had just become an assistant editor of the *Washington Post*'s "Outlook" section.

Then, in its June 1987 issue, *Newswatch* outdid itself with a fascinating account of

how National Public Radio (NPR) serves as pit-stop for many reporters between liberal political jobs and positions with the TV networks and *The New York Times*. The trail of ties tracked down with the help of the Nexis news data retrieval system illustrates how blurred the line between personal, professional, and political relationships has become for many Big Media reporters.

*Newswatch* gave this illuminating account:

A June [1987] *Washington Journalism Review* profile of CBS Morning News economics reporter Robert Krulwich revealed he was a Washington reporter in the mid-70s for Pacifica Radio, an alternative network even the *Washington Post* describes as a "beacon for the Left." After a brief stop at *Rolling Stone* he moved to [National Public Radio] where "he was instrumental in hiring several of NPR's top reporters, including Cokie Roberts." Roberts . . . reported from Athens for CBS News in the early 70s and now covers the Congress for NPR and the MacNeil-Lehrer NewsHour. . . . Fellow Wellesley College alumna Linda Wertheimer covers the Senate for NPR. Her husband, Fred, is head of the left-wing lobbying group Common Cause. Roberts is married to Steven Roberts, White House reporter for *The New York Times*.

Krulwich is married to *New York Times* business section reporter Tamar Lewin. In 1977 *Congressional Quarterly* reported Lewin's registration as a lobbyist for Common Cause. According to a June/July [1987] *Mother Jones* magazine article by Laurence Zuckerman, Krulwich's boss at NPR, National Bureau Chief Bob Zelnick, hired David Ensor, Nina Totenberg and Judith Miller. Ensor moved to his current ABC News foreign correspondent position in 1980. Totenberg is still NPR's legal reporter. . . . Miller became a reporter for *The New York Times* and is now Deputy News Editor for the Washington Bureau. . . . Until she joined the *Times* in 1977 Miller was the Washington reporter for a far-left magazine, *The Progressive*.

Zelnick left NPR in 1977 to become Executive Editor of the David Frost interviews with former President Nixon. In 1978 he moved to ABC News, since serving as Deputy Washington Bureau Chief, Moscow correspondent and Tel Aviv reporter before his current Pentagon assignment. Zuckerman wrote that Zelnick started free-lancing for NPR's evening show All Things Considered in 1972 after "working as a congressional staffer on Capitol Hill." Asked about this, Zelnick told NEWSWATCH he spent four months doing "legislative research" on lake pollution for then U.S. Rep. Henry Reuss, a Wisconsin Democrat. The 1972 "Almanac of American Politics" described Reuss as "one of the most liberal members of the House." In another interesting development, *Time* magazine just hired [*Mother Jones*] contributor Zuckerman as a staff writer.

One is surely entitled to wonder just what sorts of theories about the significance of specific "news" events are now being foisted on ABC News, CBS News, the *New York Times*, the *MacNeil-Lehrer NewsHour*, and *Time* magazine, not to mention National Public Radio, by these industrious recruits from Pacifica Radio, *Mother Jones, The Progressive*, Common Cause, and the congressional staff of Henry Reuss. (And who, if anyone, is offering any balancing alternative theories?)

The truth is that many of the media's defenders have thrown in the sponge on the issue of the personal liberalism of the overwhelming majority of the media elite. They are falling back to a previously prepared position which they intend to defend tenaciously: Sure, journalists have their private opinions, just like anybody else; and okay, those opinions are—for whatever reason—much more liberal than those of the American people as a whole. But journalists can, and do, put aside their personal preferences when they report, edit, and present the news. As Edmund Diamond put it in the March 31, 1986 issue of *New York* magazine, "Nowhere do the bias-hunters demonstrate any link between what members of elites may think and what they report."

The first thing to be noted about this contention is that the media would be the swiftest to reject it if it were offered in defense of anyone but themselves. As Fred Barnes remarked in *The New Republic*:

In trying to scotch the idea of liberal bias in news coverage, defenders of the press rely on precisely the sort of argument they would reject if made by others. The argument, cited recently by both Al Hunt of *The Wall Street Journal* and columnist Joseph Kraft, goes like this: even if most journalists are liberal, their professionalism prevents this from influencing their stories. Now, what if a judicial nominee said he was a racist but that this wouldn't affect his view on civil rights cases? Or what if the chief of the Environmental Protection Agency declared that ownership of Union Carbide stock wouldn't influence his view of that firm's toxic waste practices? Or what if a White House official said his vacation at a company's resort wasn't a factor in pressing for tax relief aiding that company? Who'd buy such an argument? Not the press.

Nevertheless, the argument that the media do not permit their private political preferences to influence their professional behavior is, analytically, a different argument than the contention that they simply *have* no such private preferences (or at least none that distinguish them from the great majority of the American people), and it must be inspected and evaluated separately.

Let us therefore turn from demonstrating the overwhelming personal liberalism of the media elite to analyzing whether that liberalism influences their work-product: the "news." Precisely what metamorphosis do the Dotty Lynches of contemporary Washington undergo on the short trip from Senator Hart's headquarters to CBS? And just how did the versatile Wally Chalmers manage to shed his identity as a member of Ted Kennedy's staff and purify his soul for service at CBS News, then smoothly resume his role as a Democratic apparatchik, fit to become executive director of the Democratic National Committee? Or do such people in fact simply remain, and behave as, liberal Democrats while working for CBS?

# CHAPTER 4

# *The Effect on the "News"*

PROVING STATISTICALLY THAT the media's demonstrated liberalism influences their handling of the news is no simple matter. The media clearly aren't going to do us the favor of admitting it, and the formidable human capacity for self-delusion makes it likely that many members of the media don't even realize it, at least not fully. A good many of them undoubtedly think their selection and treatment of stories is governed solely by their acute "news sense," where any objective observer would detect bias. And even when a member of the media knows full well that his handling of news stories is influenced by his biases, he is naturally prone to minimize that influence and make excuses for the residue.

Adding to the difficulty is the fact that evidence of bias, liberal or otherwise, is almost inevitably somewhat subjective. One man's "bias" is another man's "robust journalism," etc. Obvious as the bias may be to many thoughtful people, how can one nail it down?

One of the earliest and still one of the best efforts to do so was made by Edith Efron in her book *The News Twisters* (Nash, 1971). It is said that medieval philosophers had a high old time arguing over how many teeth a horse has, until some spoilsport ended the game by going out and actually counting them. That was essentially Efron's solution, too. As she explained it herself:

> 1. I chose to restrict myself to the prime-time nationwide news broadcasts of ABC, CBS and NBC—those which are aired between 7:00 and 7:30 P.M.—because they are known to be the major source of political information for the whole country.
> 2. I selected a set of controversial issues, on which there was strong opposing positions taken by the Republican-conservative-right axis and by the Democratic-liberal-left axis.

Specifically, I selected the three Presidential races of 1968, and a set of 10 related issues: The U.S. policy on the Vietnam War; the U.S. policy on the bombing halt; the Viet Cong; black militants; the white middle class; liberals; conservatives; the left; demonstrators; and violent radicals.

3. I chose the period of time during which these issues were being covered by network news—a period during which the networks were expected to be "fair." The exact time span of the study was determined by the nature and duration of the principal controversy itself.

Specifically: it was the critical latter two-thirds of the 90-day-long Presidential campaign period—the seven-week period starting on September 16, when the three Presidential campaigns moved into high gear, and ending on November 4, the night before the election. The electoral period provided its own cut-off date.

4. Between these polar dates, I tape-recorded the prime-time shows of each network, and had the resultant newscasts transcribed. All material was recorded, with certain exceptions noted and explained in Appendix C.

5. From the resultant body of about 100,000 words per network, I isolated all stories dealing with the chosen issues—and excerpted all "for" and "against" opinion on these issues.

The task is simpler than it may sound. Network news is an extremely nonintellectual commodity, and the opinion which it relays tends to be simple, short, highly partisan, and crudely "for" and "against." It is readily isolated.

It comes, invariably, from four sources: Presidential and Vice Presidential *candidates; politicians;* members of the *public;* and from the *reporters* themselves. In stories on the Vietnam war, there is also opinion from *foreign sources.*

The opinion appears in four clearly identifiable forms: *direct quotes,* in which an individual states his own opinion; *paraphrase,* in which a reporter condenses an individual's opinion; *narrative reports,* in which a reporter summarizes the position of a group of people; and *editorial opinion,* which appears either in separate commentaries and analyses, or within the body of a news story.

6. When all such opinion was isolated, and filed, I then counted the number of words of opinion "for" and "against," on each issue.

7. Finally, I totalled the number of words spoken on both sides of each issue.

This, in brief, was the method. It was simply calculated to reveal the pattern of opinion-selectivity by network reporters.

Efron then sets forth, in bar-graph form, the total number of words spoken for and against the three presidential candidates on the three major networks during the period under study. In the case of George Wallace, the result was as follows:

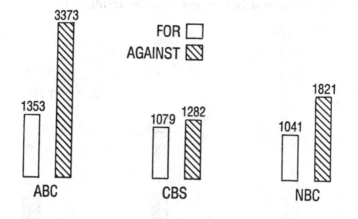

In the case of Hubert Humphrey, the graph looked like this:

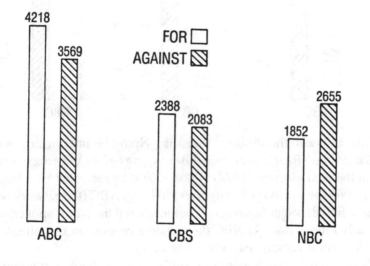

In the case of Richard Nixon, this was the result:

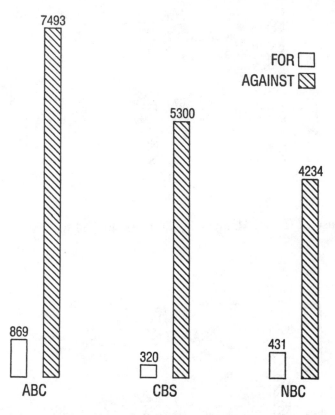

Now, how can the statistics regarding Nixon be interpreted, save as a product of bias? Bear in mind that this was long before Watergate—indeed, that in the next election (1972) Nixon would be reelected by a landslide. Yet in 1968 the words spoken *against* Nixon on ABC (the network with the smallest imbalance in this respect) outnumbered the words spoken *for* him by nearly nine to one. At NBC the negative proportion was almost ten to one. At CBS it actually exceeded sixteen to one.

There is much, much more to Efron's excellent book, but nothing in it contravenes the above analysis, or explains it on any basis save the long-recognized and inveterate hostility of most members of the media to Richard Nixon.

To be sure, it can be argued that the media's notorious dislike of Nixon is in some measure personal as well as ideological. Nixon, after all, has never been as explicit a conservative on most issues as either Barry Goldwater or Ronald Reagan (although he was always perceived as to the right of the Democrats he ran against). But that line of argument would not, even at best, exculpate the media from the charge of bias against Nixon; it would merely advance another reason for it. Moreover, there is subsequent and impressive evidence of comparable media bias against Ronald Reagan, who is not widely disliked in personal terms by the media, and as to whose conservatism there can be no doubt whatever.

Maura Clancey and Michael Robinson conducted another comprehensive study of the media's bias in reporting the "news," in connection with the 1984 presidential election, under the auspices of George Washington University and the American Enterprise Institute. In a subsequent report, they described their methodology as follows:

> Starting on Labor Day and continuing through election day, a team of five sifted through tapes from all three network evening news programs, distilling from about 200 broadcasts all the news about President Reagan or his White House; about the presidential or vice-presidential race; about lower level elections or state and local referendums. All told, we analyzed 790 stories, but for this report we concentrated on the 625 news items that dealt specifically with the presidential or vice-presidential campaign.
>
> Every piece was scored on two dozen separate dimensions, some as straightforward as length or date of the story, some as slippery as press "spin" or ideological tilt. There is no magic to what we did—our training was collective, we used specific rules, and we reached consensus on almost every decision, despite the very different political views of our group. . . .
>
> . . . Spin involves *tone*, the part of the reporting that extends *beyond* hard news. On October 12, for example, Ronald Reagan's train trip through western Ohio was hard news. But when Dan Rather chose to label the ride "a photo-opportunity train trip, chock full of symbolism and trading on Harry Truman's old turf," Rather added "spin."
>
> Throughout, we scored every story for its spin—the positive or negative implications about the candidates contained within the reporter's own words. And we used "spin" as our first and most important test of good and bad press.
>
> There are two important things to remember about the spin measure: First, when the reporter's subjective comments about objective facts went in both directions (positive *and* negative), we almost always judged the piece "ambiguous." Second, we *excluded* from our spin variable all references to the horse race, defining the spin as interpretations of the candidate's quality, *not his electability*.

Clancey and Robinson summed up their findings as follows:

> There may be some questions about the validity of our measure, but there can be no question about the lopsidedness of what it uncovered.

Assuming that a piece with a positive spin equals "good press," and assuming that negative spin equals "bad press," Ronald Reagan and George Bush proved overwhelmingly to be the "bad press" ticket of 1984. Figure 1 contains the number of news seconds we scored as good press or bad press for each of the candidates. Ronald Reagan's bad press total was *ten times greater* than his good press total. (7,230 seconds vs. 730). In other words, his "spin ratio" was ten-to-one negative.

Figure 1

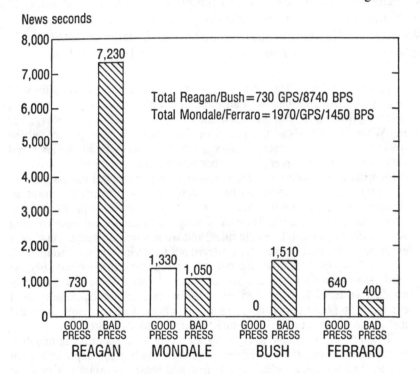

George Bush had a spin ratio that defied computation—1,500 seconds of "bad press" pieces and zero seconds of good press.

Walter Mondale and Geraldine Ferraro, on the other hand, had slightly *positive* spin ratios—1,970 seconds of good press about themselves as people or potential leaders, and 1,450 seconds of bad press. Given what we know about the bad news bias of television, the fact that anyone, let alone any ticket, got more positive spin than negative is news indeed.

This Clancey-Robinson study is all the more remarkable because the authors have over the years taken considerably more pains than Lichter and Rothman to stay on the good side of the media (or, if you prefer, have found more to be said on its behalf). For example, in a report on the 1980 campaign published by the Russell Sage Foundation and entitled *Over the Wire and on TV: CBS and UPI in Campaign '80*, Clancey and Robinson concluded:

> . . . The networks covered "the issues" objectively and actually treated liberals worse than conservatives. The networks covered liberal darling Teddy Kennedy more harshly than middle-of-the-roader Jimmy Carter during the early stages of that race, and then turned right around and treated Carter more negatively than Ronald Reagan during the rest of the campaign. In the end, the Carter-Reagan election news coverage was a mystery to those conservative press critics determined to unearth a "liberal" media.

In fact it was no "mystery." The trouble with assessing liberal bias in the 1980 campaign is that liberals were themselves sharply divided—not over the merits of Reagan, but over those of Carter. Carter had been, with the almost irrelevant exception of George Wallace, *relatively* the most conservative candidate for the Democratic nomination in 1976: a southerner, a born-again Christian, a "good ol' boy," an avowed outsider in terms of the Washington establishment. And while he certainly offended conservatives by his performance in office, his standing among liberals was scarcely any better by 1980. A significant number of them bolted the Democratic party altogether that year and cast their protest vote for the liberal-Republican independent candidate, John Anderson. Of those who remained (if the battle lines at the Democratic convention in New York that year are indicative), at least a third would have preferred to repudiate the incumbent and nominate Ted Kennedy. To speculate where the "average" liberal journalist came down in that tangle, or to demonstrate his liberal bias by his behavior that year, is understandably difficult— although the *Business Forum* survey described above (see pages 55–56) suggests that, among 162 print journalists around the country, 51 percent voted for Carter, 24 percent for Anderson, and only 25 percent for Reagan.

But Clancey and Robinson are not even prepared to concede that their own lopsided results in 1984 conclusively demonstrated a liberal bias on the part of the media. On the contrary, they suggest, "liberal bias is not the only explanation, or even the best."

Instead, they posit the existence of what they call "the four I's"— nonideological reasons for the bad press admittedly accorded Reagan and Bush in 1984. These are:

> "Impishness"—a human tendency to want to turn a walkaway into a horse race "to keep one's own work interesting."

"Irritation"—annoyance at what the media perceived as Reagan's glib one-liners and his alleged "Teflon coating" (i.e., his seeming invulnerability to criticism).

"Incumbency"—a sense that the media have "a special mission to warn Americans about the advantages any incumbent has," especially when he is winning big.

"Irrevocability"—the feeling that a double standard is justified because 1984 was the last time Reagan would ever face the electorate. Under those circumstances, giving him a bad press became "a near-messianic mission."

Defenders of the media may well wonder whether pleading them guilty to the above unpleasant set of impulses would actually constitute much of an improvement over admitting that they have a liberal bias. But they can be spared that painful decision, because "the four I's" simply don't survive careful inspection. In pure theory they might explain the media's astonishing bias against Reagan in 1984, but not one of them applies to the equally well-established instance of bias discussed earlier: the media's treatment of Nixon in the 1968 campaign.

That campaign was no "walkaway" for Nixon; it was one of the closest presidential elections in United States history—43.4 percent for Nixon, 42.7 for Humphrey, and 13.5 for Wallace. And Nixon was certainly no Reagan, either in his mastery of glib one-liners or in possessing a "Teflon coating." Moreover, he was not the incumbent, or even the nominee of the incumbent's party. And 1968 was *not* the last time Nixon could or would face the electorate. Yet the media gave him the same biased treatment that Reagan received in 1984. The conclusion is unavoidable that the media's conduct had the same basis in both cases: a liberal bias neatly congruent with the demonstrated liberal preferences of the overwhelming majority of the media elite.

The Efron study of bias in the TV news coverage of the 1968 campaign and the Clancey-Robinson analysis of the same media's performance in the 1984 campaign are the two most comprehensive surveys available on the subject, but they are not the only statistical demonstrations of a liberal bias on the part of the media.

In the *Wall Street Journal* for March 6, 1984, Holmes M. Brown, president of the Institute for Applied Economics, reported the results of a survey conducted by the IAE during the last six months of 1983. Once again the targets of the study were "the nightly news programs of the three major television networks."

The particular significance of the last half of 1983 lay in the fact that the economic news was good during those six months: The country was unmistakably emerging from the recession that had darkened 1982 and the early months of 1983, and Ronald Reagan was, quite naturally, the political beneficiary of the change. Yet here is how Brown summed up the findings of the survey:

During the entire period of the study, there were four to 15 economic-statistics stories a month. Nearly 95% of these statistical reports were positive. However, of the 104 economic stories of an in-depth or interpretive nature that were aired during this period on the three network evening news shows, 89—or 86%—were primarily negative.

The economic news was good in the second half of 1983. The coverage on network television was still in recession.

The technique, as Brown explained it, was simple:

. . . The transposition was done by concentrating on the pockets of recession within the overall recovery, thereby implying that behind the good news of falling inflation and rising employment there were black clouds of economic misery.

And he proceeded to cite examples of such distortion, drawn from all three networks:

In November, unemployment dropped sharply to 8.4% from 8.7% a month earlier, the lowest level in two years. In just two months, the total of unemployed Americans dropped well over a million.

ABC used the Dec. 2 unemployment announcement to focus on those left behind by the recovery. Although the November unemployment figures in 45 of the 50 states were down, ABC did a story that began, "Now those unemployment figures again; it's here in the Midwest that unemployment is most severe." They located two upper-middle-class men who had been unemployed for 1½ years and focused on their experiences, with a story that lasted more than four minutes. A story that began with a 0.3-percentage-point drop in unemployment ended in complete despair and talk of suicide.

Another major positive statistic during the time of the study was the increase in the gross national product. In the third quarter, it grew at a robust 7.7% inflation-adjusted annual pace, surprising even the most optimistic economists.

NBC reporter Irving R. Levine, on Oct. 22, when the GNP boost was announced, delivered one of the most negative stories of the survey. The report focused on "pockets of poverty where recovery is still just a dream," undercutting President Reagan's economic policies and their relationship to the recovery. Mr. Reagan was shown saying "virtually every sector of the economy . . . is expanding, creating new hope in a more secure future." Mr. Levine focused on the limited areas where things were getting worse, stating that "beyond small programs to retrain workers, the administration is closing its eyes to regions bogged down in recession and sees no need to alter its economic policy . . ."

Inflation continued to abate during the year. The producer price index grew by only 0.6% in 1983, the smallest increase in 20 years.

In July, the inflation rate for the first half of 1983 was announced at only 2.9%, a sharp decline from 3.9% a year before. CBS followed this news with a story featuring economist Pierre Rinfret, who said: "We kept the country in recession for three years, we've created unemployment as high as 13 million people, we idled most of the factories in this country, and put most of industry flat on its back. If you can't beat inflation with that, you can't do anything."

Such examples, however, though impressive, are not as important as the statistical totals. To repeat: Nearly 95 percent of the reported changes in United States economic statistics during those six months were positive (i.e., favorable); yet out of the 104 stories about them aired on the three networks' evening news programs, 86 percent were "primarily negative."

Once again: What is the explanation? Here we have people who have supported every Democratic presidential candidate since 1964 by margins of 80 percent or better, and who identify *themselves* as politically liberal by massive margins in poll after poll. Is it any wonder that they denied or minimized the economic upsurge in the latter half of 1983 to the best of their formidable ability? Bear in mind the very large component of wishful thinking that it is almost impossible to separate from economic analyses. These liberal journalists were not consciously deceiving their audiences. If they could have brought themselves to admit any bias whatever, they would undoubtedly have said they were simply warding off unjustified public optimism based on a few deceptive statistics, in the sure knowledge that "Reaganomics" would soon revert to form.

A somewhat narrower but still highly significant study was conducted by the Media Institute, of Washington, D.C., during March, April, and May 1985. The institute decided to focus on coverage, by the nightly newscasts of the three television networks, of two key areas in the great budget debate of that year: the Social Security cost-of-living allowance (or COLA), and defense spending. How were these issues treated?

Patrick Maines, president of the Media Institute, described the methodology of the survey as follows:

Using a research technique known as content analysis, researchers analyzed all stories mentioning proposed COLA and defense cuts. The database comprised 56 stories.

Researchers analyzed the coverage to determine its comprehensiveness and balance. A story was considered adequately comprehensive if it reported the provisions of the proposal at hand, mentioned at least one effect the proposal might have, and explained any specialized terms. Balance was determined by measuring the amount of coverage given opposing viewpoints.

Note that the Media Institute concerned itself with *comprehensiveness* as well as with the subject of our chief concern, *balance*. As it turned out, the networks received poor marks in both categories. To quote the Media Institute's report:

Several key findings emerged regarding network coverage of Social Security COLAs and defense spending:
• Over half of all network stories were not adequately comprehensive: 56.4 percent of Social Security and 65.2 percent of defense stories failed to meet even minimal criteria.
• Network coverage was overwhelmingly opposed to freezing the Social Security COLA: 66.9 percent of issues coverage opposed a COLA freeze, 23.9 percent favored a freeze, and 9.2 percent was neutral.
• Network coverage was overwhelmingly opposed to increases in defense spending: 65.5 percent of the issues coverage opposed increased spending, 31.1 percent favored increases, and 3.4 percent was neutral.

In summary, the networks offered comprehensive coverage of the COLA and defense-spending debates less than half of the time. In addition, coverage was clearly imbalanced: It opposed freezing COLAs and it opposed increased defense spending, in both cases by margins of two to one.

The results of another statistical analysis of media bias on a specific issue were announced in the spring of 1986 by the (nonprofit) Center for Media and Public Affairs, in Washington. The authors were Robert Lichter and Robert Rycroft of George Washington University, Stanley Rothman of Smith College, and Linda Lichter of the Center. (Professors Lichter and Rothman, it will be recalled, were the authors of the study of the media elite summarized on pages 48–51.)

The authors reported that there is "a gap between what the experts think about nuclear power and what the media report." They first selected at random, from *Who's Who,* the names of 679 energy scientists and engineers, and polled these individuals on their attitudes toward nuclear safety issues. Then they analyzed news coverage of those same issues, for the entire period from 1970 to 1983, on the three commercial TV networks, in the three major newsmagazines, and in the *New York Times*.

On the basis of media reports, it comes as a surprise to learn that five sixths of these energy experts rated the safety risks that presently exist in United States nuclear power reactors as "acceptable." Moreover, three out of four favored "rapid nuclear development" and would themselves be perfectly willing to live near a nuclear reactor. Finally, two out of three were "very confident" that they already knew how to solve nuclear safety problems.

Far different is the story we have been getting from our media. According to the aforementioned study, antinuclear stories have outnumbered pronuclear stories two to one in both television and newsmagazines. And a full 60 percent of all media judgments on specific nuclear safety issues have been negative.

The media achieved this impressive slant by picking very carefully the authorities they chose to cite. "Experts" critical of nuclear power outnumbered its supporters by more than two to one in newsmagazines and by a positively awesome *five* to one on the television networks.

The ancient journalistic precept that "good news is no news" may conceivably have something to do with these figures. The media would obviously adore a total meltdown, purely for its theatrical value, but alas there has never been one. (Even the ham-handed Russians, in botching Chernobyl, apparently avoided that.) But the media must be aware that, after forty years, there has yet to be in this country so much as a single radiation-related death at a commercial nuclear power plant. It is little short of appalling to reflect that American public policy on nuclear power issues must be shaped on the basis of "news" reportage so starved for sensationalism that this simple truth is not merely skewed but hustled completely out of sight in favor of alarmist reportage.

As a matter of fact, the study described above found that, of all the media investigated, only *U.S. News and World Report*'s coverage was, even by a narrow margin, pro-nuclear. As for ABC, NBC, CBS, *Time*, and *Newsweek*, their news coverage "was tilted in the anti-nuclear direction by wide margins."

Curiously enough, the environmental lobby spent the 1960s bashing utilities that burned the so-called fossil fuels (i.e., coal and oil) for polluting the atmosphere, and touting nuclear power in their legal briefs as an alternative that was both clean and safe. Then in the 1970s the "activists" suavely reversed themselves and went after nuclear power. Our liberal media, always ready for a lynching bee at the expense of American business, needed no encouragement to fall in line, and the war on nuclear power has been under way ever since. The chief casualty, as the above study demonstrates, has been the truth.

Finally, technology is beginning to make possible certain statistical analyses of media bias that would have been simply impracticable a few years ago. For example, Senator Jesse Helms is widely and rightly known as an outspoken conservative—as dependably and loudly conservative as Senator Ted Kennedy is dependably and loudly liberal. In 1984, Helms's ACU* rating (a conservative rating of votes on key issues) was 100; Kennedy's was 0. Helms's COPE† rating (reflecting Big Labor's estimate of his performance) was 8; Kennedy's was 94. To make sure that its readers were warned of Senator Helms's rightward tilt and would be able to discount for it, the *New York Times,* during the years 1984 and 1985, preceded his name *in 21 percent of all news stories* (i.e., excluding opinion pieces and editorials) with some such cautionary phrase as "right-wing," "far-right," "archconservative," or "ultraconservative." On the other hand, however, the *Times* affixed a comparable qualifying phrase to Senator Kennedy's name (signaling his rigorously liberal slant) in only 2.3 percent of similar cases.

These striking figures are available thanks to the wonders of computer science. That ingenious conservative monitor of the liberal media, *Newswatch,* hit on the idea of asking Nexis, a computerized print-media data-retrieval system, to come up with every story in the *Times* during 1984 and 1985 that mentioned either Senator Helms or Senator Kennedy. Setting aside opinion pieces and editorials, *Newswatch* then simply counted every labeling phrase that the *Times* gratuitously applied to either man.

And the *Times, Newswatch* discovered, was not by any means the only or even the worst offender in this matter. The *Washington Post* found it necessary to tag Senator Helms 22 percent of the time—but Senator Kennedy only 4.1 percent. In the case of newsmagazines, the makeup was applied with an even heavier hand: Helms was labeled 44 percent of the time in *Newsweek* and 47 percent in *Time;* Kennedy received comparable treatment only 5.6 percent and 3.5 percent of the time, respectively. Would anyone seriously contend that there is anything fair, or objective, or balanced about that performance?

---

* American Conservative Union
† Committee on Political Education

Having pretty well given up on the issue of the personal liberalism of the media elite, the media's defenders have been understandably reluctant to abandon as well their fallback contention that this does not affect their treatment of the news. But as the studies we have just discussed rolled off the presses, they have consoled themselves with certain evidence suggesting that the media are, nevertheless, well regarded or even trusted by many or most Americans. This is technically irrelevant to the question of whether bias actually exists; but, assuming it does, it is understandably comforting to the media to reflect that a large segment of the public is unaware of this, or (better yet) thinks well of the media in spite of it.

That was one conclusion of the Times Mirror study, which we have already discussed in connection with the personal political views of newspaper journalists. *Los Angeles Times* staff writer David Shaw made the point in the very first sentence of his report on the Times Mirror survey:

> American newspaper reporters and editors are substantially more liberal than the general public on a wide range of social and political issues, but readers seem largely convinced that the press does not permit this liberalism to unfairly influence its news coverage, a nationwide Los Angeles Times poll conducted over the last five months shows.

Gallup's own summary of the survey put it this way: "If credibility is defined as believability, then credibility is, in fact, one of the media's strongest suits."

Under a three-column headline, PEOPLE DO UNDERSTAND THE MEDIA (subhead: AND THEY DON'T HATE THE PRESS AS MUCH AS WAS FEARED), James R. Dickenson, a political reporter for the *Washington Post,* discussed the glad tidings in a column, or think piece, in that newspaper on February 9, 1986:

> We in the press have been sensitized for years now to the fact that many conservatives believe that there is a liberal bias in the media. We understand that while few really think that many of us actually are subversives, they do harbor deep suspicions that—at the least—we have more than our share of irresponsible opportunists who are a burden to democracy and weaken the national security. . . .
>
> Whatever the reason, we tend to worry about the First Amendment and maybe feel just a little bit sorry for ourselves. A new and provocative study of public attitudes toward the media by the Times Mirror Co. suggests, however, that our biggest mistake may be our misunderstanding of what the American people think of us. . . .

> For all the criticism and lack of talk about us, people like us to a remarkable degree.
>
> About 70 percent are generally favorably disposed toward the media. Only about 15 percent find little or nothing good about us. Ten percent of these feel alienated from every major institution and the other five are our informed, vociferous, predominantly conservative and Republican critics—who question our morality, patriotism, competence, honesty and independence.
>
> But most people like us because, for all the criticism, they think we're competent and believable—and they like the news. They like being informed.

In point of fact, the actual figures in the Times Mirror study are highly ambiguous on the subject of the public's opinion of the media. While most of the major media were given high ratings for "believability" (85 to 87 percent), and individual TV anchormen did even better (with ABC's Peter Jennings leading the pack with a rating of 90), only 55 percent of those surveyed were willing to agree that the press "generally [gets] its facts straight"; 34 percent, or over a third, disagreed. Just how do individuals or institutions whose *accuracy* is that suspect manage to score so impressively when it comes to "believability"?

A sharp criticism of the methodology of the Times Mirror poll was leveled by Accuracy in Media, a conservative organization that monitors the media, specializing in exposing liberal and leftist biases. An *AIM Report* in March 1986 took strong issue with the way in which Gallup (which conducted the poll for Times Mirror) evaluated the responses:

> . . . One question was designed to find out how the respondents rated various journalists, news programs and publications in terms of credibility. Here is how the question was put to the respondents:
>
> "I am going to read another list. This time please rate how much you think you can believe each organization I name on a scale of 4 to 1. On this 4-point scale, 4 means you can believe all or most of what they say, and 1 means you can believe almost nothing of what they say. How would you rate the believability of——on this scale of 4 to 1?"
>
> The respondents were asked first to rate a number of news organizations—TV network news departments, local TV news, Cable News Network, radio news, nationally influential newspapers, local newspapers, the Associated Press, and several magazines. They were also asked to use this same 4 to 1 scale to rate a number of prominent journalists, mainly those who appear on television.
>
> When the results were tabulated it was found that on the average, 33 percent of the respondents rated the major news sources at 4, and 36

percent rated the major TV journalists at 4. In other words, about a third of those questioned said that they believed all or most of what these news dispensers told them. This was fairly close to the findings of a poll published in April 1985 by the American Society of Newspaper Editors [ASNE], which found newspaper credibility was rated high by 32 percent and television credibility rated high by 30 percent of those polled. This poll was widely viewed as revealing a serious credibility problem for the media.

The Gallup survey commissioned by the Times Mirror Co. magically caused this problem to vanish by a very simple trick. Nearly half of the respondents in its poll had rated the media organizations and the TV personalities at 3. Unfortunately, no one had told the respondents what 3 meant. Since 4 had been defined as meaning that you could believe all or *most* of what the journalists said, 3 had to mean that you could believe much of what they said, but not *most*.

Gallup's neat trick was to pin the label of "believable" on category 3 in writing up the findings of the survey. Category 4, labeled "highly believable," was then lumped together with 3 to produce highly gratifying believability ratings for all major sources of news and leading news personalities. The ASNE had concluded that "three-fourths of all adults have some problem with the credibility of the media."

An information source that can't be trusted most of the time certainly does not deserve to be labeled "believable." The failure to define 3 for the respondents when the question was asked was a serious error. Arbitrarily labeling 3 as "believable" is deceitful and misleading. The media were so eager to proclaim the death of the credibility crisis that they failed to tell their readers and viewers about this deception in reporting the results of the Gallup survey.

Since the published findings don't disclose how many respondents said they rated the media at 1, meaning they believed almost nothing of what they say, all we know from the Gallup survey is how many respondents believe all or most of what the media say and how many do not. This would have been a more accurate way of presenting the findings. Viewed this way, here is what Gallup found.

Can You Believe All or Most of What They Say?

| | | | *Percentages* | |
|---|---|---|---|---|
| ELECTRONIC | YES | NO | PRINT | YES |
| MacNeil-Lehrer (PBS) | 43 | 57 | Wall Street Journal | 45 |
| Cable News Network | 38 | 62 | Reader's Digest | 40 |
| Local TV News | 36 | 64 | Time | 35 |
| ABC News | 34 | 66 | Newsweek | 31 |
| CBS News | 34 | 66 | Local Daily Newspaper | 29 |
| NBC News | 32 | 68 | Associated Press | 28 |
| Radio News | 30 | 70 | Nationally Influential Papers | 25 |
| All Things Considered (NPR) | 25 | 75 | USA Today | 25 |

| PERSONALITIES | YES | NO |  | YES | NO |
|---|---|---|---|---|---|
| Walter Cronkite | 57 | 43 | Geraldo Rivera | 31 | 69 |
| Dan Rather | 44 | 56 | Sam Donaldson | 30 | 70 |
| Ted Koppel | 41 | 59 | Barbara Walters | 30 | 70 |
| Peter Jennings | 40 | 60 | Bill Moyers | 28 | 72 |
| John Chancellor | 39 | 61 | Diane Sawyer | 28 | 72 |
| David Brinkley | 38 | 62 | George Will | 26 | 74 |
| Tom Brokaw | 37 | 63 | Phil Donahue | 23 | 77 |
| Mike Wallace | 35 | 65 | Jack Anderson | 17 | 83 |

It may also be wondered just how Gallup's study for the Times Mirror squares with the many polls taken, by Gallup itself and others across the years, which suggest that the American people have, in fact, a much lower opinion of the media. In 1982, for example, the National Opinion Research Center at the University of Chicago asked 1,506 people to rate eleven major American institutions in terms of the confidence they had in them, and the press came in eighth—behind medicine, science, education, organized religion, the military, the Supreme Court, and major companies. Television ranked even lower: tenth—below the federal executive branch and just above Congress.

A much more recent poll by Gallup, also commissioned by the Times Mirror Company and conducted in late December 1986 and early January 1987 (i.e., after the outbreak of the Iran/contra controversy), modified somewhat the conclusions of the first. According to the report in the *New York Times* for January 16:

> The telephone poll of 1,502 adults . . . found that believability of news organizations had declined from June 1985 levels. Respondents were asked to rank believability on a scale in which 4 indicated total or near total belief and 1 indicated total or near total disbelief.
> Sixty-six percent of those polled gave network television a positive believability rating, meaning a 4 or a 3 on that scale, as against 83 percent in the 1985 poll. The believability rating of local newspapers was 63 percent, as against 80 percent in 1985. . . .
> The personal credibility of the three television network anchors had also declined, the poll showed. Dan Rather, the CBS anchor, dropped to a believability rating of 69 percent from 81 percent in 1985. NBC's Tom Brokaw had a rating of 66 percent, as against 69 percent in 1985, and Peter Jennings' rating on ABC was also 66 percent, against 74 percent in 1985.

But these still essentially high figures were sharply challenged by others reported in the November/December 1986 issue of *Public Opinion* by Michael Robinson, academic director of the Times Mirror's "People and the Press" surveys. According to Robinson, a new survey had studied media believability as rated by three different age categories of the American national population: "Seniors" (age 50 and over), "the Woodstein generation" (from 30 to 49—the reference, of course, being to the presumed impact of the Woodward-Bernstein Watergate disclosures on this age group), and "the Post-Woodstein generation" (18 to 29 years old). The average rating of media believability was highest in the Post-Woodstein generation: 32 percent. For the Woodstein generation, media believability averaged a mere 27 percent. For Seniors, it was 28 percent. Scarcely, then, what one would call a rousing vote of confidence.

In the last analysis, however, the opinions of the public concerning such matters as the "fairness," "believability," and "accuracy" of the media are hardly very useful as evidence of the actual facts. We have Abraham Lincoln's word for it, after all, that you can fool all of the people some of the time and some of the people all of the time. Fortunately, as he went on to say, you can't fool all of the people all of the time. And in recent years, as described above, depth surveys of the personal opinions of American journalists and careful quantitative analyses of their work-product have established beyond serious dispute what common sense has told objective observers for decades: that the members of the media elite are, in personal terms, vastly more liberal, politically, than the American people as a whole; *and* that they very frequently permit their personal views to bias and distort the "news" they produce.

Exactly how is this bias and distortion accomplished? In Chapter 1 we cited various examples of bias. But such examples are only marginally useful, because any individual story can always be defended as justified by its allegedly special circumstances, or at worst dismissed as an unfortunate exception to the general rule. But there is no great mystery about the *technique,* and I will indulge in the luxury of having it described for you, not by conservative critics of the media's general liberal slant, but by liberals who rashly give the game away in their zeal to accuse conservatives of playing it.

Here is Alex Jones of the *New York Times,* describing how a *conservative* bias is allegedly smuggled into the *Washington Times,* the daily newspaper owned by Rev. Sun Myung Moon and currently edited by Arnaud de Borchgrave, formerly chief correspondent of *Newsweek:*

> In the view of many journalism critics, the paper's conservatism tends to show not so much in how articles are written but in what news is selected for publication and how prominently some articles are displayed. Articles

regarding Soviet influence and intelligence-gathering efforts, for instance, are usually prominently displayed, as are articles involving Nicaragua and Cuba.

Selectivity, moreover, can apply as much to what is said *in* an article as to the choice of which articles to run and where to run them. This was made clear by Timothy Garton Ash of *The Spectator* and *The Times* of London, reviewing Shirley Christian's *Nicaragua: Revolution in the Family* in the *New York Times Book Review* of July 28, 1985. Ms. Christian, herself a *Times* reporter, bucks the tide by nevertheless being personally unappreciative of the Sandinistas, and according to Mr. Ash her bias shows in her book:

> What she does as we go along is to put across her own views implicitly by her selection of facts and sources and descriptive touches, such as "The Sandinistas' Internal Front . . . busied themselves with new plans *from their comfortable spots in the suburban hills*" [my emphasis]. This is of course the delicate (or sly) way most professional reporters get across their own views in news stories.

"Of course." As we noted earlier, there is often no way a reporter, no matter how unbiased, can avoid choosing a particular story to cover and developing a particular theory of that story—a theory he then develops and presents through the selection of certain facts and the omission of others. The process is so inevitable that many journalists, in following it, are no doubt blissfully unaware that they are permitting their personal political biases to distort, beyond necessity or excuse, their selection and presentation of the "news."

In many cases, however, it is difficult to believe that the slanting is unconscious. Of the myriad examples that could be cited, I shall offer only one: a documentary entitled "Who's Running This War?", which was broadcast on the PBS television network's weekly series *Frontline* in March 1986. Its numerous distortions were specified in painstaking detail by television critic John Corry in the *New York Times* for March 18:

> Credit "Frontline," public television's weekly documentary series, with staying on top of the news. "Who's Running This War?" looks at the Nicaraguan rebels, the contras. Tomorrow the House of Representatives debates whether to give the contras $100 million in aid, and on Thursday it is scheduled to vote on the issue. Representatives swayed by "Frontline" are likely to vote no. "Frontline," on Channel 13 at 10 o'clock tonight, knows which side it favors.

The one-hour program looks specifically at the Nicaraguan Democratic Front, the largest rebel group fighting the Sandinistas. "Frontline" finds it to be an ineffectual fighting force, with "a notoriously bad record on human rights." Its leaders all seem to be former followers of the dictator Anastasio Somoza Debayle, and any legitimacy, or moral purpose, is not apparent. Meanwhile, its United States supporters, some of whom may act illegally, are all rich right wingers.

What's wrong with these findings is that there is nothing wholly right with them. The context is askew. The producer, Martin Smith, has taken a political position, and then selected facts to uphold the position. Journalism is supposed to work the other way around.

Consider, for example, the charge, or insinuation, that the leaders of the Nicaraguan Democratic Front are all former Somocistas. The State Department, trying to rebut charges like that, said last month that only 27 percent of the 153 "most senior military leaders" of the front were once members of Mr. Somoza's National Guard, while 20 percent were former members of Sandinista security forces; 53 percent, it said, were civilians with no military background at all.

The State Department figures may be questioned. In citing so many "senior military leaders," the State Department seemed to be reaching down to sergeant and corporal. On the other hand, "Frontline" recognizes no front leader who was not a Somocista. It is walking a very thin line.

Thus it presents Col. Enrique Bermudez and Adolfo Calero as the two principal leaders of the front. Colonel Bermudez did, in fact, support Mr. Somoza; he was his last military attaché in Washington. "Frontline" shows him as unrepentant, which, presumably, he is. Then it gives us Mr. Calero, a burly man in fatigues, whom it identifies only as the former Coca-Cola distributor in Managua. It neglects to mention that Mr. Calero opposed Mr. Somoza, who then threw him in jail.

We get a selective vision here. Facts that do not fit the political position are ignored, or else brushed off in asides. Clever film editing helps. A former rebel supporter, for instance, denounces the contras. Then President Reagan, fatuously, given the context, says of the contras: "They are our brothers—these freedom fighters."

This is followed by a quick aside by the narrator, presumably because it is not important: Since 1979, he says, the Sandinista Army has grown from 8,000 to 65,000 soldiers, equipped with Soviet tanks and helicopters, and trained by Cuban advisers; there is also a militia of 200,000.

Then back to the main argument: A contra in fatigues shouts, "War! Kill! Blood! Die!" The camera lingers; obviously, the contra is crazed. The narrator tells us then that the contras, managed by the Central Intelligence Agency, were never a military threat to the Sandinistas, and were noted mostly for "cruelty and ineptitude." In 1984, therefore, Congress cut off aid. Then, another aside:

"Despite their lack of military success," the narrator says, "problems inside Nicaragua led to a swelling in contra ranks."

The "problems" are not described; apparently they're not important either. In fact it was widely reported that the swelling of contra ranks was caused largely by Roman Catholic peasants from northern Nicaragua, who fled the Sandinistas. "Frontline" also fails to mention that, inept as the contras may have been in 1984, they still operated in one-third of Nicaragua. They withdrew after United States aid was withdrawn.

"Frontline" does note the existence of anti-Sandinista groups other than the Nicaragua Democratic Front, but declines to say anything about them. Eden Pastora Gomez, the leader of the Democratic Revolutionary Alliance, who has rejected the front, is not mentioned. The attempt by Alfonso Robelo and Arturo Cruz, both former Sandinistas, to introduce a contra code of conduct is dismissed as inconsequential. Human rights abuses by Sandinistas, meanwhile, are mentioned in only a single sentence.

Indeed the program reserves most of its scorn for Americans who support the contras, particularly John Singlaub, a retired major general, who raises financial support. He does this, "Frontline" indicates, chiefly among rich Texans and Arizona retirees. The retirees sing, "Hail, Hail, the Gang's All Here." One rich Texan, who gave $65,000 to buy a helicopter (a very small, second-hand helicopter, presumably) says that General Singlaub was "undoubtedly sent by the Lord." Contra supporters look foolish. . . .

There may be a case to be made against financing the contras, but it's not being made here.

Before ending this chapter on the demonstrable liberal bias of the media, and especially of the media elite in Washington and New York, in their presentation of the news, let us pause to note the criticism directed at this same group, for the very same reason, from a direction quite different from the conservatives': the further, harder Left.

I can remember hearing Norman Thomas complain, during the 1940s and 1950s, of the "silent treatment" the media routinely gave the activities and pronouncements of his minuscule Socialist party. And the various Communist factions, as well as miscellaneous "hard" leftists of other types, have generally voiced the same complaint. From their standpoint, of course, the explanation is simple: America's major media are firmly in "capitalist" hands and therefore part of the "capitalist conspiracy" to smother the Left. Liberals, on this view, are at best dupes of the capitalists and at worst wolves in sheeps' clothing.

Conservatives see the problem rather differently. The liberals, including those in the media, are far more sensitive to the views and actions of the hard Left than they are to the corresponding forces on the hard Right. Many, perhaps most, liberal policies in fact had their origin on the harder Left, and (as we discussed in defining "liberalism") liberals have historically found it difficult to condemn even Communists wholeheart edly, because of the assumptions they hold in common.

But it is also true that liberalism rarely does the harder Left any purely gratuitous favors: An idea originating on the hard Left must be *internalized*—i.e., made a part of liberalism's own programmatic baggage—before it will receive the affectionate attention the media elite know so well how to lavish on it.

The hard Left's complaint about media disregard is, therefore, in large part correct. The complaint, however, can be answered, and the disregard largely justified, by pointing out that these fringe activists and their movements simply don't deserve greater attention—or at any rate *much* greater attention—than they are getting. The underlying principle here is the same as that which decrees that it is permissible for major presidential candidates to be given more air time than indisputably minor contenders like the Communist candidate or, for that matter, the designee of the Libertarian party.

But it is quite a different matter for the major media in this country to distort news coverage of major-party candidates, major issues, and incumbent presidents in order to accommodate their own overwhelmingly liberal bias. And that is precisely what they have been doing for at least twenty years.

One final point: There is one political group in America that almost never protests over unfair treatment by the media, and that is the liberals themselves. It is true that from time to time some liberal organization or individual—most often a politician or a political candidate—will complain about distortions in a particular story. But a conviction that the media in general are biased against liberalism is simply not to be found in liberalism's general set of beliefs as it is in that of conservatism, and also of the harder Left. On the contrary, liberals are usually quick to praise the media, deny that the media are biased, and defend the media's claimed prerogatives against all challengers.

For them to do otherwise would be ingratitude indeed.

# CHAPTER 5

# *Who Is Behind the Media's Bias?*

DEMONSTRATING THAT THE media elite have a pronounced liberal bias and that it permeates what they produce, is one thing (or rather two); assigning the ultimate responsibility for these facts is quite another. In the last analysis, of course, the owners of America's key newspapers, major magazines, television networks, etc., are responsible for what is published or broadcast. But the good old days of the crusading newspaper owner are long gone, and. in fact the current pressure on the owners of news media is to keep their hands strictly off the editorial product, leaving this as the sacred preserve of the (hired) editors.

Some owners do precisely that, often not so much from a desire to avoid contaminating the editorial product as out of a single-minded preoccupation with the "bottom line": profitability. A good many others content themselves with choosing editors whose personal political predilections are not so far out from the prevailing center, in one direction or another, as to stir controversy. A relatively few owners, but an important few (e.g., the Sulzbergers of the *New York Times,* and the Grahams of the *Washington Post–Newsweek* complex), still exercise a major editorial influence, though even here the tendency is to do so by choosing like-minded editors and letting them have their head, rather than by attempting to dictate editorial policies directly to journalistic puppets.

In all three cases however, curiously enough, the result in recent decades has been to enhance the dominance of liberal influence in the media. From the end of World War II to the election of Ronald Reagan in 1980, liberalism seemed to most casual observers what Trilling pronounced it in 1950: "not only the dominant but even the sole intellectual tradition" in the United States. To the extent that the growth of the modern conservative movement requires modification of this assessment, its impact was not powerful enough, until very recently, to alter the intellectual climate within which the media largely operated.

Merely profit-minded owners, therefore, felt no pressure to curb the modishly liberal impulses of their editors in order to increase profits. On the contrary, in many areas of the country too vocal an editorial conservatism was actually counterproductive, diminishing advertising revenues and putting downward pressure on circulation.

An owner who was aware of these intellectual and cultural trends and affirmatively wanted his editors to respect them was, of course, even less likely to risk defying the common wisdom. For such owners, an editor comfortably in agreement with the prevailing liberalism was precisely what the situation demanded.

The few owners determined to impose their personal views on the editorial product had, however, the freedom to defy liberalism's intellectual dominance if they chose, and a few did exactly that. Practically all of these were survivors from the prewar days when (as discussed in Chapter 7) the media were predominantly conservative in both ownership and editorial product. Perhaps the most famous of these survivors was Colonel Robert R. McCormick, the crusty conservative who held his powerful regional newspaper, the *Chicago Tribune*, to a relentlessly conservative course until his death in 1955. (Since then, the *Tribune* has made its peace with liberalism.)

Another well-known conservative publisher who survived into the postwar years was Eugene Pulliam, owner of the *Indianapolis News*, the *Indianapolis Star*, the *Phoenix Gazette*, and the *Arizona Republic*. Pulliam did not die until 1975, at the age of eighty-six, and while he lived his strenuously conservative newspapers were important influences in their states, though not beyond them. Thereafter their impact declined and their conservatism, while it continues, is less outspoken.

The longest-surviving conservative among prominent local newspaper barons around the country was, of course, the redoubtable William Loeb, who did not die until 1981 and, right up to his death, employed his *Manchester* (N.H.) *Union-Leader* as a blunt instrument in political affairs that interested him. Thanks to the fact that New Hampshire's presidential primaries were the nation's earliest, Loeb occasionally managed to influence national as well as state politics to some extent—though his savage style had a tendency to boomerang, and arguably helped some of his victims as much as it hurt them. Since Loeb's death his equally conservative widow, Nacky, has continued to own the paper and keep it hewing to the right, but it is clearly a limited and transient phenomenon.

There are a handful of other local newspaper owners whose names could be added to those above, but they would not materially alter the point, which is that outspokenly conservative media owners, in the decades since World War II, have been a gradually vanishing species, confined to a few cities scattered haphazardly around the country.

One extremely important owner does, however, deserve extended mention in this context, though his relationship to the postwar liberal *Zeitgeist* stopped short of outright defiance. That is Henry Luce, the founder and longtime editor of *Time, Life, Fortune,* and the *Architectural Forum,* who launched *Time* in 1923 and ruled it without challenge until his death in 1967.

Luce is hard to classify, and probably neither the liberals nor the conservatives would care to claim him as their own. He was, on most issues, Republican and therefore relatively conservative in his sympathies, and in a few cases (notably his stubborn support for Chiang Kai-shek and the Chinese Nationalist cause) probably influenced not only Republican but United States national policies in important ways.

On the other hand, within the GOP Luce's inclinations were moderate or centrist, as opposed to distinctly conservative. Liberals were certainly pleased, if in most cases fairly silently so, by Luce's long opposition to the presidential ambitions of Senator Robert A. Taft, the Republican party's leading conservative until his death in 1953. Luce backed first Dewey and then Eisenhower against Taft (just as earlier he had backed Willkie in the 1940 convention). And later he showed little enthusiasm for the conservative movement that began gathering behind Barry Goldwater in the late 1950s and early 1960s.

Nevertheless, however we classify him, Luce was certainly a spectacular example of hands-on media ownership. Since his death, *Time* and its sister publications have trended perceptibly left, toward centrist or liberal positions on most of the subjects (e.g., China) about which their founder's views were most pronouncedly conservative. (Upon his retirement in 1987, Luce's successor Henry Anatole Grunwald cited this trend as his principal accomplishment as *Time*'s editor.)

Thus far, in discussing that minority of media owners who have exercised a specific and deliberate influence over the editorial product, we have concentrated on the few (since World War II) who have been outspokenly conservative. Others, however, have been quite as outspokenly liberal, and these, unlike the conservatives, just happen to include the owners of several of the most powerful organs of opinion in the country.

Pride of place surely belongs to the owners of the *New York Times*, if only because the *Times* is indisputably the nation's most influential newspaper. Since the demise of the moderate-Republican *New York Herald-Tribune* in 1966, the *Times* has been the essential breakfast reading of that powerful segment of America's national leadership—intellectual, cultural, and financial—that makes New York its home. In addition it is required reading for the nation's political leadership, concentrated in Washington. Third, as technology has made it possible for regional editions of the *Times* to be printed and distributed in other areas of the country, it has slowly become an important supplementary source of information for a nationwide readership not satisfied with local newspapers and what can be gleaned from the weekly newsmagazines. Finally, the syndicated New York Times Service enables other newspapers around the country to tap into much of the vast flow of national and international reportage and informed commentary produced every day by the *Times*'s large and capable staff.

The *Times* has been owned by the related Ochs and Sulzberger families for nearly a century, but it is only since World War II that its acquisition of a near-monopoly position in the New York market for serious news, combined with its symbiotic relationship to the dominant liberal elements in American society, has made the *Times* indisputably the country's most influential newspaper. Since 1963 its principal owner and its publisher has been Arthur Ochs "Punch" Sulzberger.

To say that Sulzberger's views, and those promoted by the *Times* under his direction, are broadly and explicitly liberal is entirely correct, without involving any implication that the paper's liberalism is either invariable or extreme. The *Times* is a large institution, and many influences, both internal and external, contribute to the shaping of its attitudes. But certainly Sulzberger deserves to be known as an owner in the "hands-on" tradition, and the direction in which he guides the *Times*, and in which the *Times* in turn seeks to push the country, is, in the overwhelming majority of cases, the liberal one.

Another extremely powerful family of media owners whose influence has been strenuously liberal is the Meyer-Graham dynasty of Washington, D.C. Their flagship is, of course, the *Washington Post*, which has been Washington's only commercially viable newspaper since the demise of the *Washington Star* in 1981.* In addition they own *Newsweek* magazine.

---

* The *Washington Times*, founded by Rev. Sun Myung Moon's News World Communications in 1982, is heavily subsidized and, with perhaps a hundred thousand readers, seems unlikely ever to command the advertising necessary to become commercially

\* \* \*

This combination of journalistic bases constitutes a formidable influence indeed on the Washington scene. The *Washington Post,* in particular, is even more widely read in government offices, both on Capitol Hill and at the White House, than the *New York Times.* And, even more consistently and explicitly than the *Times,* it hews to the liberal line.

In the case of the *Washington Post,* the tradition of political liberalism dates at least from the era of Agnes Meyer, the wife of the *Post*'s longtime publisher, Eugene Meyer. Mrs. Meyer passed the torch to her daughter Katharine, an able newspaperwoman in her own right, whose husband Philip Graham succeeded Meyer as the *Post*'s publisher in 1947. On Graham's death in 1963, Kay Graham assumed the title herself, and she remains the most powerful influence on the paper to this day, although her son Donald nominally succeeded her as publisher in 1979.

With both the *New York Times* and the *Washington Post* in the hands of politically liberal family dynasties and likely to remain there, a continued liberal bias in these two powerful publications seems assured. In addition, however, liberal owners, like the surviving conservative owners already discussed, exercise hands-on control of a number of more or less influential local newspapers around the country—the chief difference being that, unlike the conservatives, their number has increased rather than diminished to the vanishing point since the end of World War II. They include the Chandler family who own the *Los Angeles Times,* the Binghams of Louisville (whose family feuds appear, at this writing, to be loosening their long grip on the *Courier-Journal*), and the Cowles family of Des Moines and Minneapolis, to name only three of the better known.

But, as we noted at the outset, hands-on control of the editorial product by owners is the exception rather than the rule in American journalism, despite the conservative and liberal examples we have just cited. The large newspaper chain owners, in particular, have usually avoided it—the last major exception being William Randolph Hearst, who died in 1951. For a time his sons carried on in what they considered their father's tradition, but the recent history of the Hearst chain has reflected a growing tendency to let the local editors call the shots editorially—a trend also visible in the Scripps-Howard and Pulitzer chains. The Gannett papers, under the vigorous direction of Allen Neuharth, boast of their editorial independence; and the late Si Newhouse, who put together a

---

viable. It is a moderately influential (and outspokenly conservative) publication, however, being widely read by members and friends of the Reagan administration.

chain second only to Gannett's, was famous for leaving questions of editorial policy strictly to his editors.

The same is generally true of the owners of the major electronic media. Neither David Sarnoff (NBC) nor William Paley (CBS) sought to impose a pronounced political coloration on their networks. They did, however, allow them to be shaped editorially by producers and editors comfortable with the liberal dominance in postwar America. In the cases of both print and electronic journalism, therefore, we must in most cases turn from the owners to the editorial staffs to find the source of the liberal bias we have described.

In assessing the degree to which members of the editorial staffs of both print and electronic media are directly responsible for the media's blatant liberal bias, it will be well to remember that we are dealing with a spectrum of behavior.

In the first place, as the surveys described in Chapter 3 indicated, American journalists are heavily liberal in their personal political predilections, but they are not exclusively so: There is a conservative minority—cautious, no doubt, but not altogether negligible, even among the media elite.

In the second place, journalists vary widely in their attitudes toward their work. Some are painfully conscientious about the need for at least an effort at objectivity, the danger here being that they may actually come to believe they have achieved it. Others, equally conscientious but more highly ideologized, may feel strongly that the time is out of joint and that they, like Hamlet, were born to set it right—by selecting and putting before the American people the horrifying facts of Vietnam, or poverty, or what-have-you.

Third, journalists are at least as sensitive as the rest of us to the world around them—the intellectual milieu, the popular sociological concepts, the significant political trends. In a society as wholly dominated (intellectually speaking) by liberalism as America was between 1945 and, say, 1975, it was, as John Corry argued (see page 22), simply to be expected that professional journalists would, in the great majority of cases, share that pervasive coloration.

This tendency was reinforced, moreover, by the budding journalist's instinctive self-identification with the particular sector of society concerned with words and ideas: the sector that Kevin Phillips has dubbed "the Knowledge Industry," which just happened to be the most liberal sector of them all. Of a random ten students in a college class, four may go into one or another form of business, one may become a farmer, one a lawyer, one a teacher, one a doctor, and one a civil servant of some description. The tenth, let us assume, elects to go into journalism. By this very process of self-selection, he has already, perhaps unwittingly, identified himself with various liberal social traditions that might be thoroughly uncongenial to his classmates who chose to go into business: the tradition of the journalistic muckraker, for example.

There are still other factors at work here, which we will explore elsewhere (Chapters 7 and 8). Suffice it for the moment to note that there are perfectly comprehensible reasons for the high proportion of liberals among American journalists.

There are yet other considerations, of a personal type, that inevitably influence a journalist's ultimate attitude, however. Few careers that a person might choose to pursue have undergone so dramatic a series of changes in the past forty years as journalism, and a journalist's views and behavior will unavoidably be affected by how and when these changes manifested themselves in his particular case.

A young man or woman embarking on a journalistic career at the end of World War II, for example, was entering a profession (if we may call it that) still almost wholly dominated by the printed word. In political terms, there were plenty of local newspaper barons of both the conservative and liberal persuasions. The New York- and Washington-based media elite had not yet fully established their dominance, nor was their liberalism either as whole-souled or as near-monopolistic as it later became. The older traditions of the journalistic craft itself—especially the obligation to document or otherwise "source" every major factual assertion in a story—were still widely honored, if by no means always observed.

Forty years later, journalism had changed almost beyond recognition. The printed word had been overtaken and largely surpassed by new electronic media requiring a very different array of techniques and talents. Conservative newspaper owners were a vanishing breed, and in any case the liberal media elite, based in New York and Washington and operating through a relative handful of print and electronic instrumentalities, had established a dominance that made the opinions of local newspaper or TV station owners largely irrelevant. New technologies had given these media—especially the electronic media—immense power to influence public opinion, and the device of the anonymous informant had become the single most important weapon in every journalist's armory.

For a person embarking on a journalistic career in 1946 at the age of twenty or twenty-five, it was happily immaterial whether his ears were unfashionably large or his accent a harsh Brooklynese; what mattered was his instinct for news and his skill as a writer. But as the 1950s turned into the 1960s and television began to replace newspapers as the public's chief source of information, the important on-camera jobs in the new medium inevitably went, on rigorous Darwinian principles, to those journalists— Walter Cronkite being the most spectacular example, but far from the only one—who appealed visually to the television audience. And the off-camera production and direction of news programs tended to become the province of whole new breeds of electronic journalists who may never have interviewed a source in their lives but who knew how to visualize a story in television terms and put it on the screen. Gradually, as the 1970s came on and the older breed of TV anchormen who had begun their career in print journalism were replaced by younger successors trained in television journalism from the start, it became less and less important for the on-camera "newsman" to have any of the traditional journalistic skills. A conventionally good-looking face, an agreeable personality, and the ability to read lines from a TelePrompTer were the chief essentials, and the salaries earned by some of those with these qualifications quickly reached levels previously unheard-of in the world of journalism.

To be fair, television journalism is not by any means always, even on-camera, the refuge of the handsome dumbbell. The ability to interview a "guest" effectively is an extremely valuable quality, as the case of Barbara Walters attests. And most of the better-known anchormen, at least at the national level, pride themselves almost to excess on whatever traditional journalistic qualifications or experience they may have.

But the fact remains that journalism today is scarcely the same profession it was in 1946. The image of the eager young newspaper reporter with a notepad in his hand and a pencil behind his ear, doggedly pursuing a "scoop," has been replaced by the image of a piercingly handsome TV anchorman with blow-dried hair, Pan-Cake makeup, and contact lenses, being paid hundreds of thousands of dollars a year to read lines written for him by someone else.

It is unfortunate that most people's experience of television news is confined to this small but highly visible group of on-camera performers, because of course virtually all of the major journalistic decisions—what stories to cover, what "theory" of a story to adopt, which facts to stress (and not stress), whom to interview, etc.—are made by off-camera officials or specialist employees. It is perfectly natural, if a viewer feels that a story on the evening TV news has been distorted, for him to blame

Dan Rather, Tom Brokaw, or Peter Jennings. Who would dream of blaming Thomas Bettag, William Wheatley, or William Lord? Who, for that matter, outside the world of television, has ever heard of any of them? And yet they are, respectively, the executive producers of the *CBS Evening News, NBC Nightly News,* and ABC's *World News Tonight.* As such, they have far greater control over the content—not to mention the slant—of these programs than their three superstars. And behind and beneath the executive producers, of course, are literally scores of other important off-camera decision makers, bearing such titles as producer, associate producer, field producer, senior producer, senior broadcast producer, editor, senior editor, managing editor, foreign editor, domestic editor, assignment editor, political editor, etc.

And the decision-making hierarchy extends above the executive producers as well as below them. In the case of NBC, for example, William Wheatley's immediate superior is John Lane, senior vice-president of NBC News for all daily news coverage and programs. And over Lane, of course, is Lawrence K. Grossman, president of NBC News, which itself is simply a division of the National Broadcasting Company.

One can imagine the effect this sort of table of organization has on an old-time print journalist, accustomed to the traditional hierarchy of reporter, managing editor, editor, and publisher. The wonder is that, during the past forty years, as many of them succeeded in making the transition as did. The result, however, has been that journalism has been a rather piebald profession in the past two or three decades, in terms of the backgrounds and skills of its practitioners. Some of today's (and yesterday's) senior on-camera television news personalities have reflected the strain, insisting sentimentally on their credentials as old-fashioned reporters and resisting attempts to relegate them to better-paying but (apparently) less rewarding work.

John Chancellor, for example, the veteran television reporter who formerly served as anchorman for the *NBC Nightly News,* was widely reported to have chafed under the limitations of that job, which tended to confine him to the role of a "pointer": "Andrea Mitchell, at the White House, has the story," "And now to Rome, where Jim Bitterman is standing by with the latest developments," and so on. Tom Brokaw, Chancellor's successor as anchor, has tried valiantly to retain his reportortial credentials by combining the job of anchorman with that of a reporter on the scene. His biographical resumé, as distributed by NBC, is insistent on the point:

As co-anchor of "NBC Nightly News," Brokaw traveled extensively. In 1982, he anchored "Nightly" from various European locations when President Reagan toured France, Great Britain and West Germany. During the Lebanese War, in the summer of 1982, Brokaw anchored the news from Beirut, Jerusalem and Tel Aviv. In 1983 he traveled to Bonn for the West German elections and anchored NBC's coverage of the Pope's return to his native Poland. He also anchored a series of NBC's special segment reports entitled "Journey To The Heart of China." In January, 1985, Brokaw traveled to Geneva, Switzerland where he anchored "Nightly News" as the United States met with the Soviet Union on arms control negotiations. Before arriving in Geneva he spent time in South Africa compiling special reports on their apartheid system of government.

The CBS resumé of Brokaw's opposite number, anchorman Dan Rather, is equally insistent that its tiger is no mere "pointer":

Correspondent Dan Rather, recognized as one of the most knowledge-able reporters and analysts on the national political scene, has served as anchor and managing editor of "The CBS Evening News" since March 9, 1981.

Rather, who has reported on virtually every aspect of the American political scene, spearheaded CBS News coverage of the 1984 political year—from the whirlwind of primaries to the national conventions, from election night to the inauguration. . . .

He has travelled around the world including, most recently, to Geneva to report on the arms control negotiations (Jan. 1985) and to Cuba where he spent 14½ hours interviewing Cuban President Fidel Castro. Portions of that marathon interview were broadcast on "The CBS Evening News" and "60 Minutes" (March 1985).

Rather has reported on the crises in the Mideast and Poland, the invasion of Grenada, the succession of power following the death of Soviet leader Konstantin Chernenko, and the downing of the Korean Airlines jet, including anchoring such broadcasts as the CBS News Special Report, "Gorbachev Takes Control," a profile of the new Soviet leader (March 1985), "After the Battle: A Search For Answers," an examination of many of the questions raised by the U.S. invasion of Grenada (Oct. 1983), and a series of Special Reports on the bombing of the U.S. Marine compound in Beirut (Oct. 1983).

But this strenuous concentration on the personalities seen by the public, and their supposedly crucial skills as newsgatherers, is almost exclusively "show biz," tinctured with a cautious concern for the sensibilities of the anchors themselves. As John Chancellor came to realize, they are in fact essentially "pointers"—though their salaries, which sometimes reach six or seven figures, no doubt ease the pain.

Today, the shift of key personnel from print to electronic journalism is substantially over. The latter is now—as far as decision making is concerned—almost entirely in the hands of executives without significant backgrounds in print journalism and totally unknown to the public. These are the people who are, in the great majority of cases, directly responsible for the persistent distortions, in the direction of political liberalism, that characterize the electronic media today.

Among journalists still working with those print media whose political line is not directly dictated by their owners, the decision makers in matters of policy tend to be found in the higher ranks of the editorial personnel: the editor in chief, the managing editor, etc. Some years ago it was fashionable among liberals to argue that the press, contrary to conservative charges, was in fact overwhelmingly conservative—as evidenced by the total number of newspapers that editorially endorsed the Republican and Democratic candidates for president, respectively. By counting hundreds of rural weeklies that did in fact endorse the Republican candidate editorially, it was (and probably still is) easy to outnumber the relatively small number of elite print media that were working diligently against him. But actually the influence of local newspapers is far less than that of the liberal-dominated elites: the major weekly newsmagazines and the "national" newspapers.

Among the latter, only the *Wall Street Journal* is editorially conservative, and it is famous for a unique conflict between its news columns and its editorial page. The latter, under Robert Bartley, is a major influence for conservatism—very nearly the only such major influence in the entire field of the American media elite, both print and electronic. The *Journal*'s news columns, on the other hand, and especially the stories emanating from its Washington bureau under Al Hunt, are almost as relentlessly liberal as those of the *Washington Post* and the *New York Times*.

Below the rank of editor, in the print media, it is still occasionally possible, thanks to the nature of the medium, for a vigorous individual reporter to contribute significantly to the pervasive liberal bias. I do not know whether *New York Times* reporter Seymour Hersh was initially ordered, by Abe Rosenthal or anyone else, to investigate alleged "abuses" by the CIA in the early 1970s. Certainly the amount of space his by-line articles on the subject were given (front-page treatment literally almost every day for more than forty days) signaled a decision by his superiors to assure the story the fullest possible attention. But Hersh himself was unquestionably a major player in the game, which before it was over (and depending on one's view of the matter) either cleansed the

Agency of serious evils or gravely crippled the entire nation in its ongoing competition with the Soviet Union.

Reinforcing the personal liberalism of most members of the media elite are various rewards available to those who display a sensitivity to appropriate issues and a commendable eagerness to advance the liberal cause. Among the most prestigious and effective of these are the Nieman Fellowships at Harvard University.

The fellowships were instituted in 1937, under a bequest in memory of Lucius Nieman, founder of the *Milwaukee Journal,* to give selected journalists the opportunity to spend a sabbatical academic year at Harvard, imbibing the waters of that Pierian spring. A Nieman Fellow's principal obligations are to reside in Cambridge during the two academic semesters of his (or her) fellowship, and to complete all the work in two academic courses of his choice—one in the fall semester and one in the spring. There is no test or grade for the Fellow in these courses, but when the term is over the instructor sends a written evaluation of the individual's classwork to the Nieman office.

In addition, a Nieman Fellow normally "audits" from one to three other courses of his choice (selected from any department or graduate school), and attends various Nieman dinners and seminars. Every Fellow is assigned a faculty tutor and affiliated with one of the Harvard houses—thus facilitating interchanges with undergraduates. There are, on the average, some eighteen Neiman Fellows every year, and altogether some seven hundred journalists have completed the program.

The Nieman Foundation pays the Fellows' tuition fees, and provides them with a stipend to cover living expenses, including child-care costs if necessary. In the early 1980s, an inquiry of the foundation failed to elicit a concrete estimate of the dollar value of a fellowship, but in view of Harvard's tuition fees and the cost of living in Cambridge it can hardly total less than $15,000 or $20,000.

For this sum, the lucky Fellow is exposed for an entire academic year, in the early middle of his career, to a massive irradiation by Harvard University. It is of course a central experience in his life, and is invariably listed with pride thereafter in his curriculum vitae. (There is something rather comical, not to say downright paradoxical, about a journalist who would virtuously refuse a free ride on some airline that is inaugurating a new route, lest it contaminate his intellectual independence, bragging for the rest of his life about having received a year-long $20,000 brainwashing at Harvard. The distinction in his mind, of course, though he would be reluctant to put it this way, is that the free ride would be a crassly material benefit and therefore discreditable, whereas the rewards of a Nieman Fellowship are in large part intellectual and, in addition, put the recipient in close touch with many of the dominant philosophical and sociopolitical trends of his time.)

The atmosphere in which Nieman Fellows are selected was vividly described by Mary McGrory in an article in the *Washington Star* for May 18, 1975. Ms. McGrory was enthusing over the quality of the fellowship applicants interviewed by a Nieman selection committee on which she herself had recently sat. The full flavor of her account can only be appreciated if one bears in mind that Mary McGrory is surely in contention for the title of Most Liberal Washington Columnist of Them All:

> There were any number of times during the three days we members of the jury were interviewing Nieman Fellowship applicants that we wished the proceedings were being recorded. There are still some people out there who believe that the fourth estate is populated by hate-driven jackals who drive noble characters from office, trample on the flag, and tell anything but the truth. If those people could somehow have been brought into the smoke-filled room—four of the judges were cigar-smokers—and heard the 45 press people who told us about themselves and their work, they might have been reassured not just about journalism, but about the future of the country. There was a great deal of commitment and compassion in the polluted air. The balloting was the only unpleasant time of the experience. Strong wills clashed. . . . There were some hard feelings about lost favorites. But we were unanimous on one point: the press is in the very best of hands.

"Commitment" to what, one wonders? And "compassion" for whom? Ms. McGrory doesn't say.

Another major reinforcement of liberal attitudes on the part of the media is the Pulitzer Prizes, established under the will of the first Jospeh Pulitzer and awarded annually (for material appearing in an American newspaper published weekly or more often) by Columbia University on the recommendation of the Pulitzer Prize Board. There are prizes in Journalism, Letters (i.e., books), and Music, and while the amount of the awards ($1,000 each, save for a single gold medal for "a distinguished example of meritorious public service") is not terribly impressive, the prestige associated with them is considerable. (Not, however, universal. The distinguished critic and essayist Joseph Epstein, editor of *The American Scholar,* has declared that "for intensity of besmirchment, no single award has so covered itself with the reverse of glory as the Pulitzer Prize.")

The Journalism awards fall into fourteen categories. Aside from the aforementioned award for meritorious public service, they pretty much cover the variety of materials normally published in a newspaper, from investigative and explanatory reportage to commentary, editorials, and cartoons. As an example of what the Prize Board is likely to find "distinguished," let us review its annual awards for "commentary," a category established in 1970:

| | |
|---|---|
| Marquis Childs | *St. Louis Post Dispatch* |
| William A. Caldwell | *Bergen Record* |
| Mike Royko | *Chicago Daily News* |
| David S. Broder | *Washington Post* |
| Edwin A. Roberts, Jr. | *National Observer* |
| Mary McGrory | *Washington Star* |
| Walter W. "Red" Smith | *New York Times* |
| George F. Will | Washington Post Writers Group |
| William Safire | *New York Times* |
| Russell Baker | *New York Times* |
| Ellen Goodman | *Boston Globe* |
| Dave Anderson | *New York Times* |
| Art Buchwald | Los Angeles Times Syndicate |
| Claude Sitton | *Raleigh* (N.C.) *News and Observer* |
| Vermont Royster | *Wall Street Journal* |
| Murray Kempton | *Newsday* (N.Y.) |
| Jimmy Breslin | *New York Daily News* |
| Charles Krauthammer | *New Republic* |

Now, there are most certainly distinguished commentators in that list, and there are even three (out of eighteen) who are more or less identified with the conservative viewpoint: George Will, William Safire, and Vermont Royster. But Will is, and in 1977 (when he received the award) was even more emphatically, "the liberals' favorite conservative": a holder of elegant Tory opinions, but a dependable critic of first Agnew, then Nixon, and finally (pre-1978) Reagan, as these political figures successively became the focus of public attention. Safire was (and is) often more conservative on certain subjects than Will; but his real distinction lies in the original reportage and inside information that characterizes his column, and the acerbic style in which it is written. (He is also in the grip of various overriding preoccupations—notably Israel.) Royster is, of course, a conservative in the broad sense, and one of the grand old men of American journalism. But he is also a loner, philosophically speaking. Neither he, nor Will, nor Safire, deserves—or would, in all probability, want—inclusion in the so-called conservative movement which, originating in the early 1950s, has fundamentally altered the axis and thrust of American politics.

Where, on the Pulitzer award list, is James Jackson Kilpatrick or William F. Buckley? Yet there was plenty of room for Marquis Childs and Mary McGrory and Ellen Goodman and Claude Sitton and Murray Kempton.

An inspection of the current (1987) membership of the Pulitzer Prize Board easily explains the imbalance. The board's seventeen current members are:

| | |
|---|---|
| Michael I. Sovern, President | Columbia University |
| Frederick J. C. Yu, Acting Dean (ex-officio) | Columbia University, Graduate School of Journalism |
| Russell Baker, Columnist | *New York Times* |
| Michael Gartner, General News Executive | Gannett Company, Des Moines, Iowa |
| Hanna H. Gray, President | University of Chicago |
| Meg Greenfield, Editorial Page Editor | *Washington Post* |
| James F. Hoge, Jr., Publisher | *New York Daily News* |
| David A. Laventhol, Publisher, CEO Group Vice President | *Newsday* Times Mirror Company |
| Robert C. Maynard, Publisher and Editor | *Oakland* (Calif.) *Tribune* |
| C. K. McClatchy, President and Editor | McClatchy Newspapers, Sacramento, Calif. |
| Burl Osborne, President and Editor | *Dallas Morning News* |
| Warren H. Phillips, Chairman and CEO | Dow Jones and Company |
| Eugene L. Roberts, Jr., Executive Editor | *Philadelphia Inquirer* |
| Charlotte Saikowski, Chief of Washington Bureau | *Christian Science Monitor* |
| Claude Sitton, Editorial Director and Vice-President | *News and Observer; Raleigh* (N.C.) *Times* |
| Roger W. Wilkins, Senior Fellow | Institute for Policy Studies |
| Robert C. Christopher, Secretary | Columbia University, Graduate School of Journalism |

Presumably it will not be disputed that the presidents of Columbia University and the University of Chicago are comfortably within the liberal camp, and I doubt that Roger Wilkins, a prominent black alumnus of the *New York Times* editorial board, would very strenuously resist inclusion there.

So it goes with the rest of the members. Michael Gartner, James F. Hoge, Jr., Robert Maynard, C. K. McClatchy, and Claude Sitton are all notably liberal and in some cases positive zealots. Some of the executives on the Prize Board might conceivably qualify as centrists, but there is not a single explicit conservative on the list—nor would the presence of a token one or two change the point in the least.

If any doubt remained, however, as to the essentially liberal orientation of the Pulitzer Prize Board, it was ended by its election of Roger Wilkins as its new chairman in 1987. The significance of that choice was spelled out by Edwin Feulner, president of the (conservative) Heritage Foundation:

> Mr. Wilkins' selection sends a signal to the journalism community. And the signal it sends to conservative journalists, already a pitiful minority, is that the establishment has no damn use for them. . . .
>
> But there is more to Mr. Wilkins than his government jobs, his stint at the Ford Foundation, his years at The Washington Post and the now-defunct Washington Star: Roger Wilkins is a radical leftist. . . .
>
> No longer in the news business, Mr. Wilkins currently resides at the Institute for Policy Studies, a stridently leftist propaganda mill that embraces anti-Americanism as a child would a puppy. . . .
>
> Of course, we will be told, Mr. Wilkins alone does not select the Pulitzer Prize winner. Maybe not. But elevating him, even for a year, to the chairmanship of the Pulitzer board tells conservatives they shouldn't even bother applying.

Although magazines (other than newsmagazines) are largely outside the scope of this study, it may be worth noting that the rewards of liberalism in the journalistic arena are not confined to those who work for newspapers. An article in the *New York Times* for April 30, 1986, reported that the magazine *Science 85* had just received a prestigious award for brusquely contradicting a contention by the Reagan administration that verification of arms agreements was no longer possible solely through the use of "technical means":

> Science 85 won a National Magazine Award for articles in the public interest yesterday for its "Technology of Peace" issue of December 1985, that drew readers' attention to the scientific and political issues that underlie arms control and disarmament.
>
> The series took issue with claims within the Reagan Administration that science is no longer up to the task of maintaining the peace through its verification of arms agreement. The judges noted that a "quick response from readers and policy makers suggests that the message got through."
>
> The award was among 13 annual National Magazine Awards announced yesterday at a luncheon at the Waldorf-Astoria Hotel that was attended by nearly 1,000 magazine editors, publishers and writers.
>
> The awards, widely regarded as the most prestigious in the field, were established in 1966 by the American Society of Magazine Editors. They are financed by the Magazine Publishers Association and administered by the Columbia Graduate School of Journalism.

# CHAPTER 6

# *The Media's Response*

IN ANALYZING THE liberal bias of America's media elite, we have already had occasion to mention in passing various of the media's responses to the charge. It may be useful, however, to review, roughly in descending order of contumacy, the astonishingly wide variety of responses that defenders of the media have offered at one time or another.

By far the commonest response to the charge is to ignore it altogether. It was, as we have seen, more than four years before the important 1981 Lichter-Rothman report on the personal political preferences of the media elite elicited any serious reply whatever. The great beauty of such stonewalling is that it ordinarily requires no effort and no other party's cooperation; it can be practiced in solitude. I have, however, seen it essayed under fairly difficult circumstances. In the spring of 1984, debating the *New York Times*'s Tom Wicker at Monmouth College (New Jersey), I raised the issue of the media's liberal bias again and again, but Wicker simply refused to address it. He neither denied the charge nor admitted it; he simply and serenely ignored it. It would be interesting to know what the audience thought of this tactic. Conceivably, thanks to it, the inattentive may not even have noticed that a significant issue had been raised. After all, as Zen devotees point out, what is the sound of one hand clapping?

The second most common response of media apologists to the charge of bias is to deny it, flatly and *in toto*. Not all of the media's defenders are as iron-willed as Tom Wicker, and in addition there are occasions on which, for one reason or another, stonewalling is more or less out of the question. That was the situation on an ABC television panel show called *Viewpoint*, which aired live on the network on April 17, 1985. Ted Koppel was the moderator, and my blunt charge of media bias simply demanded a response. Hodding Carter III provided one: a straightforward and total denial. (Our exchange is set forth at the beginning of Chapter 1.) The usefulness of this tactic depends on the amount of time available to counter it. In the case of the *Viewpoint* program, we panelists were necessarily limited to short statements, and Koppel, inadvertently I am sure, complicated the problem still further when—on discovering that I wanted to cite the Lichter-Rothman report— he declared firmly that he would not permit the program to get bogged down in "statistics" (a famous bane of television hosts). The audience was left with an unsubstantiated charge and a flat denial, and was logically entitled to conclude that they canceled each other out.

But if, for whatever reason, the charge can't be ignored altogether, and a categorical denial just won't do, there are plenty of other arguments open to the media's defenders. One of the best—not because it is valid but because, like a flat denial, it takes considerable time to refute—is the contention that, even if the media elite are personally liberal by a wide margin, they rigorously suppress their own views in reporting the "news." We dealt extensively with this contention in Chapter 3, noting the impressive evidence available for its refutation. The problem is finding the *time*.

Another popular avenue of defense is to argue that the media are not really liberal, or (to put it the other way around) are not anticonservative, but are just inherently anti-"establishment" and are also driven, by the imperatives of their journalistic profession, to ferret out and stress "bad" news. A constant drumbeat of media hostility assails Reagan (so this argument goes), not because he is conservative but simply because he is president. Media defenders adopting this line will cite the very considerable journalistic hostility to those relatively liberal Democratic presidents Jimmy Carter and Lyndon Johnson as proving their point.

As already pointed out, however (page 73), the fairly severe treatment meted out to Jimmy Carter by the media in his 1980 race for reelection cannot really serve as an example of the media bashing a liberal president, because by 1980 many liberals (presumably including a proportionate number of media liberals) were so exasperated with Carter's performance *from the liberal standpoint* that they either supported Ted Kennedy's effort to take the Democratic nomination away from him, or voted for the liberal third-party candidate John Anderson, or both. To the extent that the media gave Carter a hard time in 1980, therefore, they were not disproving their liberalism but actually demonstrating it.

The same is even truer of the media's attacks on Lyndon Johnson. It is significant that contentions of a media bias *against the presidency as such* always trace the evidence as far back as Lyndon Johnson—and then stop. For John Kennedy was, of course, the darling of our liberal media. From their standpoint he could do no wrong, and the Washington press corps sedulously cooperated in concealing his numerous vulnerabilities— vulnerabilities which, from his compulsive womanizing to his grave medical problems, would instantly have been exploited to damage and if possible destroy any political figure not under the media's special and devoted protection. Where, in the case of the Kennedy presidency—the apotheosis of an imperial clan if there ever was one—was the media's alleged "inherent bias against the establishment"? Where was the media's famed "appetite for bad news"? (Or did the Kennedy White House simply not generate any bad news?)

The truth (as we shall have occasion to explain more fully in Chapter 6) is that American liberals lost effective control of the Johnson administration and its agenda in or about 1966, when Johnson's Great Society programs (which liberals of course adored) began to be over-shadowed by his increasing commitment to the war in Vietnam (a commitment inherited from Kennedy, and which liberals had therefore originally favored, but which under New Left pressure they increasingly began to oppose). It is no coincidence whatever that the liberal media elite's "inherent bias against the establishment," and therefore against the presidency, dates from precisely the same period. Since then, there has not been a president in the White House, Republican *or* Democrat, of whom liberals wholeheartedly approved, and the fact that the media have in general attacked all of them does not (once again) disprove, but in fact demonstrates, their knee-jerk liberalism.

Continuing down the scale of responses to the charge of bias, various tactical devices are used with greater or less success depending on the circumstances and the knowledgeability of the critic. Calling for defini-tions, for example, is always useful. Just what is a "liberal" or a "conservative" anyway? (See pages 43–44.) And who are these so-called media elite? Such devices are the rhetorical equivalent of a boxer going into a clinch: They accomplish nothing affirmative, but temporarily avoid further punishment.

Finally, if some concession to criticism becomes unavoidable, the media's defenders will make sure that it is kept as small and as meaningless as possible. References to identifiable conservatives in *non*elite media (local newspapers, radio talk shows, etc.) have been known to throw naïve pursuers off the track. In the past decade, however, as the conservative political tide has risen ever higher, washed over the White House, and signaled its staying power by reelecting Ronald Reagan overwhelmingly, the media elite themselves have begun to make grudging admissions that there is a new voice in the national dialogue that demands, and deserves, to be heard. The really striking point, however, is just how grudging the admissions are.

The Op-Ed page of the *New York Times,* for example, was launched in 1970 with the high-minded intention of providing space for a much wider spectrum of opinions than those to which the *Times* was either able or willing to extend the hospitality of its editorial columns. For a number of years it performed that function commendably well—perhaps, in fact, to excess, as when it published a ten-year-old's advice to Governor Hugh Carey on how to manage the affairs of the state of New York. (Fortunately, from one standpoint, it later transpired that the *Times* had been duped: The piece had actually been written by the boy's father.)

In 1973, however, the *Times* went the extra mile and hired William Safire, Richard Nixon's former speechwriter, to write two columns a week for its Op-Ed page. Since the three other regulars who appear there (Tom Wicker, Anthony Lewis, and Flora Lewis) are all passionate liberals, the expectation clearly was that Safire, an able and witty writer, would offer a relatively more conservative view of public affairs. In general, he has not disappointed in this respect—though, good Nixonian centrist that he is, he falls far short of being one of those "movement conservatives" who have revolutionized American politics in recent years.

In return for what the *Times*'s editors presumably regard as the major concession represented by Safire, however, the Op-Ed page has degenerated into a kind of liberal olla podrida on which, on the days when Safire's column doesn't appear, there often is not a single article that could plausibly be characterized as conservative (see pages 28–29). Instead, readers are treated to attacks on President Reagan's defense budget by unfamiliar writers engaged in obscure but implicitly authoritative research on the subject for some organization with a pleasant name ("Mr. Limpthink analyzes defense expenditures for the Citizens' Budget Survey Group") or to savage denunciations of the President's Central American policies by "a former assistant secretary of state for Latin American affairs" who (we are *not* told) held that post under Jimmy Carter.

Turning to the field of electronic journalism, perhaps the most notable alleged concession to conservatism has been ABC-TV's employment of George Will as a "commentator" on *World News Tonight*. Like Safire, Will is an able journalist with a trenchant mind and style, and he has acquired, both in print and on TV, an enthusiastic following which regards him as one of America's premier "conservative" spokesmen. Even more than Safire, however, Will carefully distances himself from the conservative movement as such. There is of course nothing wrong with this, either as a consciously chosen political position or as a shrewd move in career terms, but it underscores again the unwillingness of the media to yield an inch more than is absolutely necessary.

For the Washington liberal media are well aware of Will's utility as a comfortably nonthreatening conservative. The *Post*'s ultraliberal TV critic, Tom Shales, described Will in January 1987 as "the one man who has done more than anyone except possibly Reagan to make American conservatism dignified and respectable, and even chic"—explaining, a couple of paragraphs further on, that "Will represents a compassionate kind of conservatism."

But Samuel T. Francis, reviewing Will's *Statecraft as Soulcraft: What Government Does* in the Spring 1986 issue of *Modern Age*, expressed the view of many conservatives:

> Although Will is sometimes called a "neo-conservative," he is not one. Neo-conservatives typically derive more or less conservative policy positions from essentially liberal premises. Will in fact does the opposite: he derives from more or less unexceptionable premises of classical conservatism policy positions that are often congruent with the current liberal agenda. It is because he accepts, and wants to be accepted by, the "achievements" of modern liberalism that he ignores or sneers at the serious conservative thinkers and leaders of our time who have sought to break liberal idols and that he voices no criticism of the powers that support liberalism. It is therefore not surprising that his commentary is welcomed in and rewarded by liberal power centers. They have little to fear from him and his ideas and much to gain if his version of "conservatism" should gain currency. He enjoys every prospect of a bright future in their company.

As a matter of fact, Will has made a cottage industry out of being the commentator to whom Washington's embattled liberal media automatically turn whenever they feel obliged to make room for a relatively conservative opinion. A discovery and protégé of Irving Kristol's, Will (who was educated at Oxford and Princeton, and first came to Washington as a congressional aide to Republican senator Gordon Allott of Colorado) emerged onto the capital's journalistic scene under the joint auspices of William F. Buckley, Jr., and Ben Bradlee. Buckley put Will's conservative qualifications, whatever they may have been at that point, beyond effective challenge by designating him as Washington editor of *National Review* in 1972, and Bradlee followed through in 1974 by giving him a column three times a week (now two) on the Op-Ed page of the *Washington Post*.

Will's performance in those early years was artful. In general, his strategy seemed to be to take moderately conservative positions, but lace them generously with forthright attacks on pet liberal bêtes noires: notably Richard Nixon and Spiro Agnew. There being no lack of legitimate ammunition against either man, the strategy was eminently successful. After their respective resignations, however, Will's upward path must have seemed less clear. He cautiously implied that President Ford merited approval and election in his own right in 1976, and began making deprecatory references to a determined challenger, former California governor Ronald Reagan. This made it impossible for Will to continue plausibly as *National Review*'s Washington editor (since Reagan was the overwhelming choice of movement conservatives for the 1976 nomination), but he was able to explain his resignation as impelled by the obligations of a new assignment: Washington columnist for the Graham family's other major property, *Newsweek*.

Paradoxically, Carter's performance in office made it easier for Will, in the late 1970s, to strengthen his credentials as a conservative without upsetting his liberal employers at the *Washington Post* and *Newsweek*, since (as we have already noted) Carter managed to offend many liberals almost as much as he offended conservatives. By 1979, however, the national conservative tide was unmistakably setting in, and Will plainly saw no harm in letting it carry him a bit further to the right. In recent years he has carved out a comfortably idiosyncratic position as a "Tory"—a Burkean conservative with an elegant literary style to match, and a loud and profound distrust of modern American conservatism's quasi-populist components. This posture enables him to continue to remain coolly aloof from the conservative mainstream while elaborating criticisms of liberalism that are frequently quite telling. Such distinctions, however, are probably lost on the editors of *World News Tonight*, who simply know Will as a professional who can be depended on to enunciate moderately conservative views without ever going too far.

As an ABC "news analyst," Will is also on view every Sunday as a participant in *This Week with David Brinkley*. Here again ABC's implicit notion of what constitutes a fair balance of opinion is instructive. The regulars on the program are all stars of the Washington media elite, who forgather each week to cross-examine various public figures and argue vigorously among themselves on public issues. Chairman of the board is veteran TV newsman David Brinkley, who comes on as, and by this time probably is, an astringent and curmudgeonly old fellow who has seen it all so often that nothing makes him sick. Whatever Brinkley's political opinions are, he seldom lets them show on the program, preferring to ask questions and direct traffic among his fellow regulars.

Most blatantly anti-Reagan of the regulars, and therefore at least derivatively anticonservative, is ABC's chief White House correspondent, Sam Donaldson. Few Washington media personalities enrage conservatives as dependably as Donaldson, whose sharp and skeptical manner is underscored by strong features and soaring eyebrows that somehow give his face a subtly Oriental cast.

Curiously, Donaldson shows signs of sincerely believing (as we have noted many journalists do) that his obvious and offensive liberal bias is in fact merely an appearance inevitably created by a sharp nose for "bad" news. In addition, he undoubtedly remembers (though he will not discuss) his private feelings in 1964, when Goldwater's PR man Vic Gold remembers Donaldson as "the only pro-Goldwater reporter on the bus"—proof positive that his current liberalism has at least not been a lifelong passion. As a matter of fact, it is undoubtedly true that a streak of pure antiestablishmentarianism runs through Donaldson's abrasive personality: It is hard to imagine him cottoning up to any administration, even Kennedy's. But his hostility to Reagan plainly goes beyond such velleities, and makes him the quarterback of ABC-TV's vigorous liberal offensive against the President, his administration, and conservatism in general.

Will, as noted, is ABC's answer to the charge of bias. But, having recruited Brinkley (a virtual political neuter), Donaldson, and Will for their stable of regulars on the program, ABC then fleshes out the panel with a fourth member, who doesn't participate in questioning the week's guest (three are a crowd, in that respect) but joins the others for the "uninhibited" discussion that concludes the show. It tells a great deal about ABC's notion of balance that this fourth member is drawn almost exclusively from a pool of four journalists: Tom Wicker, Hodding Carter III, Jimmy Carter's White House press aide Jody Powell, and *Los Angeles Times* staffer Mary Ann Dolan. It may be true that Powell's instincts are marginally to the right of those of the other three, but any of the four represents a powerful reinforcement of the program's liberal fire-power.

And so it goes, straight through the ranks of news shows and news commentary in the major media: The overwhelming majority of commentators are blatantly liberal. Here and there a conservative has been added to the mix, often as much to add piquancy as in an effort at balance; but even in such cases the conservative will seldom be a thoroughgoing representative of the conservative movement.

Having said this much, it is only fair to acknowledge that there is occasionally an exception to the rule, and that the rule itself seems at last to be weakening somewhat, as conservatives demonstrate their clout and staying-power and as the case against the media's liberal bias grows better documented year by year.

The aforementioned ABC *Viewpoint* program (aired April 17, 1985) was one such exception. The topic, coincidentally, was media bias. To debate it, ABC introduced former Interior Secretary James Watt, Congressman Philip Crane (R-Illinois), and me—three indisputable conservatives if there ever were any—and Sam Donaldson, Hodding Carter III, and Eleanor Clift of *Newsweek,* all of whom bravely undertook to argue that the media are not, in fact, biased. The moderator was Ted Koppel, and I thought he did as fair a job as anyone could under the circumstances.

Exceptions, however, notoriously just prove the rule. William Buckley's *Firing Line*—a program which ventilates the full spectrum of opinions but is at least presided over by an indisputable "movement conservative"—has held forth in isolated splendor on the PBS television network for more than twenty years, amid what is otherwise unquestionably the most sustained leftist assault on America's TV screens ever attempted. More interesting are certain signs that the liberals who monopolize control of America's key news sources are at last gradually retreating, at least in some cases, to more defensible positions.

The reasons for the retreat—to the modest extent that there is one—are mixed. Undoubtedly one of the most important is the self-evident growth and strength of the conservative movement. It is one thing to ignore, minimize, or attack a nascent political movement, or a viewpoint that has not yet seen one of its spokesmen win national power. It is quite another to mete out that treatment to a political tide of the kind conservatism has generated in the past eight or nine years. The change is making itself felt in the corporate board rooms where ownership of the key media resides; in the editorial offices where those who actually shape the news as we receive it are mindful of the constant need to monitor every shift in the winds of public preference and opinion; and among by-line reporters and the on-camera figures on the TV news programs, whose careers might be damaged by too obvious an identification with an outmoded or unfashionable political viewpoint.

It is not an obvious shift, or a precipitate one, or even (as yet) a very widespread one. But it is there, and it is growing. One can dismiss as a mere exception to the rule ABC's aforementioned *Viewpoint* program of April 17, 1985, on which a six-person panel that was (quite exceptionally) evenly balanced between identifiable liberals and identifiable conservatives debated the issue of bias in the media. But an effort at true balance is visible every week on the syndicated panel program *The McLaughlin Group*, which is named after its feisty chairman John McLaughlin, Washington editor of *National Review*. The other regulars on the program (all journalists) are roly-poly Jack Germond, a longtime Washington political reporter who is a self-avowed liberal; Robert Novak, the glowering and bluntly conservative columnist; and Morton Kondracke, formerly of *The New Republic* and now Washington editor of *Newsweek*, whose eminently moderate brand of liberalism is often fortified by the presence of a "guest panelist" who is also a moderate liberal or even a centrist (e.g., Fred Barnes, currently a senior editor at *The New Republic*).

For every such example of an apparently genuine effort at balance, however, the nation's key media still afford half a dozen examples of sheer and obvious tokenism. George Will, as already noted, is the token conservative at ABC Television. William Safire plays a similar role on the *New York Times*'s Op-Ed page. Bill Buckley's weekly *Firing Line* has served, for over two decades, as the token conservative presence on the PBS television network.

An interesting and inherently rather well balanced PBS television program called *The Advocates*, in which I was frequently involved as the conservative advocate, did appear on PBS from 1969 until 1974, when it ran out of money. It is revived now and then for occasional specials, mostly in presidential election years. During its heyday, one subtle liberal bias built into its format was the curious requirement, imposed by its producers ostensibly in the interests of intellectual consistency, that every issue it debated must take the form of a proposal for some *action by the federal government*—which was rather like requiring a football game to be played between two teams on the understanding, however, that one of the two would have permanent possession of the ball.

As for NBC, CBS, and National Public Radio, they generally disdain even tokenism where the conservative viewpoint is concerned. *Newsweek* published a column by Milton Friedman until 1984, when he was replaced by, of all people, Paul Samuelson. *Time* magazine, as we have already noted, was quirkily conservative under Henry Luce, but his protégé and successor Henry Grunwald moved the publication into comfortable congruence with the moderate-liberal position on most issues. *U.S. News and World Report* (if we may turn aside to discuss it briefly, even though its rank as one of the media elite is debatable) was frankly conservative under its founder, David Lawrence, who died in 1973, but became carefully centrist under the staff ownership that followed, and now seems to be heading toward an explicit liberalism under its new owner, Morton Zuckerman.

To its credit, the *Washington Post*'s Op-Ed page has progressed far beyond tokenism where conservatism is concerned, carrying with reasonable frequency the columns of such staunch conservatives as William Buckley, James Jackson Kilpatrick, Evans and Novak, Jeane Kirkpatrick, and Robert Emmett Tyrrell, plus Mr. Tokenism himself, George Will, and of course a generous supply of ultraliberal decontaminants, from Ellen Goodman, Richard Cohen, and Michael Kinsley to Carl Rowan, Stephen Rosenfeld, Colman McCarthy, and Philip Geyelin. Unfortunately the news reportage of the *Washington Post* leaves even the *New York Times* in the dust when it comes to liberalism. (I cherish the memory of hearing one of the *Post*'s chief Washington political reporters introducing himself to someone in about 1975 as we all waited to appear on a television talk show. "Chalmers Roberts," he purred. *"For* impeachment *before* Watergate.")

That leaves, among the media elite, only the *Wall Street Journal* as a conservative spokesman in its more frankly editorial aspects. This is the work of its brilliant editorial-page editor, Robert Bartley, who publishes columns by conservatives of various hues, including Irving Kristol, John Chamberlain, Herbert Stein, and Suzanne Garment. But Bartley also runs columns by such liberals as Arthur Schlesinger, Jr., Michael Kinsley, and Hodding Carter III, plus the almost frantically leftish diatribes of Alexander Cockburn. (Cockburn is one of the sons of Claud Cockburn, who was one of Ireland's most prominent Communists during his middle years. The junior Cockburn, without exactly repudiating his father's views, seems to prefer a more general anti-Americanism as his basic posture, and tinctures this with a noisy sympathy for the Arab position in foreign affairs.) Here again, however, as in the case of the *Washington Post,* it is in the *Journal*'s news columns, and especially those generated by its Washington bureau, that the washing of liberalism is most diligently taken in.

It is hardly surprising, in view of the media's overall record, that one of the most promising initiatives to ensure a reasonable balance in our key media was strangled in its childhood, a few years ago, by the arrogant masters of our journalistic revels. At the time they saw little reason to countenance outside criticism, however well-intentioned or fundamentally sympathetic.

In 1971 the Twentieth Century Fund, a mainstream New York foundation, asked fourteen prominent Americans to serve as a task force "to examine the feasibility of setting up a press council—or councils—in the United States." The idea was not an altogether new one; the British Press Council had been in existence for two decades, and was generally conceded to be doing a useful job as an independent monitor of press fairness. There had, in addition, been discussions of various ideas along the same line in American journalistic circles over the years.

It seems certain, however, that one powerful spur to the impulse that flowered in the early 1970s was the famous attack on the fairness of television news by Vice President Spiro Agnew in a speech at Des Moines, Iowa, on November 13, 1969. Whatever one thought of the speech (and opinion was sharply divided: the media tended to regard it as a bald attempt at political censorship, while their critics hailed it as focusing much-needed attention on press bias), there is no gainsaying the fact that it made political bias in the media a prominent issue in the ongoing national dialogue. The media fought back savagely—with what success, at least in the personal cases of Agnew and his patron Richard Nixon, we now know; but, strategically speaking, the media were on the defensive.

It was in this atmosphere that Murray Rossant, the executive director of the Twentieth Century Fund, turned his attention to the possibility of a nationwide press council based essentially on the British model. The council would (among other things) hear out and investigate grievances against individual media, and publish its findings. It would have no "teeth"—no powers of enforcement or penalization—but it was hoped that a finding that a newspaper or television news program had been unfair in a particular instance would inspire the miscreant, and perhaps others, to be more careful thereafter.

The task force, which was composed exclusively of liberals both within and outside the journalistic profession (a saving grace in this particular instance, since it ruled out any idea that the whole thing was a right-wing plot), in due course reported that the formation of a National News Council would indeed be a desirable step. The Twentieth Century Fund and the Markle Foundation put up the money to launch it, with Rossant taking the laboring oar in selecting and recruiting members. Once again the fact that the council, as finally launched in 1973, was overwhelmingly liberal in its complexion was, in view of its mission to monitor the fairness of the media, altogether in its favor. But Rossant was aware that the conservative viewpoint on issues relating to the media could not and ought not to be disregarded completely, and that appears to have been the consideration that led him to invite me to become one of the founding members of the News Council. I served on it from 1973 until the end of 1980, working principally as a member of its Grievance Committee, the entity that investigated complaints and recommended appropriate findings to the full council.

The National News Council closed its doors in 1983, the victim of far more problems than are discussable (or, fortunately, relevant) here. When it folded, the Twentieth Century Fund sensibly commissioned a study of what had gone wrong. Patrick Brogan, an editorial writer for the *New York Daily News,* conducted the study and issued a report (*Spiked: The Short Life and Death of the National News Council,* published by the Twentieth Century Fund in 1985) which can be commended to anyone interested in the subject. But one or two aspects of the matter are highly relevant to the issues addressed in this book.

As already noted, Agnew's 1969 Des Moines speech put the media on the defensive on the issue of political bias. The generating impulse that led to the establishment of the National News Council unquestionably derived considerable momentum from that fact. If the media were under heavy attack for bias, there might after all be a certain amount of fire causing all that smoke. And whether the charge of bias was true or false, it was clearly desirable to have the charge investigated, and the media thereafter monitored, by an independent and if possible prestigious group of people whose basic sympathy for the media, and indeed whose own personal liberalism (in every case but one—mine), were beyond challenge. Add to these comforting characteristics the fact that the News Council was to have no power whatever beyond the presumed influence of its published findings, and one is tempted to feel that the council was an organization into whose lap the beleaguered media ought to have been positively eager to crawl.

But 1973—the year of the council's formation—was, by a malignant stroke of fate, also the year in which the media recovered their breath and went over to the offensive against their tormentors. It was the year when the Watergate scandal broke in full force, propelling Nixon toward ultimate impeachment or resignation; it was the year when Agnew pleaded nolo contendere to charges of accepting bribes while governor of Maryland and resigned from the vice presidency of the United States. Many conscientious journalists continued to support the concept and the work of the National News Council, but there is simply no question that the general *mood* of the media changed dramatically.

Far from being on the defensive, the media were now spectacularly, exultantly, on the offensive. They could—they did—play major roles in toppling a president and vice president of the United States. Students in schools of journalism all over the United States looked up to Robert Woodward and Carl Bernstein as having achieved the pinnacle of the profession, and dreamed of the day when they would find their own Deep Throat and topple some president as detestable as Richard Nixon (well, *almost* as detestable).

The media, in short, were simply not *interested* in self-criticism in the heady years that began with 1973. The National News Council was playing yesterday's ball game.

In addition, and quite independently of the dramatic change of mood that came over the media as a whole in and after 1973, there were influential members of the profession who were profoundly opposed, on principle, to the whole concept of a monitor of media behavior and who would have fought the idea of a National News Council whether the atmospherics were propitious or not. Perhaps the most influential of these opponents was Abe Rosenthal, managing editor (later executive editor) of the *New York Times*. Another *Times* editor, John B. Oakes (then in charge of the editorial page), had served on the original Twentieth Century Fund task force which had unanimously recommended creation of a National News Council. But Oakes apparently hadn't consulted Rosenthal, or at any rate hadn't convinced him, because Rosenthal was from the outset a determined and powerful foe of the whole concept. What's more, Rosenthal persuaded the *Times*'s publisher, Punch Sulzberger, that his view of the matter was the correct one, with the result that the most serious attempt ever made to launch a sympathetic monitoring mechanism for America's national media had to contend, from the outset, with the tooth-and-claw resistance of the nation's leading newspaper. Inquiries from the News Council staff to the *Times*, requesting the paper's version of events which had prompted someone to lodge a complaint with the council, were routinely ignored. Far worse, from the standpoint of the council's utility and viability, was the fact that the *Times*, while not necessarily refusing to carry articles on the council's findings and other activities when it deemed them newsworthy, frequently buried them in tiny paragraphs far back in the newspaper—even, on one or two memorable occasions, amid the shipping news.

Rosenthal was not by any means the News Council's only critic among prominent figures in the profession. Mike O'Neill, then editor of the *New York Daily News* and later president of the American Society of Newspaper Editors, was another. The view of critics like Rosenthal and O'Neill seemed to be (and there is no reason to doubt their sincerity) that a publication is, and ought to be, solely responsible to its readership in such matters as fairness, accuracy, reliability, and balance. Certainly they were not prepared to answer on such matters to some ad hoc group of volunteers, no matter how high-minded or distinguished.

On the other hand, a good many leading figures in the world of journalism welcomed the creation of the National News Council and lent it valuable support over the years: Richard Salant for one, then the president of CBS News; Barry Bingham, Sr., chairman of the board of the *Louisville Courier Journal;* Ralph Otwell, managing editor of the *Chicago Sun-Times;* Michael Pulitzer, associate editor of the *St. Louis Post-Dispatch;* and Norman Isaacs, the veteran journalist who was editor in residence of the Graduate School of Journalism of Columbia University, and who served as chairman of the News Council from 1977 to 1982.

Despite the support of these and many other prominent Americans in and out of the field of journalism, the National News Council never succeeded in overcoming the resistance of its critics. In addition to a general sense in the journalistic profession that the period of maximum peril (the aftermath of the Agnew speech) had passed, there was an uneasy feeling on the part of some of the council's politically liberal enthusiasts that its national mandate required it to concentrate too heavily on the derelictions of the liberal media elite ("our best," as one person revealingly put it to me) when there were plenty of conservative journalistic malefactors (e.g., Pulliam and Loeb) who deserved scourging if only the council could focus its attention on local media and local issues.

Readers interested in learning more about the problems, achievements, and ultimate fate of the National News Council are referred to the aforementioned Brogan report. The episode takes its place in this study, however, as a striking illustration of the self-satisfaction of the media (or many representatives of the media) when they came under serious criticism during the 1970s and early 1980s. Whether this will continue to be the media's attitude in some hypothetical future crisis (one of which is discussed elsewhere in this volume—see Chapter 11) may of course be questioned. For the moment, however, apprehensive friends of the legitimate rights of the media can only recall the warning of the rejected First Tempter in T. S. Eliot's *Murder in the Cathedral:*

> I leave you to the pleasures of your higher vices,
> Which will have to be paid for at higher prices.

# CHAPTER 7

# *How Did the Bias Develop?*

AS WE WILL have occasion to discuss again later (see page 152), modern scholarship makes it plain that the concept of the press as an autonomous institution committed to the ideal of objective investigative reporting arose only in the twentieth century, when the growing economic strength of major newspapers and magazines enabled them to break free from their previous dependence on political factions.

One of the concept's earliest and best-known manifestations was the group of writers criticized by President Theodore Roosevelt in 1906 as "the muckrakers," a pejorative term that soon acquired a favorable connotation among those who approved of their work. The January 1903 issue of *McClure's* magazine, for example, contained hard-hitting articles by Lincoln Steffens, Ray Stannard Baker, and Ida M. Tarbell exposing alleged wrongdoing in such disparate fields as municipal government, labor, and trusts. In the words of the *Encyclopaedia Britannica,* "The intense public interest aroused by articles critical of political and financial rings, housing, labor, insurance, and other problems rallied writers, editors, and reformers."

The muckrakers as a category had pretty well disappeared before the outbreak of World War I, but they left a permanent mark on the American journalistic psyche. There was clearly a market for hard-hitting exposes of corporate and governmental wrongdoing, provided the reporters' objectivity could be depended on. The original muckrakers had been fairly explicitly leftist in their political complexion (Steffens, for example, returning from a trip to the Soviet Union, earned a permanent place for himself in the annals of fatuity with his remark, "I have been over into the future, and it works"). But many of their journalistic criticisms were on the mark, and their technique was clearly capable of application to all sorts of situations not even highly political, let alone leftist, in their implications.

Between the wars, therefore, the tradition of independent investigative journalism grew apace. Its practitioners, of course, were no more able than their successors today (or, for that matter, than the original muckrakers) to avoid developing a "theory" or concept of the story and selecting those facts that tended to substantiate it. But there was general obeisance to the ideal of objectivity, as well as a widespread belief that every important factual assertion ought to be "sourced"—i.e., either documented or attributed to a named individual.

Insofar as political biases intruded during this period, they were at least as likely to be conservative as liberal. Certain publications were hospitable to the leftist and liberal tradition of the muckrakers, but the dominant media and their personnel—the equivalent of today's media elite—were overwhelmingly conservative.

It is true that Franklin Roosevelt's genial charm easily conquered most members of the White House press corps, which thereupon (for example) conspired to help his political managers conceal his major physical disabilities. (Photographs of Roosevelt in a wheelchair were rare until long after his death, and to this day I have only heard descriptions of the strenuous ordeal involved in seating him in a car. Compare the media's treatment of George Wallace in the 1970s, after he was crippled by a would-be assassin.) But there were plenty of major newspapers and magazines all over the country that were vehemently critical of FDR, and no lack of Washington columnists and correspondents to reflect their views.

The *New York Herald-Tribune* spoke for eastern Republicanism; Captain Joseph Patterson's *New York Daily News* was even more conservative than the *Herald-Tribune;* Colonel McCormick's *Chicago Tribune* dominated the Midwest; Henry Luce's *Time* magazine kept the country at large closely informed on what it regarded as Roosevelt's misdeeds. Pulliam, Gannett, Loeb, and scores of other locally influential newspaper publishers chimed in, while such major Washington correspondents and commentators as Mark Sullivan and David Lawrence provided ammunition from Washington itself.

Even so, however, the whole journalistic atmosphere was vastly different than it is today. A Washington reporter just starting out on his career in that city would of course try to develop personal contacts in or close to government, from whom he could obtain leads on promising stories. And those contacts would tend to group toward one end or the other of the political spectrum of that time, depending on the reporter's own inclinations. But most reporters would try to avoid at least the appearance of political bias, and their reportorial techniques were a world away from some that are common today.

It is doubtful, for example, whether the phrase "According to a source in the Administration who asked not to be identified" was ever used at all, let alone frequently, as the central basis for an investigative story in Washington in the 1930s. Certainly, anonymous sources were used and frankly cited, but the concept of citing such leaks as the chief ground for a story had just not acquired the respectability, let alone the vogue, that it enjoys today.

There is, for example, an engagingly anachronistic flavor about this dispatch from a *New York Times* correspondent in Washington which appeared on page 1 of the *Times* on February 11, 1939, as Franklin Roosevelt and his Republican opponents were arguing over the proper United States response to the approach of war in Europe:

WASHINGTON, Feb. 10—The Senate Military Affairs Committee decided today to lift, at least partially, the cloak of secrecy which has shrouded its consideration of President Roosevelt's emergency national defense programs thus far. The action was forced by a group of members who believe that the mixture of foreign policy, neutrality and national defense which has been discussed at its meetings should be made known to the public.

Committee members said that future meetings would be held behind closed doors, with members of the committee at liberty to discuss testimony publicly afterward except for portions which the full membership decided should be kept in confidence as military secrets. . . .

Senator Sheppard, chairman of the committee, did not seem enthusiastic about the new plan. He said that only a trial would demonstrate whether it would work or not. . . .

Senator Nye, who has been one of the principal critics of secrecy, expressed himself as pleased with the committee's decision. It was his understanding that practical agreement had been reached to make public the record of past testimony, including that of Secretary of the Treasury Morgenthau, Secretary of War Woodring and General Malin Craig, Chief of Staff, but this view was not shared by other members.

Each member of the committee has in his possession the printed transcript of the testimony so far. He is expected to read it between now and Monday, when the committee will meet again, with a view to determine how much, if any, of it can safely be made public.

Certainly it wouldn't take long, in the journalistic climate of Washington today, for a full copy of that printed transcript to be "made available to the *Times* by a source close to the committee."

It was only after World War II, and particularly after the first bruising encounters between the then-dominant liberal Democrats and the conservative wing of the Republican party over the issue of domestic communism and internal security, that certain journalists began to make a specialty of publishing stories based on information anonymously obtained. Not surprisingly, syndicated columnists led the way. Of these, Drew Pearson was perhaps the earliest and certainly the most prominent. Before long, in the Washington of the 1950s, Pearson was known as *the* person to whom to leak discreditable information about anybody whom one wanted to damage.

By this time the Washington press corps had begun to acquire the aggressively liberal attitudes that now characterize it. (In the field of television, one early specialist in the genre was Edward R. Murrow, whose *See It Now* television documentary was widely credited with mobilizing public opinion against the investigative tactics of Senator Joseph R. McCarthy.) But the Eisenhower administration was comfortably "moderate" on most issues from the standpoint of that day, and the impulse to savage it journalistically was not widespread among the media elite. Moreover, Eisenhower was succeeded by John Kennedy, a liberal Democrat far more to the media's taste.

Kennedy's record during his brief administration was not, in point of fact, all that liberal: He authorized the invasion of Cuba, forced the Soviet Union to withdraw its missiles from the island, sharply reduced taxes with the remark that "a rising tide raises all boats," sent the first United States forces to Vietnam, and took no major steps in the field of civil rights. But he was a Massachusetts Democrat whose heart certainly seemed to be in the right place from a liberal standpoint, and his youth, his undeniable charm, and his beautiful wife did the rest: The Washington press corps fell unashamedly in love with a president for the first time since Franklin Roosevelt.

Perhaps the best example, though by no means the only one, was Ben Bradlee, then head of the Washington bureau of *Newsweek*. In his book *Conversations with Kennedy* (Norton, 1975), Bradlee retired, one hopes for good, the image of the Washington reporter as a neutral, objective observer of the American political scene. Even before Kennedy was nominated by the Democrats in 1960, Bradlee had become his personal friend. He was quick to recognize the rarity and the potential value of the perspective this afforded him:

> There came a time when I understood that I had a unique, historical access to this fascinating man. Not the access of those who worked so closely with him and created with him the public record—the Bundys, the Sorensens, the

O'Donnells, the O'Briens, the McNamaras. Nor the access of many who had known him longer and better. But the unique access of a journalist who saw him after the day's work was done, who saw him relaxed and anxious for companionship and diversion, eager to interrupt his sobering duties with conversation, gossip, and laughter. And I knew enough of history to know that the fruits of this kind of access seldom make the history books, and the great men of our time are less understood as a result. [p. 10]

So Bradlee continued to play the dual roles of reporter and friend, with the perfectly predictable result. Of the 1960 election, he writes:

. . . But however much I had tried to be fair and objective in my reporting of the campaign, I now wanted Kennedy to win. I wanted my friend and neighbor to be president. It wasn't that I didn't like Richard Nixon. I had covered him for several weeks during the campaign, and I just didn't know him. I never got close to understanding him. [p. 31]

But what about the media's famous fallback contention that, however much they may personally like or dislike an individual, they don't let that fact influence their reportage? Bradlee spares us such cant. Describing an occasion on which candidate Kennedy bragged to the editors of *Newsweek* that during the primary campaign he was "going to goddamn well take Ohio, for openers," Bradlee continues:

That line never appeared in print. The press generally protected Kennedy [a *frisson* of caution may have assailed Bradlee here, for he adds] as they protected all candidates, from his excesses of language and his sometimes outspokenly deprecatory characterizations of other politicians. [p.18]

But the strain of insisting that the media treated all candidates equally soon becomes too great; after citing a couple of examples of Kennedy's undiplomatic candor about his fellow politicians, Bradlee admits the media's double standard:

. . . Kennedy sometimes referred to Lyndon Johnson, and truly without hostility, as a "riverboat gambler," and often as "Landslide," a reference to the time when LBJ was first elected to the Senate by a majority of eighty-seven votes. He liked Stuart Symington as a human being, and felt the 1960 Democratic convention would most likely turn to Symington if they stopped him, but he stood in less than awe of his intellectual ability and said so often and bluntly to reporters. Other politicians said the same things about Kennedy, of course, but *the press appreciated Kennedy for his openness and protected him,* while the press reacted skeptically to other candidates. [p. 18] [Emphasis supplied.]

That Bradlee's personal friendship with Kennedy was a gold mine for a journalist goes without saying. Doubters are referred to Bradlee's book. Kennedy deliberately let Bradlee have valuable information before the rest of the media received it, and Bradlee's opportunity to gain insights into the President's attitude toward individuals and issues was matchless. Of course, such a relationship also had its perils: More than once Bradlee was temporarily exiled from Kennedy's inner circle for some supposed journalistic misdeed. But his book is a graphic account of how personal and journalistic motives can become interwoven.

It is never more so than in its thunderous silence about Kennedy's obsessive womanizing. This unappealing aspect of Kennedy's personality was known, during his years in the White House, to every Washington journalist worth his salt—as well, for that matter, as to every politician and indeed every ordinary gossip within the Beltway. It is a fair question whether such information is in fact relevant in commenting or reporting on a public figure, but the trend in recent years has certainly been running in favor of "the people's right to know." Assuredly, if any president after Kennedy had had as many assignations with as many women as he did, both in the White House itself and elsewhere, the journalistic impulse to publish the story would have overpowered any residual doubts about its relevance.

But "the press . . . protected him," and as late as 1975 when his book was published Bradlee (now editor of the *Washington Post*) was protecting him still—even though, by that late date, the "Camelot" image was already acquiring considerable tarnish. In Bradlee's case, the tendency was humanly understandable: He and his wife had been friends of the Kennedys *as couples,* and it was scarcely conceivable that Bradlee, at any later date, could bring himself to gossip about the adulterous activities of his old crony, however aware he had been of them at the time. But this simply illustrates the depth of Bradlee's commitment to the Kennedys, and how easily it outstripped any journalistic obligation he may have felt. The situation of Kennedy's other friends and admirers in the Washington press corps differed from Bradlee's chiefly in degree, rather than in kind.

But a time was drawing near when the media's attitude toward the presidency would change dramatically. And given the by now overwhelmingly liberal bias of the media, it is not surprising that the change coincided precisely with the break between Lyndon Johnson and liberals in general.

In succeeding John Kennedy, Johnson undertook the probably hopeless job of pleasing, or at any rate charming, America's liberals as much as

Kennedy had—a task not made any easier by the clashes that quickly began occurring between Johnson and such powerful members of JFK's inner circle as Attorney General Robert Kennedy. For a time, however, open warfare was avoided, and Johnson actually enjoyed a distinctly friendly press. Certainly the liberals, including those in the media, vastly preferred him to Barry Goldwater, and the treatment accorded Goldwater by the media in the 1964 election campaign faithfully reflected that preference.

In addition, Johnson's early legislative initiatives met with enthusiastic liberal approval. Even before the 1964 election, he had steered important civil rights measures through Congress; and after his landslide defeat of Goldwater he launched a vast expansion of the nation's welfare system, in such varied fields as housing and urban development, education, and medical care for the elderly. Johnson was, in fact—despite a folksy southwestern manner not all that congenial to most liberals—well on his way to a high place in the liberal pantheon of eminently satisfactory presidents when Vietnam brought him down.

Ironically, it was not under Lyndon Johnson that American military involvement in Vietnam began. And in the 1964 election campaign he took care to leave the impression that, in his peace-loving administration, it would assuredly not expand. In point of fact, however, even before the campaign was over Johnson was quietly planning to escalate American involvement in the struggle between North and South Vietnam. During 1965 and 1966, America's commitment doubled and redoubled, though Johnson, most unwisely, never asked Congress for a formal declaration of war, or took any other effective steps to mobilize American public opinion behind the war effort. In the words of the *Encyclopaedia Britannica*, "Strident student opposition to both war and the draft system spread to include liberals, intellectuals, and civil rights leaders." And, it might have added, the media.

In the light of hindsight, we can see that a development of truly monumental significance was taking place. Prior to 1965, with negligible exceptions and differences in degree, the Washington press corps (and the media elite generally) were broadly sympathetic to the successive occupants of the White House. From 1965 forward, they moved into increasingly explicit and outspoken opposition to the presidents chosen by the American people. Today it has been not far short of a quarter of a century since America has had a president of whom the media, and liberals generally, wholeheartedly approved.

It has been suggested, by Kevin Phillips and others, that at least in the ten years beginning in 1965 the media and various other groups in American society—the major foundations, the state and federal bureaucracies, and the educational establishment—began to regard themselves as collectively the vanguard of a brand-new class in the American society, destined to challenge certain older social structures (notably business, but also conservative blue-collar labor) for dominance. On this view, as Jeffrey Hart remarked in *National Review,* the growing welfare constituency, to which liberals were of course devoted, served to legitimize the actions of the new-class vanguard in much the same way that the interests of the "proletariat" served to legitimize the actions of the Leninists in the Russian Revolution.

Certainly the performance of the media in the decade 1965–1975 lent plausibility to this "new class" speculation. The Vietnam War was, of course, the dominant issue as long as it lasted. On the battlefields of Indochina, the ever-increasing technological capabilities of television made it possible to bring the horrors of war into every American living room in a way that had simply not been possible even as recently as the Korean War. But, though technology was part of the story, it was far from being the whole of it. The decision of American journalists concerning what to stress and what to disregard—i.e., their "theory" of the story—was far more important. And the performance of America's journalists in Vietnam set new and positively awesome records for tendentiousness.

One does not have to be of any particular opinion on the general subject of the Vietnam War to acknowledge this. No one who was watching American television or reading American newspapers at the time can ever forget the emotional impact of the photographs of "burning bonzes," or a child ablaze with napalm, or the pistol-to-head execution of a captured guerrilla. Was the Vietnam War the first in our history in which such things occurred? Was it even, for all the conceded improvements in the technology of wartime news coverage, the first time that such tragedies and/or atrocities were ever witnessed and recorded by American newsmen? Not at all.

What was different about the Vietnam War was the fact that, for the first time a large and influential segment of the American society was profoundly opposed to a war in which the country was engaged *and* was able to wage a powerful and effective propaganda campaign against it with the help of media representatives who enthusiastically shared that opposition.

Of course the battlefields were far from the only place where the media placed their influence at the disposal of the war's opponents. On the home front, the practice of publishing documents and information from unidentified sources hostile to the war effort began to take on unprecedented dimensions. At home too, every antiwar demonstration was accorded lavish television coverage. The whole custom (now sanctified by time) of staging mass events of one sort or another on behalf of liberal causes in good weather in the spring and fall originated in this period, and twenty years later there are superannuated former "peaceniks" who still remember those early marches as "the good old days" and who are still casting about nostalgically for an emotional substitute.

But it was in Vietnam, and not on some remote and bloody hilltop but in Saigon itself, that the American media most dramatically outdid themselves in misreporting, for squarely political purposes, an important story and thereby materially influenced the course and outcome of the Vietnam War.

Thanks to Peter Braestrup and others who have researched the subject intensively, we now know that the Communists' "Tet offensive" of February 1968 was, from their own standpoint, an unmitigated disaster. The North Vietnamese invasion of the south was getting nowhere, and the Tet offensive—a coordinated series of all-out attacks on numerous cities and military targets in South Vietnam, including Saigon itself—was launched in a desperate effort to acquire the essential strategic initiative. The attempt failed spectacularly. But the focus of the media was on Saigon, where Communist commandos made a daring (though futile) attack on the United States embassy, briefly penetrating its grounds; and this foray, extensively reported in the American media without any adequate context, was used by CBS's Walter Cronkite and other commentators to make it appear that American and South Vietnamese forces had suffered a devastating setback.

From being a bone-crunching defeat for the Communists, the Tet offensive was quite simply transformed, by the American media, into an American and South Vietnamese disaster which demonstrated and ultimately came to symbolize the "unwinnability" of the war. Less than two months later Lyndon Johnson announced that he would neither seek nor accept his party's renomination for president that year. The media had reason to feel that they had played a noteworthy part in his decision.

But the dramatic break of liberals generally, and of the media in particular, with Lyndon Johnson turned out to be only a minor-key prelude to the battle that broke out between the media and Richard Nixon when the latter was first nominated and then elected President of the United States in 1968.

The hostility between Nixon and the media was partly a by-product of the hostility of liberals generally toward Nixon. This dated from at least 1950, when then-Congressman Nixon ran against Congresswoman Helen Gahagan Douglas for the United States Senate, and was sharply faulted by critics for allegedly imputing Communist sympathies to her.

Nixon won the election, and may have rehabilitated himself to some extent in liberal eyes by serving as leader of the pro-Eisenhower forces in the California delegation at the 1952 Republican National Convention in Chicago—a key delegation which Governor Earl Warren was trying to keep behind his favorite-son candidacy at a time when Eisenhower (whom the liberals were rooting for) was straining every nerve to defeat Robert Taft. Certainly Nixon pleased the Eisenhower camp, which rewarded him with the vice presidential nomination.

The campaign itself, however, included an incident which revived and reinforced the liberal dislike of Nixon. Once Taft had been defeated by Eisenhower for the Republican nomination, liberal sympathies were free to rally around Eisenhower's liberal Democratic opponent, Adlai Stevenson. Disarray in the Eisenhower camp was therefore good news, and Nixon inadvertently caused a very considerable amount of it when, in mid-campaign, the vice presidential nominee was disclosed to have been the beneficiary of a "secret campaign fund" contributed by business backers during his 1950 race for the Senate.

There was nothing illegal about the fund (indeed, it quickly transpired that Stevenson had had one too, during his race for the Illinois governorship), but in the superheated atmosphere of the campaign appearances counted for more than mere facts. Nixon proved that he realized this by going on national television and making an emotional appeal for understanding that included everything from a reference to his dog Checkers to a mention of his wife's "good Republican cloth coat"— a sly dig at the mink coats which figured in scandal charges against the outgoing Truman administration. National sentiment shifted to Nixon's side in the controversy and he survived it—but his reputation among liberals, including the media, for "trickiness" was heavily reinforced.

One later episode may have helped Nixon's reputation among the liberals somewhat, but probably not much. When Eisenhower finally decided, very late in the day, to break with Senator Joseph McCarthy, it was Vice President Nixon who (on Eisenhower's orders) actually signaled the administration's displeasure with McCarthy in a nationwide radio broadcast on March 13, 1954.

But the liberal dislike of Nixon never really died, and as he became the front-runner for the 1960 Republican presidential nomination in the late 1950s, at a time when conservative sentiment in the country was beginning to organize and grow and Nixon felt obliged to stay on reasonably good terms with these new forces, the old liberal distrust of him returned in full vigor. New York governor Nelson Rockefeller was now the liberals' favorite to succeed Eisenhower as leader of the Republican party and, if the party must win in 1960, as president of the United States.

With conservative support, Nixon won the Republican nomination— only to lose narrowly to John Kennedy in November. Back in California, he wrested the 1962 gubernatorial nomination from conservative Assemblyman Joseph Shell, but was then defeated by Democrat Edmund G. "Pat" Brown in the general election. It was after that bitter blow that Nixon, despairing of ever winning high office again, briefly dropped his guard and affirmed his own reciprocal bitterness toward the media by announcing, at his "last press conference" that "you won't have Nixon to kick around anymore."

In the ensuing years, however, Nixon, having moved east and become a partner in a Wall Street law firm, edged back into the Republican and national limelight—introducing Barry Goldwater to the 1964 Republican convention that had just nominated him, campaigning tirelessly for Republican candidates in every state in the off-year elections of 1966, and ultimately declaring himself a candidate for the 1968 presidential nomination.

Few developments could have been better calculated to rouse the hostility of the media. Their old enemy was abroad again, and closing in on the White House. Having, like liberals generally, broken with the presidency as an institution while it was still held by Lyndon Johnson, they had no difficulty whatever in combining their new animus against the presidency with their ancient animus against Nixon.

We have already noted (pages 67–70) the media's truly monumental bias against Nixon in the 1968 campaign, as demonstrated by Edith Efron in her book, *The News Twisters*. The evening news programs of the three commercial television networks expended (by actual word count) many times as much wordage on hostile coverage of Nixon as on any that could conceivably be described as sympathetic.

To recapitulate briefly: ABC, where the unfavorable word count exceeded the favorable by nearly nine to one (7,493 to 869), was actually the best-balanced network of the three. In the last seven weeks of the campaign, which was the period under review, NBC aired just 431 words favorable to Nixon and 4,234—or nearly ten times as many—that were critical of him. But CBS walked off with the roses in this bias derby, by broadcasting just 320 favorable words about Nixon and 5,300 that were hostile: a ratio of better (or worse) than sixteen to one. Not even George Wallace, let alone Hubert Humphrey, encountered anything approaching such an overwhelming barrage of negativism.

But the American people—not for the first time—reacted very differently than the media to the choices before them. While 13 percent of them cast their ballots for Wallace, a narrow majority of the remainder still preferred Nixon over Humphrey. Richard Nixon had made it to the Oval Office at last, and the media would now have Nixon to kick around again for at least four years.

They set to work with grim enthusiasm. Their principal weapon was the anonymous informant—an instrument already honed to razor-sharpness during the latter years of the Johnson administration, but positively made to order for badgering, thwarting, and just generally tormenting Richard Nixon.

For after all, the advent of a Republican presidential administration—the first in thirty-six years, if you didn't count Eisenhower (and there was precious little point in counting him)—initially changed the occupants of only a few hundred government jobs at most. In every department and agency, not to mention Congress, both branches of which remained solidly in Democratic control, virtually every job below that thin top layer was held by someone who had obtained it under Democratic auspices. Moreover, the vast majority of such people enjoyed Civil Service status, which made it all but impossible to move them and quite impossible to fire them.

Of course, many—perhaps most—of these government employees were willing to serve their new bosses loyally, at least in the sense of discharging their duties with reasonable neutrality and competence. But large numbers of them were, in personal terms, liberal ideologues who privately detested the new President, his policies, and his appointees. How long do you suppose it took these disgruntled federal employees and the Washington media elite to find each other and make common cause against the Nixon presidency and all it stood for?

Not long. From the very outset, the Nixon administration was plagued by leaks carefully designed to weaken it and thwart its policy initiatives. It was not that such leaks had not occurred in prior administrations; they had. Nor, as the media were quick to stress, were officials of the Nixon administration itself by any means innocent of such practices. (Henry

Kissinger in particular acquired a formidable reputation as one of Washington's prime sources of anonymous information.) Rather, it was the *quantity* of the leaks, and the deliberate effect they had on the formulation and implementation of policy, that were new.

As a matter of fact, there is nothing to prevent a reporter from inventing a "source" out of whole cloth. According to Mel Grayson, a former Associated Press reporter and assistant night city editor at the old *New York Herald-Tribune,* that is exactly what many of them do:

> As a former newspaper and wire service reporter I realize that the reason many newsmen refuse to name their sources is that there aren't any sources. The reporters made the whole thing up: It's all fiction. In other cases there are sources, but the sources are so unqualified to be sources that for a newsman to reveal them would be to expose himself as either a fool or a charlatan.

Grayson's charge, which was understandably not all that popular in journalistic circles, received spectacular confirmation in 1981 when Janet Cooke, a reporter for the *Washington Post,* received a Pulitzer Prize for her touching description of the plight of "Jimmy," an unidentified eight-year-old heroin addict—a story which subsequent investigation revealed to be pure fiction.

Nevertheless, genuine anonymous sources do exist, and in one agency and department after another, employees opposed to the existing or prospective policies of the Nixon administration leaked information or documents, or both, to their friends in the media. The latter, in turn, were able to use them as the basis for stories suggesting that things were going badly, or that this or that proposed change would have disastrous results, or that a particular named individual was responsible for such and such blunders, etc.

Jack Anderson, to take only one example, was able to tell his readers of secret discussions concerning United States policy toward India and Pakistan that took place in the ultrasensitive National Security Council—reports that seriously damaged American relations with India, the largest and perhaps most important nation in the Third World.

Undoubtedly the most famous such leak, however, was that of the so-called Pentagon Papers—forty-seven volumes of classified documents, originating during the Johnson administration and dealing largely with the growing United States military involvement in Vietnam, which were "made available" to the *New York Times* and certain other publications in 1971.

The valid impact of the Pentagon Papers, insofar as they had any, was merely to confirm what was already widely known: that Johnson had privately been planning to escalate American military participation in the Vietnam War even before the 1964 election, at the very time he was accusing Barry Goldwater, the Republican nominee, of such plans and depicting himself as the "peace" candidate. In the overheated atmosphere of 1971, however, millions of people who never read a line of the Pentagon Papers were sure they disclosed all manner of sordid derring-do behind the scenes in the United States government, including the Nixon administration.

From the standpoint of President Nixon, the situation had its ironies. He had no particular obligation, or inclination, to protect the confidences of his Democratic predecessor. On the other hand, he did feel a general obligation to defend the principle of the confidentiality of classified documents, even though it was undoubtedly true that many of the Pentagon Papers were overclassified or ought never to have been classified at all. In addition, the Pentagon Papers' forty-seven volumes contained copies of a considerable number of communications between Washington, Saigon, and elsewhere which, if published, would un-questionably enable the Russians to break the codes in which they had originally been transmitted. This, in turn, would enable them to decode many other messages transmitted in those same codes at around the same time, it being the practice of most major powers to record and file even messages they cannot immediately decode, in the event of just such a future break as publication of the Pentagon Papers would provide.

So Nixon ordered the Justice Department to seek an injunction against publication of the Pentagon Papers by the *Times* or anyone else—the sort of "prior restraint" on a news medium that our courts are understandably reluctant (though not, in a proper case, absolutely unwilling) to impose. The basic issue was whether publication of the documents would do "irreparable damage" to the interests of the United States. The media, closing ranks behind the *Times,* sought to suggest to the public that prior restraint on publication would be, or ought to be, unconstitutional per se. For the courts, their lawyers added the more persuasive argument that, in this particular case, publication would not in fact result in irreparable damage to United States interests anyway.

It is not widely known that, to strengthen this latter argument, the *Times,* while continuing to pose as the foe of all prior restraint, quietly agreed, in private negotiations with the administration, not to publish certain parts of the Pentagon Papers that would jeopardize the security of American codes, as described above.

Under those circumstances, the media were able to persuade the courts, including the Supreme Court, that publication of the remaining Pentagon Papers would not irreparably damage the legitimate interests of the United States (as distinguished from Lyndon Johnson's reputation for probity), and thus did not constitute a proper occasion for an injunction.

The final chapter of the Pentagon Papers controversy opened later in 1971, when Daniel Ellsberg, an MIT professor and research analyst for the Rand Foundation to whom the documents later known as the Pentagon Papers had been made available for purposes of a historical study of the Vietnam War, was identified by a colleague as the individual who leaked those documents to the media.

It is rather comical these days to see Ellsberg (who was indicted for violating the Espionage Act but never convicted) posing, at well-paid appearances on college campuses, as a heroic whistle-blower who sacrificed his career and risked prosecution to disclose to the American people documents demonstrating the existence of massive perfidy high in the government. The truth, of course, is that there is no evidence that Ellsberg ever planned to suffer the slightest inconvenience as a result of leaking the Pentagon Papers to the media. He was still posing, in discreet silence, as an innocent academician when a colleague who happened to know about his responsibility for the leak disclosed the facts to the federal authorities. Ellsberg was thereupon dragged, kicking and screaming as it were, into the limelight, where he has flourished ever since.

Statistical evidence on the subject of leaks is, in the nature of things, extremely difficult to obtain. But one interesting analysis, based on a poll of 786 readers of the magazine *American Politics* who described themselves as politicians, Capitol Hill staffers, attorneys, or lobbyists, appeared in the August 1987 issue of that publication. Not surprisingly in view of the growth of the phenomenon as we have traced it, the magazine reported that "the highest overall percentages of leakers were found among those who identified themselves as Democrats (33 percent), liberals (36 percent), lobbyists (37 percent), those aged 35–54 (34 percent) and men (30 percent)."

By the early 1970's, the leak was firmly established as perhaps the media's principal weapon for waging journalistic battles. Even before the flap over the Pentagon Papers, however, the media had been put on notice that their war with the Nixon administration was going to be a two-sided affair. The new President moved with characteristic indirection, but there can be no doubt that he knew about in advance, and thoroughly approved, Vice President Spiro Agnew's famous attack on the news programs of the commercial television networks on November 13, 1969.

Agnew had his own reasons for resenting the media. As the Republican candidate for governor of Maryland in 1966 he had been the media's favorite, since his Democratic opponent was a segregationist who ran on the slogan, "A man's home is his castle." As governor, however, Agnew had antagonized the media by calling in Maryland's black leaders during the riots that followed Martin Luther King, Jr.'s, assassination in April 1968 and warning them sternly that violence would not be permitted.

Agnew quickly sensed, and resented, the change in the media's attitude toward him. He was, however, probably not prepared for the job the media proceeded to do on him when Nixon chose him as his running mate in 1968. The crowning blow was the incident of "the Fat Jap."

One of the reporters on Agnew's vice presidential campaign plane was a corpulent Japanese American known affectionately to one and all as the Fat Jap. During a stop in Las Vegas, various members of the accompanying press contingent overindulged, and when Agnew reboarded the plane the Oriental in question was snoozing peacefully in his seat. Passing him, Agnew inquired jokingly, "Did the Fat Jap have too much to drink?"

Nothing came of the incident at once. But a few days later, when the Agnew plane arrived in Hawaii (whose population is approximately 40 percent Japanese American), reporters aboard the plane leaked the anecdote to the local media, which predictably played it as an example of Agnew's insensitivity to racial jibes and of his contempt for Japanese Americans in particular. Within days the story was all over America.

A little of that sort of thing goes a long way, and Agnew was on the receiving end of a great deal of it. By the time he settled into the vice presidential offices in what is now the Old Executive Office Building, Spiro Agnew knew what he thought about the media.

So it was "no accident," as the Marxists like to say, when Agnew rose to address a meeting in Des Moines, Iowa, on November 13, 1969, and announced, "Tonight I want to discuss the importance of the television news medium to the American people." The speech was largely written by Patrick Buchanan, an outspokenly conservative member of Nixon's personal staff who had gotten to know Agnew well when he was assigned as a speechwriter to the Agnew campaign staff during the fall of 1968. In retrospect, it strikes one as a frank but thoughtful criticism of the news programs of the television networks:

. . . No nation depends more on the intelligent judgment of its citizens. No medium has a more profound influence over public opinion. Nowhere in our system are there fewer checks on vast power. So nowhere should there be more conscientious responsibility exercised than by the news media. . . .

The purpose of my remarks tonight is to focus your attention on this little group of men who not only enjoy a right of instant rebuttal to every Presidential address, but more importantly, wield a free hand in selecting, presenting and interpreting the great issues of our nation. . . .

What do Americans know of the men who wield this power? Of the men who produce and direct the network news—the nation knows practically nothing.

Of the commentators, most Americans know little, other than that they reflect an urbane and assured presence, seemingly well informed on every important matter. . . .

The views of this fraternity do *not* represent the views of America. . . .

As with other American institutions, perhaps it is time that the networks were made more responsive to the views of the nation and more responsible to the people they serve.

It is easy in retrospect to imagine how this blunt language must have sounded to that "little group of men . . . who produce and direct the network news"—the executive producers and other decision-makers in the show-producing hierarchies described in Chapter 5. For the first time in history, their key role in the presentation of news was being spotlighted—and spotlighted, moreover, by none other than the Vice President of the United States. And his message to the American people was that "the views of this fraternity do *not* represent the views of America."

Agnew knew the charge that would be leveled against him and sought to defuse it in advance:

I am not asking for government censorship or any other kind of censorship. I am asking whether a form of censorship already exists when the news that forty million Americans receive each night is determined by a handful of men responsible only to their corporate employers and filtered through a handful of commentators who admit to their own set of biases.

Surely without much hope of success, Agnew concluded with an appeal to the media to set their own house in order:

Tonight, I have raised questions. I have made no attempt to suggest answers. These answers must come from the media men. They are challenged to turn their critical powers on themselves. They are challenged

to direct their energy, talent and conviction toward improving the quality
and objectivity of news presentation. They are challenged to structure their
own civic ethics to relate their great freedom with their great responsibility.

Even without the woozy syntax of that last sentence, it would be
obvious that Agnew must have realized he was asking a lot. In point of
fact, he was boldly calling public attention to the unremitting liberal slant
of the evening news programs and declaring that they "do not represent
the views of America." As both sides realized, something very like a
battle for control of America was under way. And while its dimensions
and even the identity of some of the participants might be obscure, it
seemed clear that the institution of the presidency was on one side of the
battle, while America's media elite were squarely on the other.

# CHAPTER 8

# *From Advocacy Journalism to Attack Journalism*

BETWEEN WORLD WARS I and II, and more particularly after World War II, investigative journalism began to take on increasingly the aspect of what came to be called "advocacy journalism"—i.e., journalism designed to advocate a particular viewpoint or a particular action. That investigative journalism could have such an aspect had been apparent as early as the era of the "muckrakers" at the beginning of the century. That it almost inevitably did so became apparent as the century wore on.

The advent of *Time* magazine in 1923 undoubtedly did much to advance and expand the process. From *McClure's* magazine at the turn of the century through *Collier's, The Saturday Evening Post,* and many other publications that carried nonfiction articles, journalists had long been able to advocate specific viewpoints on all sorts of issues. As a newsmagazine, however, *Time* undertook to summarize for its readers all of the important news stories of the past week. Simply as a practical matter—to make these summaries interesting and intelligible to the reader—it was necessary to adopt a dramatic "theory" of each story and report primarily those facts that supported it. The result was that complex events were simplified for the sake of explication and (all too often) adorned with a moral for the edification of the innocent.

Thus, "clean-jawed young" Senator So-and-So would find himself thwarted in some noble endeavor by "crusty octogenarian" Senator This-and-That, but after various vicissitudes right would triumph—or (equally dramatically) suffer defeat. The technique was astonishingly versatile and the details infinitely plastic, but the result was deadeningly familiar: *Time*'s version of events, supplied and supported by its worldwide network of correspondents, frequently became the accepted one, and its views on major questions often prevailed.

Certainly Henry Luce's detestation of the Chinese Communists, and his long personal friendship with Chiang Kai-shek, were a major factor in keeping the United States from recognizing the Communist regime for thirty years after it had conquered the Chinese mainland. And Luce's strenuous support for Dwight Eisenhower for the Republican presidential nomination in 1952 may well have been the decisive factor in Eisenhower's extremely close and hard-fought battle with Senator Robert Taft. (The present author, as a Young Republican, attended the convention in Chicago to root for Eisenhower, and remembers how the press-run of *Time*'s issue scheduled to come out during the critical week when the convention was held was advanced by a day or more to make sure the delegates saw it before they began voting.)

Of course *Newsweek,* when it appeared, copied *Time* in this as in so much else—though, given its ownership, it could be counted on to follow a much more liberal line.

The point is that advocacy journalism was well established as a journalistic tradition long before the media elite broke with the imperial presidencies of Lyndon Johnson and Richard Nixon. By the early 1970s, however, leading liberal journalists had moved into a political role so openly, and expanded their "investigative" techniques so dramatically, as to warrant a brand-new name for what they were doing. "Advocacy journalism" had become "adversary journalism" or even "attack journalism," and the decade of the 1970s was to be the golden age of the media as challengers for greater power and vastly enhanced status in the American society.

The major battle and chief triumph of the media in this era was, of course, the forced resignation of Richard Nixon from the presidency in the wake of the Watergate scandal. There were, to be sure, many other forces and influences involved in the struggle. The liberal elements which had dominated the Democratic party for four decades were deeply divided over the problem of how to deal with the novel issues and forces brought to the fore during the 1960s by the so-called New Left. At the Democratic convention in Miami Beach in 1972 the accommodationists had carried the day, nominating Senator George McGovern, who proceeded to campaign on a platform well to the left of any that had previously been endorsed by the Democratic party. The result was a landslide defeat, in which Nixon carried every state but Massachusetts. Both the Democrats as a party and the liberal movement more generally were searching desperately for some means of counterattack on which to base a comeback, when Watergate offered itself for their consideration.

But it was the media that had the most justification for regarding themselves as the principal winners in the whole vast Watergate controversy. For the two major parties were forever battling for power and seeking to upend one another, whereas Watergate and the Nixon resignation marked the first time that the media as an independent institution entered a major national fray and, to all appearances, emerged as the victor in its own right.

One must add that qualifying phrase "to all appearances" because there is, curiously enough, grave doubt that the media in fact had much to do with exposing the truth about Watergate and thus forcing Nixon's resignation. They did, to be sure, give lavish coverage to the trial of the Watergate burglars before federal judge John Sirica, and they reported intensively the subsequent congressional hearings as these probed ever closer to the truth of Nixon's brief but vital (because technically criminal) cover-up of the facts. But the American public believes that the Watergate scandal was exposed by the diligent investigative reportage of Robert Woodward and Carl Bernstein of the *Washington Post* (which received the Pulitzer Prize for 1973 as a result), and this is largely a myth.

Anyone who saw *All the President's Men*, the motion picture that heroized Woodward and Bernstein (played by Robert Redford and Dustin Hoffman, respectively), will remember the dramatic sequence at the very end of the picture in which a wire service ticker types out news reports of one indictment and conviction after another. The obvious implication was that the reportorial derring-do that had constituted the stuff of the preceding scenes—the dashes in and out of the *Post*'s newsroom, the interviews with White House staffers, the secret meetings with Deep Throat in shadowy underground garages, etc.—was directly linked, in cause-and-effect fashion, to the subsequent convictions.

But in fact, as the film implicitly admitted by failing to spell out the connection, the convictions in the Watergate cases were not a result of the investigations conducted by Woodward and Bernstein. The two reporters correctly suspected that there was more to the story than the White House had disclosed, and diligently pursued such leads as were suggested to them by Deep Throat, etc.; but there is no reason to suppose that anyone in the Nixon administration would ever have spent a night in jail as a result of anything they uncovered. It was Judge Sirica who, by imposing "provisional" maximum sentences on the convicted Watergate burglars and then giving them several weeks to think about it before "confirming" the sentences, induced one of them—John McCord—to talk. McCord implicated Jeb Magruder, Magruder implicated John Mitchell, Mitchell implicated John Ehrlichman, etc., etc. Sirica rewarded McCord by reducing his "provisional" sentence of forty years in prison to four months.

But "perception," meaning what is believed to be true about something, is for many purposes more important than the truth itself. Thus, as we saw, although the Tet offensive was in fact a devastating defeat for North Vietnam and the Vietcong, it was perceived and portrayed in the United States as a grave setback for our own forces, and played a major role in President Johnson's decision not to run for reelection. And, although Woodward and Bernstein—or for that matter the media as a whole—had in fact little to do with uncovering the Watergate scandal, the perception was, and largely still is, that these journalistic Davids toppled the presidential Goliath—a conviction that remains to this day the principal zircon in the diadem of the Imperial Media of the mid-1970s.

A far more legitimate claim of media influence can be made on behalf of Seymour Hersh, the *New York Times* reporter who drew a bead on the CIA in December 1974. On December 22 of that year, in a page 1 story in the *Times* under his by-line, Hersh charged that the Agency had "illegally" conducted intelligence operations in the United States. I take considerable pride in the fact that, in a column written the very next day for release December 29, I predicted what was about to happen: "You will be hearing an awful lot about 'illegal' CIA activities in the U.S. on your favorite TV news show, in your favorite newsmagazine, and on the front page of your local newspaper. That's the way 'news' is managed, you see."

As it turned out, I was understating the situation. The *Times* proceeded to give Hersh's analyses of alleged CIA misbehavior unprecedented emphasis, running stories on the subject under his by-line on page 1 almost every day for well over a month. Under such circumstances it didn't take long for what William Buckley calls "the echo-chamber effect" to manifest itself.

First, the rest of the media took up the cry. Other papers, quickly followed by the newsmagazines, began to develop fresh aspects of the basic story, or related stories. And where the media went, the politicians were sure to follow: Within a matter of weeks, both the House and the Senate had launched probes of the CIA's alleged misdeeds, and President Ford, not to be outdone, had appointed a presidential commission to inquire into the matter, headed by Vice President Rockefeller (and including, as one of its members, former Governor Reagan of California).

The outcome of all this furor, as we now know, was a series of major modifications (or "reforms") in the operating procedures of the CIA. Some were imposed statutorily; others were brought about by administrative edict. In addition, there was a major shake-up in personnel, reaching into the Agency's highest levels.

Whether these changes were for the better can be, and has been, hotly debated. (Charles Lichenstein, our deputy ambassador to the UN in the early 1980s, told a conference on terrorism held in Tel Aviv in January 1986 that "I reserve a very special ring right in the heart of hell for those of my countrymen who, in the orgy of recrimination and self-doubt of the mid-70s in the United States, systematically and deliberately dismantled the intelligence capabilities of the United States—and particularly those capabilities that are most critical to the success of the effort of which I speak, namely, counterintelligence and covert operations.") But few, I think, would today deny that the impact of Hersh's articles and their sequelae was enormous, or that they had major and lasting effects on this country's intelligence policies and capabilities.

It was during the 1970s, incidentally, and partly as a result of the fresh attention being paid to the media in general, that certain individual reporters and commentators began to benefit, in quite explicitly material terms, from their own cults of personality.

Of course, from the days of Walter Lippmann forward prominent reporters and commentators had cultivated loyal followings of their own, and sometimes even become minicelebrities in their own right. But it was only with the growth of television news programs and talk shows— beginning, of course, with *Meet the Press*—that the public in large numbers began to notice and admire the personalities of specific journalists. Walter Cronkite was only the earliest and most trusted of a series of anchormen on the evening news to develop a nationwide fan club. In the field of TV commentary, the late Edward R. Murrow had pioneered the genre as far back as the 1950s with his scathing coverage of Senator Joseph McCarthy, while on the right Bill Buckley's *Firing Line* has survived since 1966.

But it was in the 1970s that the marketing of journalistic celebrities really hit its stride. Reporters like the *Washington Post*'s Robert Woodward and Carl Bernstein were immortalized in motion pictures (*All the President's Men*), while such knights of the press conference as CBS's Dan Rather earned their spurs in rhetorical combat with the President of the United States.

More sedately but no less successfully, a whole series of commentators began imprinting their personalities on the public consciousness through talk shows. CBS's *Face the Nation* followed the format of NBC's *Meet the Press* in focusing on the questioning of one public figure per week. But other programs—Martin Agronsky's *Agronsky and Company*, for one—dispensed with the public figure, and allowed its resident commentators to pontificate without any interference whatever. Gradually, all of the formats increased their intensity, probably reaching some sort of Ultima Thule in CNN's *Crossfire*, where one or more "guests" are mercilessly badgered "from the left" or "from the right," and the syndicated *McLaughlin Group*, where four journalists abandon all pretense of objectivity and go for each other's jugulars under the expert management of John McLaughlin.

Such TV assignments are profitable in and of themselves, for the relatively few lucky journalists and/or commentators who land them. But they pale into insignificance when compared to the sums many of these "TV personalities" are able to earn on the lecture circuit, as a result of their high visibility. It is a curious fact that most audiences (typically, business conventions or college students) are far more captivated by the sight of a familiar television personality in the flesh, and by the opportunity to listen to his (or her) rambling reminiscences on politics, than by the chance to hear a truly distinguished but less familiar expert in the very same field.

The result has been a handful of new millionaires. According to Eleanor Randolph in an article in the *Washington Post* dated April 18, 1987:

> A smart columnist, who also manages to do well on television, can easily earn $150,000 a year. There have been estimates that a few—Evans and Novak, George Will and John McLaughlin—can gross close to $1 million in a good year. . . . [A]s columnist Jack W. Germond put it, "Who says journalists have to take a vow of poverty?"

The Randolph article continued:

> Television stars, in line with their salaries, command the largest fees and give the fewest number of speeches.
> The $12,000 to $15,000 range is for anybody that's visible—Ted Koppel, Dan Rather, Charles Kuralt, George Will," said Alan Walker, a leading agent for speakers. "If you have to start explaining who these people are, then the ability to ask these big fees goes down immediately." . . .

Other favorites, according to agents and organizers of events that pay the fees, are Hugh Sidey, Mark Shields, John McLaughlin, Jack Germond and "any television anchor or correspondent who has the time to do it," as California agent Ruth Alben said.

"There is a big market for news media people now," Alben adds. "They are just as celebrated as movie stars, in some cases even more so." . . .

"The speeches, that's where you're really printing money," said one journalist who moved into the limelight recently. "Anybody who's any good at this can do it without even looking at notes. It's a snap."

The advent of the Carter administration did little to soften the aggressive mood of the media elite, now in full career as a major and relentlessly liberal influence on the political scene. As already discussed (page 73), Jimmy Carter was far from being the liberals' beau ideal. He was, in fact, as we noted, a relative conservative in Democratic terms: an avowed outsider implicitly hostile to the Washington establishment, a born-again Christian from the always-suspect South. His presidential honeymoon with the media was notable for its brevity, and by the summer of 1977 they had zeroed in on the issue whereby they intended to teach Mr. Carter who was boss in this town: His close friend and budget director, Bert Lance.

Despite Carter's loyal and quite open efforts to save him, Lance was forced to step down as budget director on September 21, under fire from both the media and congressional critics, and under indictment as well, for various alleged malfeasances in his capacity as an officer of a Georgia bank in the early 1970s. It is almost irrelevant for our purposes, or those of the media, that a jury of his peers subsequently acquitted him of all these charges. What mattered, in terms of the power distribution in Washington, was that the media had quickly established their ability to inflict a damaging blow on the new President.

What effect this demonstration had on the subsequent course of the Carter administration is difficult to gauge. Certainly the influence of Carter's inner circle of Georgia "good ol' boys" (Lance, Charles Kirbo, Griffin Bell, etc.) seemed to diminish thereafter. On the other hand, Carter never seemed able, or perhaps never tried very hard, to satisfy the liberals that he was in any satisfactory sense "their man." In addition, it slowly became apparent that, quite independently of doubts about his ability to pass an ideological litmus test, Carter simply lacked qualities of leadership that were crucial to an effective presidency. By the end of his term, it required a major exercise of presidential muscle to force the Democratic National Convention to renominate him, and a full third of the delegates refused almost to the end. By that time, however, the

golden age of the Imperial Media was over—one of the chief victims of
a major sea-change in American politics.

It has been impossible to describe the development of America's
modern media elite without making occasional reference to the slow but
steady growth of the modern conservative movement that paralleled it,
but we can hardly do justice here to that long and interesting story.*
Suffice it to say that by the late 1970s the long hostility of our liberal
media to every serious manifestation of the conservative movement was
being reciprocated with interest. Increasingly, the conservative movement
was demonstrating that it was able to take care of itself—and not only
take care of itself, but assume the political leadership of the country. In
1980 it did just that, under the leadership of a man with whom the media
found themselves dismayingly ill-equipped to cope.

Many conservatives had, of course, believed for a quarter of a century
that the liberal media elite were their sworn enemies; the Goldwater
campaign alone had furnished enough examples of their tactics to satisfy
anyone on that score. And as early as 1969, in his Des Moines challenge
to the television network news programs, Vice President Spiro Agnew
had signaled conservatives' readiness to do battle with these formidable
adversaries. But Agnew's own downfall, followed by Nixon's, had not
only stopped that effort in its tracks but vastly increased the power and
prestige of the media vis-à-vis the forces then in a position to take them
on. As we saw in Chapter 6 (pages 115–119), it was impossible, in the
early 1970s, to obtain general acceptance by the media of even such
broadly sympathetic monitoring for basic fairness as was offered by the
National News Council.

By 1980, however, the national mood was very different. With the
election of Ronald Reagan, the stage was set for a battle royal between
the media elite and those forces, both old and new, that challenged their
claim to a new and vastly more powerful position in the American
society.

Squaring off against Reagan in the election campaign of 1980, the
media decided that his most readily accessible vulnerability was in the
matter of gaffes—verbal blunders, resulting in either simple misstatements or outright factual errors. At a minimum, such errors suggested
that Reagan was just too old for the presidency (he would turn seventy
less than a month after his inauguration); at worst, they implied that he

---

* Anyone wishing to pursue it is referred to my own account, *The Rise of the Right* (New
York: Morrow, 1984).

was recklessly indifferent to the facts of particular cases. The media vacuumed Reagan's speeches and casual remarks for such gaffes, and gleefully contradicted them with the results of their own diligent ex post facto research.

But Reagan responded by amiably owning up to various unintentional misstatements and successfully defending other assertions as not mistakes at all. Gradually it became apparent that the American people just didn't mind this man's slips of the tongue, or even his acknowledged factual errors. They believed they understood him, and they felt comfortable with him, and on Election Day they made him President of the United States by 45 states to 5 and 489 electoral votes to 49, with almost 2.7 million more votes than his two opponents (Carter and Anderson) combined.

Throughout Reagan's first term, the media grappled strenuously but unsuccessfully with this "Teflon" President, to whom no criticism could be made to stick. His press conferences became the journalistic equivalents of bullfights, in which media matadors competed to see which could vanquish this formidable adversary. Throughout, Reagan's personal style remained modest, low-keyed, and earnest, but also tinged with humor, usually at his own expense. Grudgingly, in partial explanation of their failure to damage Reagan seriously, the media adopted his admirers' enthusiastic description of him as the Great Communicator. On November 6, 1984, he proved his right to that title by winning reelection 49 states to 1.

At that point, a good many conservatives were beginning to suspect that the media—and for that matter the liberals generally—had been overrated as adversaries. Granted, Ronald Reagan was clearly something pretty special when it came to winning the hearts of the American people; but it no longer seemed quite so impossible to win national elections, even with the major media solidly in the opposition's corner. To many conservatives, it was a blessed relief to know that there were at least some things the media couldn't always do.

Then came the Democratic capture of the Senate in the off-year elections of 1986, hotly followed by the explosion of the Iran/contra controversy. Suddenly it seemed like Watergate all over again, with a beleaguered President and his top aides under heavy attack by a congressional investigating committee and impeachment clearly on everyone's mind if not (yet) on everyone's tongue. And in the Democrats' corner once again, focusing national attention on the controversy and using every aspect of it to inflict maximum damage on the President, his administration, and the Republican party, were the media.

The Iran/contra controversy is too large a subject to go into here at any length. Nor, probably, could anything short of an elaborate numerical and textual analysis of the reportage of the affair—if that—establish beyond dispute the role played in it by the media. Certainly the whole episode was legitimately newsworthy, and the media can hardly be criticized just because they covered it intensively.

But one example can, perhaps, serve as illustrative of many that conservatives would cite as demonstrating the media's passionate bias on the subject. Throughout the course of the investigation, various organizations (e.g., the *New York Times* and CBS, jointly) commissioned polls to test public opinion on various aspects of the matter. The pollsters early discovered that, if they asked people whether President Reagan was telling the truth or "lying" when he denied knowing of the diversion of arms sale proceeds to the Nicaraguan resistance, a majority of those with an opinion would opt for the latter formulation. This fact was used, time and again, to produce headlines in which the two words (REAGAN . . . LYING) were splashed across the nation's front pages and intoned on the evening television news programs with all too evident relish.

No effort was ever made (why paint the lily?) to offer those questioned a broader choice of alternatives, or a less corrosive teminology. They were simply invited either to accept Mr. Reagan's assurances, lock, stock, and barrel, or to protect themselves against the dangers of naïveté in the whole complex situation by opting for the only other choice given them. Those who had been successfully maneuvered into guessing that Reagan was "lying" were not even asked whether they would think less of him for doing so in those particular circumstances. The media had their prize: REAGAN . . . LYING; REAGAN . . . LIAR.

It would be interesting to know just how often, prior to the Iran/contra controversy, the media had linked the name of an incumbent president with the word "lying" or "liar" in a headline or even in a sentence in a news story. My impression—not supported, I admit, by any research—is that it occurred rarely, if ever. Previous presidents, even those detested by the media, were generally distanced, in news stories, from such bluntly disparaging terminology.

In any case, as the hearings ended in mid-1987, it had become apparent that, damaging as the whole affair had unquestionably been to Mr. Reagan and his administration, it was *not* "Watergate all over again." The President's Teflon covering had clearly been punctured to some uncertain degree; his political momentum had definitely been slowed (though the Democrats' recapture of the Senate had left him very little momentum anyway). But he was still President, still well liked—and his handling of the presidency still approved—by a majority of the American people. If the media were clearly more formidable than they had seemed after Reagan's overwhelming reelection in 1984, they were equally clearly not invincible: The exciting (or nerve-wracking) process of catching a Republican President in some misdeed, subjecting him to savage congressional investigation and media abuse, and then impeaching him and removing him from office, was apparently not, after all, going to be a really dependable substitute for winning presidential elections the old-fashioned way.

Moreover, although the carefully narrowed focus of the investigation did not permit much consideration of the larger implications of the Iran/contra affair, thoughtful observers had not lost sight of these. There remained serious questions to be discussed concerning the viability of American political processes (especially in the field of foreign policy) and the role of the media in regard to them. Before we turn to those, however, let us pause for a moment to consider from a strictly legal standpoint the current privileges and immunities of the media.

# CHAPTER 9

# *The Media's Privileges and Immunities*

IF THE AVERAGE reasonably well-educated American were asked to describe the historical role of the press in our society, he might well respond approximately as follows. From the outset, the Founding Fathers recognized that the press had a special and essentially adversarial role in American society: the precious responsibility of aggressively investigating and informing the people about public topics, so that the people in turn could manage their affairs intelligently. By the First Amendment, therefore, the Framers conferred upon the press (subsequently expanded to include the electronic media as well) certain special privileges and immunities, to assist them in discharging this responsibility.

Of these, perhaps the most important is the privilege of a reporter to keep confidential the identity of a person who imparts information to him. Without this privilege, which is analogous to the familiar common law privileges that protect communications between doctor and patient, attorney and client, priest and penitent, husband and wife, the task of a reporter would be impossible, since obviously information would be vastly more difficult to obtain.

Almost equally important, however, are the media's historic immunity from prior restraints on publication and the immunity of editorial offices from search warrants. These provide the minimum conditions under which the media can be expected to function in a free society. If the media overstep their bounds, the proper remedy is the libel laws.

The privileges and immunities thus conferred upon the media by the First Amendment have, throughout most of our national history, functioned reasonably well, enabling the media to play their special role of informing the public. Recently however, commencing with the Nixon administration and specifically with Vice President Agnew's attack on the media in his Des Moines speech in November 1969, a major effort has been launched to limit or even eliminate entirely these vital privileges and immunities. The struggle is still under way, with the Supreme Court divided on the issue. Fortunately a majority of the justices still usually, like the Founders, recognizes the special role of the media and their consequent need for a special constitutional status.

That, to repeat, is roughly the summary that many reasonably well informed people would offer, or at any rate comfortably subscribe to, if asked about the role of the media in the American society. (I was told several years ago, by a professor of political science at a well-regarded Pennsylvania college, that he had always "assumed everybody took it for granted.")

The only trouble with this summary is that it is, in its entirety and in precise detail, the exact opposite of the truth. We will deal with the various assertions in order.

1. The whole concept of the media as having a special, basically adversarial role in the American society is largely a twentieth-century phenomenon. As a young Harvard scholar, Stephen Bates, recently wrote, describing the development of the press:

> During Stage One, prior to the Stamp Act [1765], the press was essentially a bulletin board for news and opinions. Thereafter, during Stage Two, the press became a partisan megaphone, with each newspaper amplifying the views of a particular faction. Stage Three, when economic strength combined with the norms of objectivity and the ideology of investigative reporting, arrived slowly and unsteadily during the twentieth century. That stage allowed the press to become, for the first time, [an] autonomous institution. . . . To suggest that the Framers were familiar with such a press is inaccurate; to suggest that they envisioned its ultimate appearance is incredible.

2. The proposition that the Framers, in view of this alleged special role of the press, intended, in drafting the First Amendment, to confer special privileges and immunities on it is even newer, having sprung full-blown from the brow of Justice Potter Stewart during a Law Day address at Yale in 1974.*

* Reprinted in *Hastings Law Journal*, Vol. 26 (1975), p. 631.

3. The first time it ever seems to have occurred to a lawyer to invoke the First Amendment as justification for the alleged "privilege" of a reporter to conceal the identity of a source was in 1958. The argument was raised by the attorneys for a *New York Herald-Tribune* reporter named Marie Torre, who had been cited for contempt for refusing to disclose the identity of a source in a libel suit in the federal district court in New York. It was promptly and unanimously rejected, and Ms. Torre jailed, by the United States Court of Appeals for the Second Circuit (on which, by coincidence, Judge Potter Stewart happened to be sitting—his novel interpretation of the First Amendment apparently not having yet congealed). *Certiorari* was denied by the Supreme Court of the United States.

The ordinary rule is that anyone in possession of information relevant to a judicial proceeding (e.g., a grand jury investigation or a criminal trial) can be compelled to come forth with it, on pain of contempt of court. Some media partisans argue, however, that this requirement does not, or ought not to, apply to the media because there is a negotiable conflict between such clear-cut constitutional provisions as the "fair trial" clause of the Sixth Amendment and the press immunities Justice Stewart believes the Framers incorporated in the First. A majority of the Court's members, however, have declined to accept this analysis, and therefore the *Branzburg* case (1972), though muddied somewhat by the obscure concurring opinion of Justice Powell, remains the latest constitutional word on this issue. In that case the Court held that a reporter could indeed be required to reveal a confidential source to a grand jury, at least where the information was relevant and material and the reporter was its only possessor.

In at least twenty-six states, state legislatures have passed "shield laws" which seek to protect journalists from the obligation to reveal their sources in appropriate cases, but the courts (as in the celebrated Jascalevich murder case in New Jersey, when *New York Times* reporter M. A. Farber went to jail rather than hand over interview notes to the trial judge) have simply declared such laws unconstitutional to the extent that they clash with the "fair trial" clause of the Sixth Amendment or other provisions of the Constitution. (That legislatures pass such laws anyway, simply as a way of toadying to the media, is a memorable commentary on the respective senses of responsibility of the legislative and judicial branches of government.)

In states without such shield laws, reporters believed to possess relevant and material information not otherwise available are routinely required to testify in criminal cases. An article in the *New York Times* for January 9, 1987, reported from Rockland, Maine:

> A Maine judge today charged a New Hampshire newspaper reporter with contempt of court for refusing to testify in a murder trial here.
>
> Justice G. Arthur Brennan of Superior Court allowed Robert Hohler, 35 years old, a reporter for The Concord Monitor in New Hampshire, to leave the Knox County Courthouse in this coastal town without posting bail but said he would have to return later for a jury trial on the charge of criminal contempt.
>
> Mr. Hohler said he was exempt from being subpoenaed to testify because the First Amendment protected reporters.
>
> A state Assistant Attorney General, Thomas Goodwin, sought Mr. Hohler's testimony about statements made by Richard Steeves in an interview in June 1985, shortly after Mr. Steeves was charged in the fatal shooting of an acquaintance, Russell Bailey. . . .
>
> In court today, Justice Brennan said the prosecution had met the three conditions that allowed the courts to compel a reporter to testify: the state showed that Mr. Hohler's testimony was material and relevant, as well as necessary or critical to its case and that the information was not available from other sources.
>
> "The jury would be very well served hearing this evidence," Justice Brennan said.

Even in states without shield laws, however, some thoughtful and highly respected reporters have considered the First Amendment entirely adequate to protect the interests of the media. Clark Mollenhoff, for example, perhaps the dean of American investigative reporters, opposes shield laws, arguing that whatever privileges legislatures confer legislatures can later take away. And Anthony Lewis, the liberal *New York Times* columnist who used to cover the Supreme Court beat for the *Times*, astonished a Princeton audience several years ago by similarly speaking out against special privileges for the media.

4. Whatever the justification for the alleged "reporter's privilege" may be, it cannot be its analogy to the four recognized common law privileges mentioned earlier, for the alleged analogy simply doesn't hold water. In the case of all four common law privileges the identity of the communicator (client, patient, penitent, spouse) is known; what we don't know, or what at least is not admissible in evidence, is the substance of the communication. In the case of the "reporter's privilege," the situation is reversed: We know the substance of the communication—indeed, it is blared around the world; what we don't know is the identity

of the communicator. Does this distinction matter? It matters enormously, of course, for unless we know the communicator's identity we have no way of judging his qualifications for making those newsworthy assertions: his honesty, his accuracy, his motives, his bias (or lack of it), etc. Indeed, as the case of *Washington Post* reporter Janet Cooke demonstrated, we cannot be sure that he exists at all.

5. Although protection of a source's identity may well encourage him to be more forthcoming with information, it is nonsense to contend that a reporter's job is rendered impossible if such protection is not offered. Many an old-time reporter prided himself on making sure that every substantial factual assertion in a story was "sourced"—i.e., either established by specified documentary evidence or attributed to a named individual in a position to know the facts. As discussed in Chapter 7, confidential sources were, until relatively recently, used principally to *locate* news stories rather than to substantiate them. The recent tremendous upsurge in stories or specific items of information attributed to "a source who asked not to be identified" is a direct result of the media's shift, in the mid-1960s, from basically investigative to more frankly adversary journalism.

As an example of the current overuse of confidential sources, one could not do much better than cite a Washington dispatch by the *New York Times*'s Stephen Engelberg, dated December 23, 1986, and carried at the top of the right-hand column on page 1 of the *Times* the next day. Virtually every source cited in it was anonymous.

The significance of the story lay in the fact that it appeared soon after President Reagan had publicly denied that the sales of arms to Iran were designed as a *quid pro quo* for the release of our hostages in Lebanon and had declared instead that they were intended to facilitate an approach to relatively moderate and potentially pro-American forces in Iran.

The first two paragraphs of the story read as follows:

> In a memorandum written at the beginning of the United States arms sales to Iran, the Director of Central Intelligence explicitly described the program as a trade of arms for hostages, according to a high ranking Government official who has seen the document.
>
> In addition, the official said, the memo written by William J. Casey said that if the matter became public, President Reagan was prepared to portray the secret operation as a political opening to Teheran.

Now, unless English has lost its ordinary meaning, these paragraphs make two major assertions:

1. That in this memorandum CIA Director Casey explicitly described the program as a trade of arms for hostages, but

2. That (also according to the memorandum) if the matter became public, President Reagan was prepared to portray the secret operation as a political opening to Teheran. ·

If, therefore, the memorandum existed, and said what it was purported to say, it not only refuted Mr. Reagan's description of the transaction's purpose but characterized him as "prepared" to make a false statement about it.

This deadly document, however, had apparently not actually been seen by Engelberg. Indeed, according to the article, "It could not be learned to whom the memorandum was addressed." In fact, as the article admitted, the document's very existence depended on the unsupported assertion of "a high ranking Government official who has seen the document." The official was not identified.

Engelberg's efforts to verify the existence of the document were unavailing: Anonymous "senior officials at the White House and Justice Department said they had not seen the memo and one Congressional official who has read many of Mr. Casey's other memos said it was out of character with them."

Nevertheless, Engelberg found other anonymous sources who offered indirect support for the existence of such a document: "Several Congressional sources said the operatives for the initiative, including a retired C.I.A. official, George Cave, have testified that they believed the policy was to trade arms for hostages."

In addition, also anonymously, "A senior White House official, who said he doubted the existence of the Casey memo, acknowledged, however, that National Security Council staff members wrote memos in the last year that mentioned hostage releases as an objective for the program."

Engelberg also cited "a senior White House official who asked not to be identified" as suggesting that, while an opening to Iran was undoubtedly the chief objective of those making policy, the memo might have originated lower down the line.

In short, Engelberg was unable to name a single person who was willing to vouch for the alleged memorandum's existence, or to cite, even anonymously, any supporting source who would go so far as to say it sounded plausible that Casey would write such a memorandum. Nevertheless the *Times* ran this mishmash of anonymous and contradictory assertions as its lead story, in support of the proposition that the President had misdescribed the real purpose of the arms sales and that his CIA director had explicitly affirmed in writing the President's intention to do so if the sales became public knowledge.

Thus far have we come from the grand old journalistic rule that every major assertion in a story must be sourced.

Questioned about the article in August 1987, Engelberg at first was uncertain whether the document had ever subsequently come to light. On further reflection he believed that it had, and recalled that it wasn't "phrased quite the way I said. There was a nuance that was different." Finally, consulting a copy of the report of the Tower Commission, he identified a document quoted therein as the one in question, and on reading it expressed satisfaction with the way in which his article had described it.

This document, which is quoted in part in the paperback edition of *The Tower Commission Report* (Times Books, 1987), is a memorandum from CIA director Casey to deputy CIA director John McMahon, dated December 10, 1985. Casey is summarizing a meeting he had had with the President, former NSC director Robert "Bud" McFarlane, and perhaps others. He notes that McFarlane

did not have a good impression of Gorbanifehr [sic] and recommended that we not pursue the proposed relationship with him. He recommended that we pursue the relationship with others representing the moderate forces in the Iranian government, talking and listening to them on a purely intelligence basis but being alert to any action that might influence events in Iran.

2. Everybody supported this in our round-table discussion. Other options which Bud had suggested were to let the Israelis go ahead doing what they would probably do anyway, and hope we get some benefit, or to mount a rescue effort. The President argued mildly for letting the operation go ahead without any commitments from us except that we should ultimately fill up the Israeli pipeline in any event, or the Congress will do it for us. He was afraid that terminating the ongoing discussions, as Bud had speculated they might, could lead to early action against the hostages. The trend of the succession [sic—discussion?] of this was that it was a little disingenuous and would still bear the onus of having traded with the captors and provide an incentive for them to do some more kidnapping, which was the main burden of the argument against going forward on the program. The President felt that any ongoing contact would be justified and any charges that might be made later could be met and justified as an effort to influence future events in Iran. I did point out that there was historical precedent for this and that was always the rationale the Israelis had given us for their providing arms to Iran. . . .

4. As the meeting broke up, I had the idea that the President had not entirely given up on encouraging the Israelis to carry on with the Iranians. I suspect he would be willing to run the risk and take the heat in the future if this will lead to springing the hostages. It appears that Bud has the action. [Pp. 197–198]

Compare this rather rambling memorandum with the Engelberg article's flat opening statement that Casey, in it, "explicitly described the program as a trade of arms for hostages," and that Casey "said that if the matter became public, Mr. Reagan was prepared to portray the secret operation as a political opening to Teheran."

It is not a question of whether such meanings can be tortured out of Casey's words. The conversation was obviously a fairly disjointed one in which various options, objectives, and dangers were discussed. On the most hotly contested point, the memo says flatly that Mr. Reagan believed that "any charges that might be made later could be met and justified as an effort to influence future events in Iran." Engelberg's anonymous inform-ant, reading the memorandum (if this is indeed the document he read), understood this as implying that Mr. Reagan was willing, if necessary, to falsify the public record as to the purpose of the sales. Certainly that was Engelberg's understanding, and the one he conveyed to the readers of the *Times:* The President, he paraphrased the memorandum as saying, was "prepared to portray" the operation as a "political opening."

But, just as certainly, the memo is capable of a far more innocent interpretation: namely, that Mr. Reagan felt that the justification of the operation on diplomatic grounds was not only possible but perfectly legitimate. Small wonder that Mr. Engelberg's first recollection was that the President's point was not "phrased quite the way I said," and that there was "a nuance that was different."

And that, of course, is one of the fundamental weaknesses of the anonymous leak as a journalistic device: We are not able to question, or even evaluate, the unknown informant. What kind of person is he? What are his motives? Under what circumstances did he see the memo? How long did he study it? We know now how ambiguous the memorandum is; but we didn't know it when the *Times* published Stephen Engelberg's unsourced story. At the time we were simply told that a document existed in which William Casey asserted that President Reagan was "prepared to portray" the Iran operation as something it wasn't.

6. The media's supposed "immunity from prior restraints on publi-cation" is as fictitious as the so-called reporter's privilege. Ordinarily,

any individual or organization that proposes or threatens some action that will do "irreparable damage" (i.e., damge not compensable by a money payment) to another can be enjoined from performing that action. But some media representatives contend that the media are, or ought to be, free from all such "prior restraint," and they cite the Supreme Court's decision in the Pentagon Papers case as supporting the proposition that they are indeed immune to it. But the Court held no such thing. It simply weighed the *New York Times*'s interest in the publication of the Pentagon Papers against the government's interest in the security aspects of the matter and concluded that in this particular case (and after the *Times* had privately agreed not to publish certain portions of the papers) no irreparable damage would be done by permitting publication.

In a subsequent case involving *The Progressive* magazine, which proposed to print an article allegedly telling readers how to construct an atomic bomb, the courts granted an injunction despite the passionate contention of *The Progressive*'s partisans that it had not been shown that irreparable damage would result from publication.

Media partisans tend to interpret the irreparable damage test as requiring proof that the world will vanish instantly in a blast of flame if an injunction isn't granted. This is incorrect. As stated above, damage is "irreparable" whenever it cannot be adequately compensated by the payment of money—the ordinary relief in a civil action.

7. The third major contention of certain media partisans, in this matter of privileges and immunities, is that the First Amendment renders the media immune from a reasonable-cause search warrant. Unfortunately for this theory, the Supreme Court has quite recently ruled to the contrary. As in the case of other kinds of information, anyone in possession of documentary or other physical evidence relevant to a legal proceeding such as a grand jury investigation or a criminal trial can ordinarily be required and if necessary compelled to produce it, on pain of contempt. If a judge finds there is reasonable cause to believe that the possessor might conceal or destroy such evidence if ordered to produce it, he can issue a search warrant authorizing the police to search the premises where the evidence is believed to be located and to take possession of it if it is found.

The Supreme Court in the *Zurcher* case (1978) ruled that the premises of the undergraduate newspaper at Stanford were subject to search on such a warrant. (The authorities suspected the editors of the *Stanford Daily* of possessing photographs of a rioting mob that had injured nine policemen.) The ensuing journalistic hullaballoo was so great that the Carter administration rushed through Congress a bill (PL 96-440) exempting journalists from such searches, so far as their "work products" are concerned, unless they themselves are suspected of criminal activity— a great tribute to the power of the media, but merely additional evidence that the special privileges and immunities claimed for them are not to be found in the First Amendment.

Incidentally, although it is not germane to the central question, the point is worth making that these demands for special privileges and immunities for the media raise almost endless problems so far as concerns their application. For one thing, just what (or who) are "the media"? The term obviously covers ordinary newspapers and newsmagazines, and radio and television stations (or at least their news departments), and apparently also undergraduate college newspapers like the *Stanford Daily*. (Presumably it also covers me, as publisher of a journal of opinion, and anyone I choose to designate as a reporter for *National Review*.) But how about the food editor of a small-town weekly, or the offices of a corporate conglomerate that happens to own a newspaper?

And while we are on the subject of corporations, let us pause to consider certain further complexities that these entities introduce into the question. Any corporation that publishes a newspaper is already clearly exempt, under the First Amendment, from having its editorial endorsements or its coverage of particular political candidates treated as illegal corporate contributions. But there is widespread opposition, in certain journalistic circles, to the acquisition of newspapers or other journalistic properties by any corporation not exclusively or primarily engaged in the business of journalism. To what extent ought such corporations be accorded the special privileges and immunities claimed by the media?

8. The assumption that the libel laws are a sufficient protection against wrongdoing on the part of the media is obviously absurd. They do not even apply to any falsehood the media may publish, however egregious and however misleading to the public, unless that falsehood provably damages some specific individual. They will not, under the *Sullivan* rule proclaimed by the Supreme Court in 1962, apply even then if the individual is a public official—or is, alternatively, a "public figure" (i.e., someone who "thrusts himself into the vortex of controversy").

The *Sullivan* case simply illustrates how difficult it became, in the long heyday of liberalism, to inflict a serious penalty on a major totem of the liberal establishment—in this case the *New York Times*. Under then-prevailing law, the *Times* had clearly libeled Sullivan, an Alabama law-enforcement official who had become enmeshed in a civil-rights controversy. Sullivan sued the *Times*, and won a jury verdict of $200,000 in damages. The judgment was affirmed on appeal—until, that is, it reached the Warren Court. The Court thereupon obligingly rewrote the libel law to provide that, in the case of a public official, it was no longer enough to prove that the alleged libelous statement was indeed false, and also damaging; it was now necessary to prove in addition that the falsehood was "malicious"—or, in other words, was published with knowledge of its falsity, or with a recklessness so great as to be tantamount to an indifference as to whether it was false or not.

This remarkable measure of special protection for the media has subsequently been fleshed out by the Court in other cases. By the mid-1960s it had been extended to cover libels against the aforementioned "public figures" as well. And subsequent cases in recent years have tended to expand still further the protection afforded by the rule. For example, the plaintiff is now required to prove the falsity of a damaging statement (rather than requiring the defendant to prove its truth) in any matter of "public concern," and libel suits by public officials and public figures must be dismissed before trial unless the evidence suggests that they can prove libel with "convincing clarity." The result has been, for practical purposes, to eliminate the libel laws altogether from the arena of debate over public issues, and confine them to libels committed against private individuals in matters of purely private concern.

From time to time, of course, some public figure succeeds in convincing a jury that the defendant harbored actual malice toward him and that some false statement about him therefore falls even within the rigid requirements of the *Sullivan* rule. That was the achievement of Barry Goldwater in the late 1960s, after his defeat in the presidential election of 1964, when he persuaded a jury that publisher Ralph Ginsburg had libeled him to the tune of $75,000. Ginsburg had polled several hundred psychiatrists (none of whom had ever examined Goldwater, and therefore ought to have known better) as to whether Goldwater was mentally competent to serve as president, obtaining a gratifyingly high percentage of nos. The jury apparently thought Ginsburg knew very well that his methodology was faulty, and concluded that his defamation of Goldwater met the *Sullivan* test.

Much more recently, former Mobil Corporation president William P. Tavoulareas won libel damages of $2.05 million in 1982 against the

*Washington Post,* which had charged that Tavoulareas used his money and influence to further his son Peter's shipping career. That verdict, however, has subsequently had a rather checkered career of its own. It was, to begin with, overturned by trial judge Oliver Gasch. It was then restored, on appeal, by a 2 to 1 vote of a three-judge panel of the United States Court of Appeals of the District of Columbia in 1985. Two years further on, however, the same Court of Appeals sitting *en banc* (i.e., the full court, rather than a three-judge panel) reinstated Judge Gasch's decision setting the verdict aside and granting judgment to the *Post.* The court ruled that Tavoulareas was a public figure, and that although portions of the article were false and defamatory Tavoulareas had failed to prove actual malice by clear and convincing evidence. As of this writing, the case remains on further appeal.

Late in 1986 a federal jury in Las Vegas awarded entertainer Wayne Newton a verdict of $19.2 million against NBC for defaming him in broadcasts linking him to organized crime.

Two other famous libel suits had outcomes less satisfactory to the plaintiffs, though not without their lessons for the defendants too. Israeli general Ariel Sharon and American general William Westmoreland undertook to prove actual malice in libel actions against *Time* magazine and CBS respectively. Both cases were immensely complicated and lengthy, and their results were far from clear-cut.

The Sharon suit went to the jury, which ultimately concluded that certain statements about General Sharon in a *Time* article were indeed false, and that *Time* correspondent David Halevy had acted "negligently and carelessly" in reporting the information on which the statements were based, but that the plaintiff had not proved that *Time* published the statements with actual malice, in the sense that it knew they were false or had serious doubts as to their truth.

General Westmoreland settled his case against CBS before it went to the jury, under circumstances in which many observers believed he would have prevailed if he had persisted, and in return for the issuance by CBS of a statement that many of his supporters regarded as far from sufficiently apologetic.

The net result is that these two cases cut both ways. News organizations are on notice that public figures with the resources to wage a long and expensive battle can still from time to time entangle them in costly litigation over things they have written or broadcast. Public figures, on the other hand, have discovered that suing a powerful corporation like *Time* or CBS is no small task, and that collecting money damages from one, even if it has published something highly defamatory and extremely harmful, may be almost impossible.

The *Sullivan* rule enjoyed great popularity among the media for a good many years, since it was the Supreme Court's most explicit (in fact, very nearly its only) suggestion that the media enjoyed a special constitutional status in the American society. In recent years, however, this posy for the press has turned out to have a serpent under it. If the media can be held liable for a libel against a public official or a public figure only if the defendant can be proved to have acted "maliciously," then the mental processes of the defendant at the time of the alleged libel (including internal memos, television outtakes, etc.) are clearly subject to probing by the plaintiff's attorney, as he seeks to prove malice. And the media have been extremely reluctant to produce such memos, outtakes, etc.

We are near the frontiers of the law here, but enough has been said to dispose of the notion that the libel laws provide, or are even intended to provide, an adequate remedy for any but a rare minority of the media's potential misdeeds.

We also saw (pages 115–119) how unwilling many important representatives of the media were to countenance even the benign monitoring conducted by the toothless and sympathetic National News Council between 1973 and 1983. The only form of remedy for most media wrongs that survives today is the institution of the ombudsman, where that exists. This is an individual employed by the newspaper itself (it is almost always a newspaper—e.g., the *Washington Post*) to evaluate complaints about the paper's performance and, if necessary, criticize it in its own pages. But ombudsmen are few and far between, and the reason is summed up in a witty insight of the late Willmoore Kendall: "For the New York Times to criticize itself," Kendall declared, "would be ontologically inconceivable."

9. From what has already been said, it can be seen that the alleged privileges and immunities of the media, far from being coeval with the Constitution and enshrined in the First Amendment, have been invented and asserted only recently—in most cases in connection with the media's recent bid for greater power and status in the American society. And the battle that has broken out since their assertion, far from being an attempt by the Nixon administration, or the conservatives, or what-have-you, to wrest ancient rights from the media, is basically an attempt to keep the media's bold bid from succeeding.

What remains to be considered, in connection with the media's claim to these rights, is what kind of a society we would have if they were granted—especially the so-called reporter's privilege.

In Venice to this day one can see the stone lions' mouths, or *boccaleoni,* in which Venetians were formerly encouraged to deposit anonymous denunciations of their fellow citizens, for the information of the Council of Ten. The efficacy of this vicious system was never challenged, as far as I know, and undoubtedly its defenders argued that its anonymity had to be protected, for otherwise those with knowledge of wrongdoing would be unwilling to divulge it. It was in reaction to such repellent techniques, however, that it was long ago laid down as a rule in our judicial system that an accused person shall have the right to confront his accuser.

Of course, our media have somewhat modified the Venetian system. In cautious Venice only the Council of Ten heard the accusation, at least until it had been investigated thoroughly. Today the world hears it at once—often with little investigatory verification or none. And in Venice the stone lions were rigorously nonselective: They told the Council of Ten absolutely everything they heard. Today our journalists are more discriminating: They tell us only what they want us to know (i.e., what is relevant to their "theory" of the story).

Do we really want to encourage the sort of national atmosphere that would develop if we became a nation of informers, each leaking anonymous tidbits to his favorite reporter? Is it even self-evident that such a system favors the disclosure of the truth?

Fortunately the media's bid for these new and highly dubious privileges and immunities has not gone unresisted, even within the profession of journalism itself. As already noted, Clark Mollenhoff, a Pulitzer Prize winner who is now a professor of both law and journalism at Washington and Lee, has declared that shield laws are undesirable (for what legislatures grant, legislatures can also take away) and that anonymous sources should rarely if ever be used as the stated basis for the central facts of a news story.

And the courts, by and large, have stood firm too, refusing to diminish the fair-trial requirements of the Sixth Amendment to make way for these aggressive new extrapolations of the First. In the case of the Supreme Court, the margin has not been great—5 to 4 in some of the most important cases—but thus far it has proved sufficient, and it seems unlikely that any further Reagan appointees will do much to tilt this balance in favor of the media.

It may be wondered, in closing, how any concept of the media's role in our society as ludicrously inaccurate as that with which this chapter opened can attain the vogue that that one enjoys. The reason is simple: The case for it is set forth, simply and repeatedly, in the media themselves, whereas the case against it (i.e., the traditional interpretation of the First Amendment and of the media's role thereunder) is contained in court decisions that not one person in a thousand ever reads. Moreover, the media's staying power is far longer than the public's memory: When the media win a court case, we all hear about the victory; when they lose, "the issue" (in the words of the *New York Times* upon one such melancholy occasion) "remains unresolved."

Fortunately the judiciary's staying power is as great as the media's.

# CHAPTER 10

# *Reactions to the Media's Bias*

OBVIOUSLY, THE LIBERAL bias of the major news media has not gone unnoticed. We have already discussed (Chapter 6) the various ways in which the media have responded to the charge of bias. Now however it is time to ask, not what the media's critics have charged, or how the media have responded to the charges, but what concrete efforts the media's critics have made to remedy the situation.

One possible approach can be dismissed at the outset as impractical and in any case undesirable. There is no reason in the world why American corporations should feel obliged to sponsor television programs that consistently, in fictional presentations, depict businessmen as villainous, stupid, uncaring, or just generally venal. Nor is a business sponsor out of bounds if it expresses opposition to scenes involving pornography, unnecessary violence, hostility to religion, and the like. But a sponsor that sought to influence the presentation of the *news* would be inviting a firestorm of criticism. The media cherish their independence in this respect, and would undoubtedly resent and reject any effort on the part of a sponsor to use his economic clout as a means of bringing about reforms—even manifestly desirable ones—in their news departments.

There are, however, several less objectionable ways in which the media's critics have attempted to cope with the problem of political bias in the news. Basically, five different courses have been pursued. We will consider them separately.

### The Fairness Doctrine

In general, the First Amendment has served well to protect the print media from any very egregious governmental efforts to limit their freedom. But almost from the outset the federal government recognized that the situation of the electronic media was different in one important respect. Anyone can publish a newspaper or magazine, but the number of wavelengths available for the use of radio and television stations is limited by technical considerations. Accordingly, the government assigns these wavelengths to private citizens, to be used for private profit, under a license which can be withdrawn for proper cause.

As early as 1929, just two years after the creation of the Federal Radio Commission, the FRC denied the application of Great Lakes Broadcasting Company for a license modification. The company's broadcasts were known to be one-sided to the exclusion of other viewpoints, and the FRC declared: ''Broadcasting stations are licensed to serve the public, and not for the purpose of furthering the private or selfish interests of individuals or groups of individuals.''

The Federal Communications Commission replaced the FRC in 1934, and in 1941 it renewed the license of the Mayflower Broadcasting Company of Boston only after obtaining its promise that station WAAB would not editorialize in the future. The FCC stated:

> A truly free radio cannot be used to advocate the causes of the licensee. . . . [T]he broadcaster cannot be an advocate. Freedom of speech on the radio must be broad enough to provide full and equal opportunity for the presentation to the public of all sides of public issues. Indeed, as one licensed to operate in a public domain the licensee has assumed the obligation of presenting all sides of important public questions fairly, objectively and without bias. The public interest—not the private—is paramount.

In 1946 the FCC issued a ''Blue Book'' (officially entitled ''Public Service Responsibility of Broadcast Licensees'') which discussed the handling of controversial issues in rather vague terms:

> Probably no other type of problem in the entire broadcasting industry is as important or requires of the broadcaster a greater sense of objectivity, responsibility and fair play. . . . Accordingly, the carrying of such programs in reasonable sufficiency and during good listening hours is a factor to be considered in any finding of public interest.

In 1949, attempting to clarify the ambiguities in the Blue Book, the FCC published a ''Report on Editorializing by Broadcast Licensees.'' This directive, which became known as the Fairness Doctrine, has been the touchstone of federal interest in this issue ever since. It directed broadcast licensees ''to operate in the public interest'' and ''(1) to devote a reasonable amount of time to the coverage of controversial issues of public importance; and (2) to do so fairly by affording a reasonable opportunity for contrasting viewpoints to be voiced on these issues.''

Understandably, the Fairness Doctrine has never been terribly popular with broadcasters. In addition to limiting whatever inclinations they might have to use their stations to promote particular viewpoints on public issues, it is forever entangling them in controversies with members of the public who feel, rightly or wrongly, that their own views aren't getting enough airtime. Moreover, broadcasters argue that the existence of the Fairness Doctrine tends to encourage what veteran correspondent Bill Monroe has called ''blandness, timidity and don't-rock-the-boat fear of government.''

On the other hand, exponents of views that do not in fact receive much attention from the major networks have usually regarded the Fairness Doctrine as critically important, and this has been true of advocates of views both left and right of those held by the broadcasters. Russell Hemenway, director of the ultraliberal National Committee for an Effective Congress, described it as ''a hell of a big stick for us''; while on the right Phyllis Schlafly, the one-woman dynamo who blocked the Equal Rights Amendment, doubts that ERA could ever have been defeated without the access to the electronic media that the Fairness Doctrine assured.

In recent years, however, the Fairness Doctrine has come to be pretty much of a dead letter, thanks to an unusual coalition of political forces. Mainline liberal broadcasters and their allies on the relevant committees of Congress have generally looked with disfavor on rigorous enforcement of the Fairness Doctrine, being, with good reason, quite satisfied with the current liberal bias of the major electronic media. And during most of the Reagan administration they enjoyed the active cooperation of President Reagan's original appointee as FCC chairman, Mark Fowler.

Fowler is a sincere and earnest libertarian, opposed on principle to all government interference with broadcast content. Under his management, accordingly, the FCC all but abandoned any attempt to enforce the Fairness Doctrine, let alone expand it. In a 1985 report the commission condemned the doctrine as unnecessary and probably unconstitutional, but deferred to Congress on the question of whether it ought to be abolished outright.

Instead, Congress early in 1987 passed a Fairness in Broadcasting Act that sought to write the doctrine into statute law. The bill's margins in both chambers were impressive (302 to 102 in the House and 59 to 31 in the Senate). But the attempt failed when President Reagan, siding with the libertarian conservatives, vetoed the bill. Noting that "in any other medium besides broadcasting, such Federal policing of the editorial judgment of journalists would be unthinkable," Mr. Reagan pointed—as the FCC itself had in 1985—to "the recent explosion in the number of new information sources such as cable television" which, he declared, "has clearly made the 'fairness doctrine' unnecessary." In fact, he asserted, "It is, in my judgment, unconstitutional."

Reed Irvine's conservative *AIM Report* promptly denounced the President's action:

> The idea that these people will be fair in the absence of any legal obligation to air all sides is simply laughable. Even though it has not been enforced by the Reagan FCC for the past six and a half years, the Fairness Doctrine still has some influence on individual radio and television stations around the country, prompting them to offer time to individuals or groups who disagree with broadcast editorials or complain that coverage of an issue has been one-sided. In the absence of any fairness requirement, broadcast licensees will be free to use their stations to ride their personal hobby horses without restraint. This added power may well increase the value of stations to their owners. It is unlikely to add to public enlightenment or to the enrichment of the debate on public affairs in most cases.

On August 4, 1987, nonetheless, the FCC, under Fowler's equally libertarian successor as chairman, Dennis Patrick, finally voted 4 to 0 to abolish the Fairness Doctrine altogether. In view of the lopsided congressional majorities in its favor only months earlier, however, the battle may not be over. If Mr. Reagan's successor in the White House is willing to sign a bill establishing the Fairness Doctrine as the law of the land, its eventual fate will probably have to be settled in the courts.

At least for the moment, though, it is safe to say that the Fairness Doctrine does not represent, for the electronic media (to which alone, be it remembered, it applies), even a partial solution to the problem of media bias. Critics of such bias will have to look elsewhere.

### Jawboning

The simplest way in which private critics have tried to modify the media's liberal bias is by complaining loudly about it. And, curiously enough, this technique has had its successes. After all, the media are far from monolithic, and various parts of them are more responsive to justified complaints, or to pressure whether justified or not, than others.

It is a fact, however, that, during the 1960s, with remarkably few exceptions, conservative spokesmen were treated as curiosities, rather like a two-headed calf, when they were given airtime or editorial space at all. Only the vice-presidential jawboning of Spiro Agnew, in his Des Moines speech in November 1969, managed to break through the prevailing journalistic complacency on a broad front and induce a part of the media to strive for something at least approaching better balance in their presentation of the news. Thereafter, especially in the realm of news analysis (e.g., on Op-Ed pages, TV panel shows, and the like), it became almost obligatory to have the conservative viewpoint represented, along with others more congenial to the media.

In general, therefore, it is probably true that the major media have shifted a few inches toward center in recent years as a result of vigorous jawboning (as distinguished from other causes, including those discussed in this chapter, and the media's own belated and grudging recognition that conservatism is today inescapably a "presence in the room" of American politics). But jawboning alone can never accomplish anything very much, let alone anything very enduring. Something more will be required, if the American media are going to achieve the kind of balance that they profess to honor, and that alone can justify their claim to the affection and respect of the public.

## Internal Monitoring

From time to time friends or thoughtful representatives of the media, recognizing the justice of complaints of bias, have sought to remedy the problem by one or another form of internal monitoring process.

Perhaps the simplest is the "ombudsman," a functionary whose Swedish origin is implied by the name. As far as I am aware, the concept has thus far been adopted only by a few newspapers, and not by any newsmagazine or any of the electronic media, though the principle certainly seems capable of application in such cases.

In any event, an ombudsman is simply a member of the paper's staff who is assigned, full-time, to the task of receiving and evaluating complaints against the paper. If in his opinion a complaint is justified, he will be given space in which to say so, at appropriate length. Since the ombudsman is almost always an experienced journalist with a reputation for judiciousness and fair-mindedness, he can usually be counted on to possess the objectivity to do his job reasonably well.

Of course, the ombudsman's mandate ordinarily includes evaluation of all sorts of complaints against the paper, including malice and sheer inaccuracy as well as political bias. But such a functionary—where one exists at all—is at least a step in the right direction, as far as political bias is concerned. A problem ordinarily can't be solved until it is recognized as one, and the mere existence of an ombudsman acknowledges, usefully, that the paper can err.*

Another internal monitoring device that some media sympathizers and some media themselves have favored is not "internal" to the particular newspaper, magazine, or network itself, but rather internal from the standpoint of the media as a whole—i.e., does not involve monitoring by any individual or institution extrinsic to the media themselves. This is the "press council." Once again, as in the case of the ombudsman, the device is addressed at least as much to remedying other forms of media misbehavior as to dealing with instances of political bias, but press councils have concerned themselves with this subject among others.

The leading contemporary example of the species is the British Press Council. An excellent discussion of this organization is annexed as an appendix to Patrick Brogan's aforementioned report on the National News Council (page 116). To quote from it:

> The [British] Press Council had a more official paternity than the National News Council. It was fathered upon the Mother of Parliaments by the National Union of Journalists, at whose urging the first Royal Commission was set up in 1947. It recommended the establishment of a press council, to be financed by the newspapers and to act as a public watchdog for journalistic impropriety. The proprietors and editors opposed the council, but Parliament insisted, and the council came into existence in 1951. However, it was given little money, and all its members came from the press. . . .
> The council's first decade was a period of total neglect, and it might have died unmourned and unnoticed, like the [National] News Council after its own first decade. There was, however, another Royal Commission in 1962, chaired by Lord Shawcross. He went for the jugular. If the press refused to set up a proper press council, with adequate funding and lay members, Parliament would do it for them. . . . Fleet Street took the hint. A reconstituted Press Council set up shop, with Lord Devlin, a retired judge of great eminence and independence of mind, as its chairman.
> Under Devlin's brisk leadership, the Press Council increased steadily in

---

* *The New Yorker* magazine, in contrast, for many years had no device whatever for correcting errors—not even so much as a Letters column. The rather engaging implication was that *The New Yorker* was simply above making errors. On those rare occasions when correction was absolutely essential, a new article would be published in the magazine under the title "Department of Amplification."

influence throughout the 1960s. It published annual reports, entitled "The Press and the People," in which succinct accounts were given of the council's more important findings, and managed to win the grudging acceptance of newspapers and the confidence of the general public. . . .

The Press Council serves the British press well, far better than it deserves. Under the blaring headlines, and despite the naked ladies, the wild sensationalism, and the unscrupulous political slanting of the news, the British press operates within strict limits, partly set by the laws of libel, far stricter than those in the United States, [and] partly by the accumulated case law of the Press Council. [The press] may trivialize every issue and sensationalize everything, but it tries to be fair. It no longer maligns ordinary citizens, because if it does, they will complain to the Press Council, which will oblige the offender to print a retraction. There is now a workable and reasonable code of journalistic ethics in Britain.

Not all assessments of the performance of the British Press Council are quite so enthusiastic. Paul Johnson, writing in the July 19, 1986, issue of *The Spectator,* summed it up this way:

The press is unpopular primarily because it is inaccurate and intrusive, usually in conjunction. Vast numbers of people can give an instance, from their own experience or that of neighbours, friends or relations, of bad press behaviour. With this in mind, the voluntary system of discipline embodied in the Press Council was set up, in order to forestall some kind of compulsory control by parliamentary statute. It appeared to work for a time but must now be regarded as a failure. The council itself no longer carries much authority, primarily because of changes in its composition. The journalistic heavyweights who once made it respected have departed. The lay membership, as often happens in such bodies, inclines increasingly toward the Left, and the council is thus becoming identified with causes the Left holds dear. I finally lost confidence in the council when it sought to censor an editorial critical of homosexual behaviour.

Nevertheless, the British Press Council survives, as testimony to the possibility (however unsatisfactory in practice) of this particular form of internal monitoring of the media's behavior.

There have been efforts to create state press councils in various states of the United States, but as of 1987 the only one extant was in Minnesota. The Minnesota Press Council was founded in 1971, and changed its name to the Minnesota News Council in 1977 when it expanded its jurisdiction to include electronic as well as print media. Consisting of twenty-four members (half from the media and half from the public) and chaired by Judge John Simonett of the Minnesota Supreme Court, it functions on a budget of about $65,000 a year and boasts just one full-time employee: its executive director, Tom Patterson.

Financed by private contributions (a third of them from the Minnesota media), the council conducts public hearings on complaints against the media. Its only sanction is the publicity generated by its holdings, but Patterson asserts that the local media are largely cooperative.

In 1986 the MNC received 134 complaints—a record—and about 10 percent of these reached the hearing stage. The council also played a part in reaching a mediated settlement in another 10 percent; the rest, typically, were dropped by the complainant somewhere along the line. (The council requires complainants to sign a waiver of all rights to seek other redress, including suits for libel.)

The only effort to monitor the major American media nationwide, on an essentially internal basis, was the National News Council. As already described (pages 115–119), the council was founded in 1973 in response to the flood of criticism of the media's political bias that began with and followed from Vice President Agnew's Des Moines speech of November 1969. Despite generous financial support from several foundations, and the cooperation of certain segments of the media, it expired ten years later owing to the inveterate hostility of other important media players.

There are several reasons for the different outcomes of the British and American attempts to monitor the press internally. Perhaps most important, the First Amendment to the U.S. Constitution expressly bars Congress from enacting any law abridging the freedom of the press, whereas the power of the British Parliament to do so is technically unrestrained.

In the second place, and almost equally important for the moment, the de facto alliance between the major American media and the forces of political liberalism—in Congress, in the state legislatures, and in the country at large—assures the media of passionate support for their asserted prerogatives whenever these are threatened.

These considerations make it far from certain that the major American media will ever unite in consenting to effective internal monitoring of their performance. And that, of course, simply increases the pressure for a fourth kind of approach to the problem of media bias: some form of external monitoring.

## External Monitoring

In a sense, of course, an attempt to remedy media bias by means of external monitoring is simply a specialized form of jawboning. But we confined our discussion of jawboning (above) to criticisms of the media which did not involve sustained or systematic observation and criticism. It is those that do that we will now review, under the head of "external monitoring."

The indisputable doyen of American media-watchers is Accuracy in Media (or AIM, for short). AIM was founded in 1971 by Reed Irvine, and is supported financially by the contributions of individuals who approve of its strenuous criticism of the media's liberal and/or leftist bias. Irvine serves as chairman of the board, and also edits its semimonthly bulletin, *The AIM Report,* which commenced publication in 1972.

AIM's criticisms are often dismissed by the media and their defenders on the ground that Irvine's own strong conservative predilections are obvious—as indeed they are. But this excuse serves merely to spare the media the necessity of answering Irvine's criticisms on their merits, which are usually substantial.

A given issue of *The AIM Report* will typically concentrate on one specific instance, or set of instances, of slanting in the presentation of news. The December-A 1986 issue, for example, described in detail the generous and friendly attention given by the three commercial TV networks to the reunion in Spain of a few members of the Abraham Lincoln Brigade to observe the fiftieth anniversary of the outbreak of the Spanish civil war.

The brigade consisted of Americans who had volunteered to fight on the "loyalist," or Republican, side of that war, against the ultimately victorious forces of Francisco Franco. Historically the brigade's veterans have depicted themselves as simply early antifascists, who perceived in the Spanish conflict a sort of test run for World War II, which quickly followed it. This view, however, obscures, and is intended to obscure, the fact that the Spanish forces opposing Franco were dominated and led by the Spanish Communist party, and that the Abraham Lincoln Brigade was similarly led, dominated, and largely populated by American Communists.

Irvine takes the networks sharply to task for adopting the sanitized view of the Abraham Lincoln Brigade. He describes ABC's coverage of the story as follows:

. . . The segment was introduced by anchorman Peter Jennings saying, "Fifty years ago, to be a member of the Abraham Lincoln Brigade and fight against fascism was regarded by some Americans as a romantic and important adventure."

Pierre Salinger, the former press secretary to President John F. Kennedy and now a correspondent for ABC proceeded to tell us about that "romantic and important adventure," utilizing interviews with a few of the men who made that sentimental journey to Spain. Prominent among them was a veteran former Communist Party official, Steve Nelson. Without being identified as a long-time Communist, Nelson was shown saying, "To me, the Spanish Civil War and the fight there was the most important thing in my lifetime, not because I was in it, but because it was the first major fight against fascism."

That was followed by Pierre Salinger saying, "And fight they did, against the wishes of the American government, outmanned and out-gunned. Nearly a third of them died and were buried on Spanish soil. It was here at Bruneti, on the road to Madrid, that the Americans were plunged into one of the bloodiest battles of the war. For some, the return brought back strong memories, buried for half a century."

Irvine quotes still more of Salinger's lachrymose tribute, which described the veterans as "from the left, to be sure, but not in every case." Salinger concluded on the following proud, sad note:

> . . . There were no brass bands, no parades for the survivors of the Abraham Lincoln battalion. The reunion was today as it was 50 years ago, a private journey, made of conviction, supported by belief, and ending in the personal satisfaction of knowing they showed the world the face of its enemy and sounded the alert."

Irvine promptly fired off a letter to ABC News president Roone Arledge, asserting that ABC News should have informed its viewers that the international brigades, including the American Abraham Lincoln Brigade, were organized and run by Communists, and that many of those who joined were profoundly disillusioned when they discovered that the Stalinists in Spain were imprisoning, torturing, and even summarily executing their ideological rivals on the left—the Anarchists, members of the Partido Obrero de Unificación Marxista, and anyone suspected of Trotskyism. In the letter, Irvine said, "We pointed out that this had been exposed many years ago by the British writer, George Orwell, in his great book, *Homage to Catalonia,* which was based on what Orwell had personally seen and heard as a volunteer in Spain."

Irvine then turned to similar critical analyses of two CBS programs on the brigade's reunion. On CBS's *Sunday Morning,* to cite one example, Charles Kuralt introduced the segment with this eloquent tribute: "But the ideals that the Abraham Lincoln Brigade was dedicated to—freedom and the struggle against tyranny—made them comrades of a world that found itself at war with those same tyrants just a few years later."

Irvine summed up as follows:

These programs by ABC and CBS have again demonstrated how easily TV
network news can be used to disseminate propaganda favorable to the
Communists. Rather than do even superficial research and seek out
knowledgeable individuals who could tell the story of the Spanish Civil
War and the International Brigades from a non-communist viewpoint,
ABC and CBS relied exclusively on Communists or former Communists
who still appear to follow the party line, misleading their audiences by
perpetuating old myths.

In a multilithed insert in the same issue of the report, Irvine listed the
names and addresses of the top officers of various major corporations that
advertised on the offending segments and urged his readers to write letters
of protest to them. "They will tell you," he predicted, "that they have
no control over the content of programs of this type, which is true. You
should point out that they have the right and the duty to let the network
know that they don't like to see their ads on news programs that are used
to disseminate blatant propaganda of this type."

In the insert, Irvine also reported that Salinger had replied to his letter
to ABC concerning its version of the story:

. . . Salinger correctly points out that he had noted that the Republican
government in Spain had been backed by Russia and that the Communist
parties around the world had offered help forming the international
brigades. He had mentioned that many who joined the brigades were
Communists. Salinger said this was enough "to clearly establish the Soviet
and Communist participation in the Abraham Lincoln Battalion." He
claimed that Steve Nelson had been adequately identified as a Communist.
Superimposed over his picture on the screen were the words, "Steve
Nelson, Commissar, Lincoln Battalion." Salinger thought that was enough
to inform viewers that Nelson was a Communist Party leader.

The Communists did not merely "participate" in the Abraham Lincoln
Brigade; they organized it and ran it. The "many" Communists who were
mixed in with those "adventurers, political activists and some pacifists"
actually comprised 80 percent of the total. To suggest that the average
viewer would catch the words "Commissar, Lincoln Battalion" superimposed on Nelson's picture and immediately understand that this man was
a high official of the Communist Party for most of his life is fatuous.
Salinger, who said he was well acquainted with the history of the Spanish
Civil War, did not dispute the charge that his piece had given the
Communist version of the war and the role of the international brigades.
He didn't dispute our refutation of that version. He said only that it was not
possible to tell the whole story in three-and-a-half minutes. No one would

deny that, but it leaves unanswered the question of why it was considered appropriate to mislead viewers with the Communist version rather than telling them as much of the truth as could be fitted into the available time.

Patient, precise, implacable, and (usually) imperturbable, Reed Irvine has become a distinct hairshirt to America's liberal media elite in the past decade. He seldom misses the annual meetings of the owner-corporations, in which he has thoughtfully bought a few shares to assure himself a voice and a vote. The harassed executives try hard to rise above him, but they seldom manage to ignore him altogether.

A far younger and in some ways even livelier conservative monitor of the nation's liberal media is *Newswatch* (recently renamed MediaWatch) a monthly eight-page newsletter launched in 1986 and published by the Media Research Center. The publisher, heading a staff of seven editors and "media analysts," is L. Brent Bozell III, a son of one of William F. Buckley's brothers-in-law; the chief editor is Brent Baker.

Like *The AIM Report*, *Newswatch* monitors the media from an explicitly conservative perspective. But it would be quite wrong to assume that its criticisms can for that reason be dismissed easily. Every monthly issue of the publication discusses a score or more of recent examples of the media's liberal bias.

The November 1986 issue, for example, opened by noting in three paragraphs the media's sympathetic coverage of the fiftieth-anniversary reunion of the Abraham Lincoln Brigade, which had been the entire topic of the December-A 1986 semimonthly issue of *The AIM Report*. It then pointed out that October 1986 had also been the thirtieth anniversary of the Soviets' crushing of the Hungarian Rebellion, and observed that in this case the TV networks, instead of praising the ideals of the defeated rebels, "preferred to focus on [Hungary's] current comparatively high standard of living, despite the fact that thousands who fled to America are available for interviews to recount their experiences."

The second page of the newsletter carried a review of Robert Lichter's then just-released book, *The Media Elite: America's New Power Brokers* (Adler and Adler). Noting that the book "has provided more evidence documenting the media's pervasive liberal bias," *Newswatch* summarized three in-depth content analyses that Lichter set forth at length. The review concluded by quoting some furious liberal reviewers, and adding, "In the ultimate insult, neither *The New York Times* nor *Washington Post* considered the book worthy of review. What better evidence of a media elite?"

Page 3 announced the recipient of the "Janet Cooke Award" ("in honor of *The Washington Post* reporter who won the Pulitzer Prize for 'Jimmy,' a story about an eight year old heroin addict which was later proven totally fictitious"). Every month, *Newswatch* awards the honor to "the most outrageously distorted piece of reporting masquerading as fact."

The November 1986 Janet Cooke Award went "to NBC News Paris correspondent Jim Bitterman for an October 25 Nightly News segment on the death of President Samora Machel of Mozambique." The report described Mozambique as verging on collapse because of what Bitterman described as

South African backed guerrillas who leave in their wake burned out villages and brutally tortured villagers as evidence of their growing strength. One of their favorite methods of terrorizing the local people is to cut off ears, lips, and limbs to frighten victims from supporting the government.

When *Newswatch* reached Bitterman in Paris, he admitted that he personally had never been to Mozambique, and that the entire story was based on the account of a French free-lance journalist who "has been reliable in the past." Neither Bitterman nor *NBC Nightly News* spokesman Andrew Freedman, however, would disclose the name of the French free-lancer. (Apparently the modern heavy reliance on anonymous sources got totally out of control in this case: Not merely the source but the reporter was anonymous!)

*Newswatch* condemned Bitterman for "trying to duck responsibility for an incredibly one-sided and misleading report he irresponsibly passed off as fact."

Pages 4, 5, and 8 contained nearly a dozen short paragraphic analyses of various recent media derelictions: The notorious anti-Reagan bias of UPI White House reporter Helen Thomas; the close association of certain NBC and ABC newsmen with the liberal *New Republic* and the far-left *Nation* magazine, as evidenced by the articles they wrote for these publications; a "meaningless change" made, after numerous protests, by the producers of a PBS series which "glorifies Qaddafi"; the assertion of ABC's Sylvan Rodriguez, without providing any evidence, that Seattle archbishop Raymond Hunthausen "is generally acknowledged to reflect the views of a majority of the 360,000 Catholics in his archdiocese"; and so on.

Pages 6 and 7 of the November 1986 issue of *Newswatch* were given over to a detailed "study" of television news coverage of the November 1985 Reagan-Gorbachev summit in Geneva:

> . . . While the Soviets travelled to Geneva in an effort to block any further development of the Strategic Defense Initiative (SDI), dubbed "Star Wars" by the press, President Reagan declared his priorities to be Soviet human rights abuses, arms pact violations and aggression abroad. Then, talks about an arms agreement. Which agenda did the American networks follow? A *Newswatch* study found they pursued the Soviet one.

The heart of the *Newswatch* "study" was a statistical table setting forth the number of minutes, between November 1 and November 22, 1985, that the evening news programs of the three networks had collectively devoted to the United States and Soviet positions.

It turned out that the leading item on the American agenda, Soviet human rights violations, had received 28:30 (28 minutes and 30 seconds) of discussion, distributed as follows: 5:55 "Pro-U.S./Anti-USSR," 16:10 "Neutral," and 6:25 "Anti-U.S./Pro-USSR".

SDI, the major item on the Soviet agenda, received more attention on American television networks. It received 37:30 of discussion, distributed as follows: 3:55 "Pro-U.S./Anti-USSR," 19:34 "Neutral," and 14:01 "Anti-U.S./Pro-USSR."

As for Soviet versus United States military buildups (i.e., the problem of arms control), the coverage was wildly lopsided. There wasn't a single second of coverage that could be characterized as "Pro-U.S./Anti-USSR." "Neutral" coverage added up to 7:20. The remaining 8:59 were "Anti-U.S./Pro-USSR."

So much for a single issue of *Newswatch*. In addition to publishing twelve issues a year, the editors commenced in December 1986 a two-minute weekly radio commentary on the media's liberal bias, to be broadcast on the 150 stations of the conservative Radio America syndicate.

Publications like *The AIM Report* and *Newswatch* are, of course, comparatively small, but their influence may be greater than even they realize. Like Admiral Mahan's "fleet in being," their chief successes may be not what they affirmatively accomplish so much as what they deter the media from attempting. However much they may scoff at such right-wing gnats, ABC's Roone Arledge and Pierre Salinger can hardly have enjoyed *The AIM Report*'s close analysis of their reverent approach to the Abraham Lincoln Brigade. And you can be sure that Jim Bitterman hasn't quite forgotten that he was the recipient of one of *Newswatch*'s Janet Cooke Awards for his inexcusably casual handling of the facts in reporting the civil war in Mozambique from three thousand miles away.

As a result, it is probably safe to say that external monitoring of the media by such conservative publications as *The AIM Report* and *Newswatch* is having some effect. Moreover, the effect may be cumulative, as such organizations gain a larger audience and the media become convinced at last that they aren't just going to go away.

In addition to explicitly conservative efforts to monitor the media, there are recent evidences of centrist and even liberal interest in doing so.

On February 28, 1987, the Center for Media and Public Affairs (Robert and Linda Lichter, codirectors) announced the launching of *Media Monitor,* a periodical that the center stated "will analyze coverage of breaking stories in the form of regular reports that are accurate, fair, and timely." It expressed the hope that the *Monitor*

> can help fill the gap between academic scholarship and journalism by presenting scientifically valid media analysis in readable form to journalists and the general public. Over time this research will build a body of knowledge that can enhance media performance and increase public understanding of the media's vital role in a free society.

The first issue of *Media Monitor,* dated March 1987, concentrated on TV news coverage of the Iran/contra story to that point, including the Tower Commission report. The study examined nightly network news broadcasts for one month after the arms sale story broke on November 4, 1986. It concluded that "coverage of the Iran/contra story was massive and relatively balanced, but relied heavily on unnamed sources."

The final paragraph of the first issue asserted:

> This study is not intended to decide the debate over media fairness. How scientific evidence is interpreted depends on the reader's own values. Our goal is more modest—to provide a sound basis for judgment and, perhaps, further debate. At the least, the results suggest that reality is often more complex than partisanship will admit.

The third issue of *Media Monitor,* dated May 1987, was devoted largely to the anniversary of Chernobyl, and to a comparison of the major media coverage of the Chernobyl accident with a CMPA poll of American scientists. It concluded that whereas the scientists overwhelmingly regarded Chernobyl as "a Soviet anomaly," the media portrayed it as "a portent of domestic [i.e., U.S.] disaster."

The fourth and final page of the May issue offered some early statistics on reactions to the withdrawal of Gary Hart from the race for the Democratic presidential nomination.

There is evidence that liberals, at least of the sterner variety, may themselves be preparing to enter the lists of those who monitor the media. According to Jonathan Rowe, writing in the *Christian Science Monitor* for May 21, 1987, "Ralph Nader is launching a media newsletter this fall." If his purpose is to contend that America's major media aren't liberal enough, he must be insatiable indeed.

In any event, as with simple jawboning and internal monitoring, it is obvious that external monitoring will not be sufficient, in and of itself, to compel the major American media to abandon their liberal bias and offer a reasonably balanced presentation of the news.

That is why certain analysts of the problem have come up with yet another solution, more drastic and far more difficult.

## Outright Takeover

In the late 1950s, when *National Review* had just been founded and was serving willy-nilly as a sort of clearinghouse for all kinds of projects of interest to the conservative movement, its editor Bill Buckley was frequently approached by fellow conservatives who were understandably incensed at the liberal bias of the media and thought they had found the perfect solution: Let conservatives buy outright control of one of the major media and change its political orientation. One of the most persistent advocates of this course, as I recall, was a Texas dentist, and his target of choice was the Columbia Broadcasting System. CBS stock was on the open market, and he simply proposed to assemble a consortium of conservatives wealthy enough and concerned enough to buy a controlling interest and replace William Paley as the dominant force on the board and in management.

There was nothing inherently impossible about the idea—as Laurence Tisch demonstrated in 1986 when he did precisely that (though with motives more entrepreneurial than ideological). But Buckley felt the proposal was impractical, for at least two reasons.

For one thing, the amount of money that would have to be committed to the project would be enormous. (Tisch and his colleagues reportedly spent $830 million over a period of fourteen months to acquire 24.9 percent of the stock of CBS.) In the fragile circumstances of the infant conservative movement, and bearing in mind too the enormous drain such an effort would impose on the time and energies of the individuals qualified and willing to mount such a drive, Buckley felt (rightly, in my opinion) that such an attempt would constitute an unjustified diversion of scarce resources, assuming it could be mounted at all and even if it succeeded.

But secondly, Buckley seriously doubted whether such a project could possibly succeed. In the first place, even if a takeover bid was successful, the swift response of America's liberal intelligentsia, including the rest of the media, would be to try to discredit the network under its new ownership. Without admitting their own bias (which, as we have seen, they practically never do), the media would have permanently affixed "right-wing" or "ultraconservative" or some other pejorative adjective to the name of the born-again CBS, to warn the unwary that it was purveying biased "news."

In the second place, it is highly doubtful that the basic thrust of a large news organization could be permanently transformed from liberal to conservative by a mere change of ownership, in the absence of fundamental shifts in the intellectual atmosphere of the entire society—what Buckley calls the *Zeitgeist*, or "spirit of the age," and John Corry (page 22) described as "the dominant culture."

Probably every era has its characterizing spirit—a set of unspoken underlying assumptions that effectively limit what can be said and done without encountering seriously disabling disapproval. What makes the life of the mind so exciting, of course, is precisely the fact that such assumptions do change over time—are challenged, overthrown, and replaced by others (which in their turn define the characterizing spirit of the succeeding age).

From the early decades of this century until very recently, the underlying assumptions that dominated the intellectual life of the American society—almost without serious challenge—were the liberal assumptions. In such circumstances, liberal views were bound to prevail wherever ideas mattered, and this most certainly included the media.

But not only the media. The nation's colleges and universities were an earlier and even more obvious target. But perhaps the most dramatic example of the power of liberal assumptions to overwhelm theoretically conservative control was afforded by the nation's major foundations.

Most of the country's leading private charitable foundations were created by multimillionaire businessmen whose own political and economic views would qualify as conservative by almost anyone's definition: John D. Rockefeller, Sr., Andrew Carnegie, Henry Ford, John D. MacArthur, etc. Yet the foundations created by these men have been taken over by trustees and administrators of a predominantly and outspokenly liberal inclination, and serve today as major financial resources of the liberal intellectual establishment.

Were these takeovers the result of a conspiracy, or conspiracies? Probably not, at least in most cases. The foundations were, however, entrusted to academics and other intellectuals deeply imbued with the "spirit of the age"—and that spirit was liberal.

Similarly, any network or newsmagazine or major newspaper taken over by conservatives with a conscious intention to alter its political bias would (assuming, implausibly, that it somehow survived its predictable denigration by the liberals) nevertheless have to employ, and act through, journalists of quality if it hoped to earn and deserve respect. And during the past half century or more, these have, overwhelmingly, been liberals for the reasons outlined above. Slowly but inexorably the organization would bend with the prevailing wind—witness Colonel McCormick's *Chicago Tribune* or David Lawrence's *U.S. News and World Report,* after their deaths.

Finally, what, even, if it didn't? Do conservatives really want simply to replace a liberal bias in the news media with a conservative one? Certainly these pages have not advocated such an outcome. The real ambition of those who value a free press ought to be, not a pronounced bias in any direction, but a reasonable balance in the presentation of the news.

Nevertheless, the outright takeover of some major news medium has continued to be the ambition of certain conservatives. A few years ago Senator Jesse Helms, the redoubtable North Carolina Republican, lent his name and prestige to one such effort. Once again the target was CBS.

Fairness in Media (the name Helms gave the project) was an offshoot of the National Congressional Club, Helms's umbrella organization for the financing of political campaigns and other worthy ventures. Again the intention was simply to buy enough CBS stock to acquire working control, and there was a good deal of inside humor about the look Dan Rather would have on his face when summoned for the first time to meet his new employers. But the project never got very far, in part because it was upstaged by Georgia entrepreneur Ted Turner's own subsequent bold bid to buy CBS (financed, it was alleged, largely by high-yield securities known as "junk bonds") and in part because of the protective measures adopted by the incumbent CBS owner and management to protect their control against all uninvited takeovers. Ultimately William Paley, the longtime owner of CBS (through a controlling stock interest in the neighborhood of 10 percent), acquiesced in the takeover bid of Loew's Laurence Tisch, who graciously consented to share control of the network with Paley.

Since these developments, Fairness in Media had lingered "in limbo," in the words of one individual familiar with its affairs. There will probably be protests lodged on its behalf at future CBS shareholders' meetings, and at this writing it is still appealing, before the FCC, against the above-described protective measures adopted by CBS's management. But it seems likely that, in setting its sights on CBS, Fairness in Media bit off considerably more than it could chew.

So, of course, did Ted Turner. Many conservatives wished his effort well, regarding "the Mouth of the South" as a principled conservative himself, if not quite in the same league with Jesse Helms. But in recent years, to the astonishment of many observers, Turner has become deeply interested in various investment opportunities behind the Iron Curtain, and has collaterally become an outspoken advocate of warmer relations between the United States and the Soviet Union. Moscow, for its part, has shown a lively reciprocal interest in Turner, evidently perceiving him as a valuable potential resource in the American business community—on the order, perhaps, of a younger Armand Hammer. At any rate, their mutual admiration was apparently behind the Goodwill Games which Turner organized and televised in Moscow in the summer of 1986.

Needless to say, such antics have cooled conservative enthusiasm for the idea of Turner taking over CBS, or anything else for that matter, and also illustrate some of the perils of putting one's trust in any particular individual to turn a network around—as distinguished from the far longer and more difficult but infinitely sounder policy of changing the *Zeitgeist* itself.

Turner's bid also caused alarm in quite a different quarter. Ever since the end of World War II and in some cases even earlier, ownership and thus ultimate control of the three major broadcasting networks had remained in the hands of a relatively small group of people who were, at a very minimum, quite content to watch the liberal bias in their networks' news presentations develop into the phenomenon it has become today. Almost without thinking about it, the impression grew and became fixed that this agreeable state of affairs would go on indefinitely—that William Paley, for example, would continue to rule in the CBS empyrean more or less forever.

Turner's hostile takeover bid, therefore, loosened a great many rooted assumptions at CBS and elsewhere. And when Capital Cities Communications actually did proceed in that same year (1985) to buy ABC for $3.5 billion in a friendly takeover, many liberals long accustomed to unchallenged possession of on-screen jobs and key producerships and editorships at all three networks sensed the ground shifting, or at least threatening to shift, beneath their feet.

As matters transpired, the concern was at the very least premature. Laurence Tisch is, if anything, a bit more pronouncedly and outspokenly liberal in his views than William Paley. And while Thomas S. Murphy, chairman of Capital Cities, is believed to be a good deal more conservative, personally, than longtime ABC chairman Leonard Goldenson, the advent of the new bosses at ABC has thus far had no perceptible ideological effect; the emphasis has been on cutting costs.

Nevertheless, the old confidence that nothing could change in broadcasting circles has unquestionably been shaken. Perhaps an outright ideological takeover, à la Helms, need not be seriously feared. But how many Ted Turners may be out there, on the lookout for a vulnerable network? And who can be sure that the next corporation to stage a takeover will be as indifferent to a liberal bias in news presentations as Capital Cities appears to be?

A fear of this unknown future probably underlies most of the halfhearted efforts that America's commercial networks have made in recent years to clean up their act. But that fear alone is no more a sufficient answer to the problem of liberal bias in the key national media than jawboning or internal or external monitoring.

The truth is that the problem is almost no longer describable as a simple matter of unfair political bias on the part of an important national institution. We are dealing here with the fundamental problem of the distribution of forces within the American society. The historic role of the media has been changing before our eyes. The media no longer are—if they ever were—objective observers of the political conflict. They are highly partisan participants in it, allied with the other institutional supporters of liberalism, and they will have to be recognized, challenged, and defeated as such, or allowed to prevail and participate in a renewed liberal dominance of the American society.

Where we may be headed is suggested by the imaginary scenario that follows.

# CHAPTER 11

## *Scenario*

*The power of the media not merely to influence but to determine and even make events is growing. That is bound, in the end, to lead to a popular demand that it be subjected to more democratic control.''*
—Paul Johnson, *The Spectator*, November 1, 1986

AT 10:00 A.M. EST on Saturday, February 15, 1989, the President of the United States addressed the nation. His talk was carried on all major television and radio networks. It was brief and dramatic:

My fellow Americans: As you know, our relations with Nicaragua have deteriorated gravely in recent years. The Sandinista regime, having consolidated its hold on the country after Congress ended military aid to the contras, has stepped up its pressure against its non-Communist neighbors. Guerrilla forces based in Nicaragua, and supplied by Communist nations through that country, are gravely threatening the freely elected government of El Salvador through repeated bombings in its capital, San Salvador, and are also active in Honduras and Guatemala. I regret to say that there is evidence that revolutionary forces inspired by the Communist bloc are preparing to strike in our closest neighbor, Mexico, in the near future.

The United States has repeatedly warned Nicaragua and its Communist allies that it cannot tolerate the steady, indefinite expansion of communism by force northward through Central America to our very border. In particular we have made it clear that the introduction of new weapons systems in that area would not be permitted, since they would fundamentally alter the strategic balance there and compel a reevaluation, and probably a major reduction, of this country's global military commitments.

Despite these warnings, Nicaragua and its supporters in the Communist bloc have persisted in their attempts to destabilize the free and democratic countries to the north. And I very much regret to say that last week, in express disregard of our solemn and repeated warnings, three squadrons of Soviet-made MiG-29s—the most modern and deadly fighter planes in the Soviet arsenal—arrived at Nicaraguan military air bases in what is very clearly an attempt to change fundamentally the military balance in Central America.

Under these circumstances, the United States is left no choice but to act before the situation becomes even worse and perhaps gets out of control altogether. Accordingly, after consultations with the National Security Council, the Joint Chiefs of Staff, the relevant Cabinet members, and leaders of both parties in both Houses of Congress, I have directed the armed forces of the United States to occupy the territory of the Republic of Nicaragua and secure it for the forces of freedom, in preparation for early elections to choose a new government. Operations to that end began just a little over four hours ago, and will continue until the assigned objectives have been achieved.

I am confident that these steps will meet with the full approval of the American people, and that they will also be endorsed by Congress if they are still proceeding in sixty days when congressional approval of the overseas deployment of United States forces is required by the War Powers Act. Meanwhile, today our hearts are with our soldiers, sailors, airmen, and Marines, on whom so much depends. Let us pray that casualties on both sides will be light, that the battle will be over shortly, and that all of Central America will soon know, once again, the blessings of freedom.

Thank you, and God bless America.

The first attacks of American forces—by landing craft on the Atlantic and Pacific coasts of Nicaragua, by land across Nicaragua's border with Honduras, and by parachute and helicopter onto certain small airfields which could then be used to fly in supplies—were almost uniformly successful, and the mood in the White House and the Pentagon was described as one of "cautious optimism." In Congress, only a handful of extreme leftist congressmen condemned the operation, while many in both parties praised it. A majority of members of the House and Senate, on both sides of the aisle, acknowledged privately that there seemed little else the President could do, in view of the brazen deployment of the MiG-29s.

The major media too, during that first week, contented themselves with reporting the military operations, with due regard for the security of troop movements, etc. In fact, just about the only discordant notes came from foreign sources. In a special emergency session the UN Security Council, by an overwhelming margin, condemned the American attack. The nations voting for the resolution included some of America's closest allies, but the resolution was technically void because the United States representative vetoed it.

Reaction throughout the Communist bloc and the Third World was vociferously anti-American from the start. There were riots and anti-American demonstrations in almost every capital; bombs exploded near the American embassies in six countries, and three U.S. Information

Agency libraries were set ablaze. In NATO Europe, the gloom was intense; the conviction was almost universal that the United States had committed a disastrous blunder. The British prime minister insisted on suspending judgment until the situation became clearer, but was hooted down in the House of Commons.

These negative reactions were, of course, duly reported to the American people by the media, but they had little effect as long as the news from the battlefronts remained consistently upbeat.

During the second and third weeks of the invasion, the various fronts were stabilized. United States forces had consolidated their hold on much of the Atlantic coast of Nicaragua, as well as on a smaller segment of its Pacific coast, and also over a portion of its northern sector where Nicaragua borders Honduras. However, it had become apparent that the Sandinista armed forces, including their "international" component, weren't going to be any pushovers. The Sandinistas were digging in grimly around Managua, Estelí, and Granada, and their large and well-equipped army was giving a good account of itself in pitched battles with United States forces. The U.S. Navy had, of course, effectively blockaded the country the moment hostilities began, and the Air Force could claim air supremacy over the battlefronts most of the time, though antiaircraft missiles had managed, by the Pentagon's own admission, to shoot down six United States helicopters and three troop carriers.

Now, however, opposition to the invasion was increasing and mobilizing on the domestic Left. By mid-March demonstrations—small at first, but growing in size and number—were being staged in almost every major American city, and there were "teach-ins" or other protest actions on virtually every college campus. Television coverage of these was, of course, intensive. Abroad, too, the protests (and the riots, and the bombings) grew; one American military attaché was gunned down as he stepped out of his car.

In Congress, now, there was grumbling in the cloakrooms and the corridors. How long, exactly, did the President expect members of Congress to take this heat? Was this operation going to be a quick, surgical strike, on the order of a bigger Grenada, or was it going to drag on for years, like Vietnam? Just how important was Nicaragua to American security anyway? It had been Communist-controlled, for all practical purposes, since 1979, yet the world hadn't vanished in a blast of flame, had it? Certain prominent liberals in both the House and the Senate told their countrymen, on the evening news programs of the major TV networks, that the President owed the American people an explanation.

What, exactly, was the *goal* of this invasion? The people of Nicaragua certainly weren't welcoming our soldiers with open arms. Besides, three squadrons of fighter planes were scarcely much of a threat to American sovereignty in the skies. "How many more American soldiers," one senator demanded, "will have to be shipped home in body bags before we learn why this invasion was necessary, or call a halt to it?"

Meanwhile, in El Salvador, guerrilla forces launched a massive campaign of terrorism, and the country's chief executive was assassinated. His successor declared a national state of emergency.

On March 20, on the recommendation of the Joint Chiefs of Staff, the President authorized the commitment of thirty thousand additional combat troops, to augment the initial invasion force of fifty thousand, and called up elements of the Reserve and the National Guard. This, however, simply increased the protests in Congress, in the country at large, and abroad. "Where will it all end?" demanded one of television's most prominent anchormen, who thereupon decided to use that question as his sign-off words every night.

And now, as March drew toward a close and the enemy, though slowly giving ground, fought with desperate intensity, the mood of the American people turned somber. Casualty reports were now a familiar phenomenon, and every sizable American city counted its dead and wounded. On television, the grim reality of war was brought home to the public every night by newsmen the vast majority of whom had opposed the invasion, at least privately, from the very start.

From a crater carved by an exploding shell of the battleship *New Jersey*, fired during the early days of the invasion, one TV correspondent picked up a fragment of shrapnel and held it out toward the camera.

"This particular shell did no damage," he explained with a smile. "It landed here, in an empty field. The only losers were the taxpayers who paid for it in the first place. But another shell"—and here he gestured with the shrapnel—"scored a direct hit over there. On an orphanage."

One of the battleship's sixteen-inch guns had indeed, it seemed, by accident hit an orphanage in a nearby town where enemy soldiers were holding up the American advance. The scene now shifted to a makeshift hospital, where nursing nuns were caring for children injured by the shell. They had nothing to say to the American TV crew, but their looks—and the sad-eyed faces of the children—told volumes.

On another network that evening, the reporter was interviewing wounded American soldiers. Most of them were pretty matter-of-fact about it all. One young man with his arm in a sling just wanted to say hello to his folks back home. Another, who had lost a leg, was less exuberant. The war, he said, was "pretty bad." The camera moved on.

There was straight battle reportage too, of course: camera footage of American soldiers scurrying forward across a road and through a line of trees. ("The gooks are over there," a big black sergeant explained.) There was the sound of shots, and pictures of some sort of smoky fire. Then the reporter appeared onscreen: The village had been taken. Two American soldiers were dead. On, tomorrow, to the next village. But, "Where will it all end?"

By the beginning of April, five weeks into the invasion, polls indicated that most of the American people still supported it, but the percentage opposed had grown from 17 percent in late February to 26 percent in mid-March. Now it stood at 39 percent. In Congress, the rumbles had become a roar. Most congressmen, like most of the public, still supported the invasion, but they were growing increasingly uneasy as April 25 drew nearer—the sixtieth day of the operation and the one on which the President must, by law, recall America's troops unless Congress had by then authorized their continued deployment abroad.

Public uneasiness was heightened by a sharp increase in Soviet military activity in the neighborhood of the Persian Gulf. Suddenly it seemed possible that what had begun as a quick, relatively painless military operation on our southern flank might escalate into a global conflict, with incalculable consequences.

The savage week-long battle for possession of Nicaragua's capital, Managua, which ended in victory for the Americans on April 7, was nevertheless depicted on American television as a disastrous defeat, because American casualties had been high. Closely paraphrasing Pyrrhus, one TV newsman declared that "one more such 'victory' and we will be ruined." His camera crew took Americans, watching horrified in their living rooms, on a grim tour of a road on the city's outskirts. Clearly visible were the bodies of seven American soldiers killed by a land mine. "I talked to this boy yesterday," the reporter mused, gesturing. "He was going to be married in September."

Another of the bodies was identified as that of Corporal Harry Flint, twenty-two, of Rochester, New York. The scene switched to Rochester, where, by one of those miracles of modern television, Harry Flint's mother could now be seen, "live," watching this very program. A camera closed in tight on her homely face—puffy and red from weeping. But she was composed now, as she began to speak in a high-pitched, querulous voice.

"Harry loved the Army," she began. "He really loved it. I know, if he had to die, this . . . he would have"—her chin was trembling now— "I only hope, somehow, that some good comes of all this killing. I didn't want"—and now the eyes brim and overflow—"to lose my boy." She covers her sobbing face with her hands.

(In December 1989 a special citation for distinguished reportage was awarded to the director of that program by a committee of the television industry.)

By coincidence it was later that very evening that another network carried an interview with the Nicaraguan foreign minister, taped earlier in the day through the facilities of the Canadian Broadcasting Corporation in Toronto. He was a mild-mannered, bespectacled man who spoke excellent English. He described mournfully the carnage the American invasion was causing in his country, and demanded reproachfully, "What have we done to you, to deserve this?" The interviewer raised the matter of the MiG-29s, only to be told that America's invasion proved why they were necessary—a point the interviewer seemed unable to refute. "Leave us in peace," the Nicaraguan begged; "we wish you no harm."

In vain the administration strove to remind the public of the stakes in this battle: Was Central America going to become a forward base of the Soviet empire, armed with its most advanced weapons (and requiring, therefore, correspondingly advanced defenses), or wasn't it? The daily inundation of news from the battlefronts rubbed the public's nose in the human tragedy that war has always been—but which it had never before, even in Vietnam, so vividly and constantly been seen to be. As one furious general pointed out, a viewer watching the war on TV in his own home—morning, noon, and night—actually heard far more gunfire than the average combat infantryman, and saw more American corpses.

Television was, of course, the major medium that shaped American opinion, but the print media were not to be disregarded. And even radio, which receives far less attention than television but retains a vast audience and is dominated by producers, directors, and writers with exactly the same spectrum of leftist and liberal political attitudes, did its Herculean share. (One New York radio station began every news report from the battlefronts with the deadpan phrase, "On the Nicaraguan killing-ground . . .")

By mid-April, America was a nation torn asunder. A little over half of the public sincerely believed that unless the invasion was carried through to a successful conclusion, the Soviet Union would have succeeded in planting a forward military base in America's own backyard, ready to

create still further trouble in Mexico and elsewhere. About 40 percent
(the rest "didn't know") believed, equally sincerely, that no possible
military or diplomatic objective could possibly be worth the slaughter
unfolding before their eyes on the evening news programs. In Congress,
which was controlled by the opposition party, it now appeared that
narrow majorities in both Houses were prepared to deny authorization
(required, after sixty days, by the War Powers Act) for the invasion to
continue after April 25. The President was staring disaster—military for
the nation, political for himself—in the face.

On the morning of April 18 he summoned the owners of the major
television networks, newsmagazines, wire services, and national newspapers to the White House for an all-day, off-the-record discussion.
(Verbatim accounts of its key parts were published and broadcast the next
day.)

"Ladies and gentlemen," the President began somberly, "I have
asked you to come here to consult with me because this nation faces a
crisis that is truly constitutional.

"None of us wishes our country ill. If we disagree, it is over means,
not ends. I ask you, therefore, to believe me when I say that my military
and civilian advisers and I—this administration, if you will—sincerely
believed, and continue to believe, that the introduction of Soviet MiG
Twenty-nines into Central America represented a threat so grave that it
warranted an immediate military response. I may add that this belief was,
at least until the middle of March, common ground between the two
major parties, including the great majority of congressmen in both. That
is why there was, in the beginning, as little opposition to the invasion, in
Congress, as there was.

"But in the nearly two months since the invasion began, there has been
a dramatic swing in public opinion. Although the military operations are
succeeding and my military advisers tell me that we will prevail,
casualties have been somewhat higher than expected and we are about
four weeks behind our timetable. Far more ominously, public support for
the invasion has fallen from over eighty percent at the outset to only a
little over fifty percent today, and polls indicate that many of its critics are
not only against it but furiously so.

"The reason is perfectly plain. Modern technology, which is nobody's
fault, has made it possible for the news media to cover a war more
rapidly, more intensively, and more vividly than ever before in history.
The coverage of the Vietnam War, to which many people, rightly or
wrongly, assign responsibility for America's failure to finish that job, was

not half as effective, in terms of its impact on the home front, as the coverage of this invasion has already been.

"Now, the freedom of the American press is a precious thing. Certainly neither I nor any responsible member of my administration wants to infringe on it. Ordinarily, in any case, you can generally figure in politics"—and here the President permitted himself a weary smile— "that pressure from one side will tend to be canceled out by pressure from the other.

"But, in the case of the major American media and this invasion, the fracture line runs, not through the media (which are now in almost unanimous opposition to it), but between the media and certain of their allies on the one hand and, on the other, those groups and forces in American life that have normally supported me.

"Well, there's nothing wrong with that." (Another smile.) "I've been in this game too long to be surprised by, or angry at, opposition. But, ladies and gentlemen, we are approaching a point at which our media, dominated by people who are still in the minority politically, may nonetheless be able to impose their political will, thanks to the virtuosity of the news technologies they control. And I'm not sure that would be democracy.

"I have called you together, therefore—the people who, in effect, control what the American people see and hear about this war—to ask you to modify your reportage. I am not asking you to say or do anything that is false, or to suppress anything that is relevant. I *am* asking you to make your coverage better balanced, and to avoid taking cheap shots with what George Will once called 'the pornography of grief.' My military advisers estimate that we should be able to complete this operation by mid-July, but we can't do it by April twenty-fifth. Unless Congress authorizes continuation of the operation it will fail, Nicaragua will remain Communist, all of our dead will have died for nothing, and Communist efforts to seize control of the rest of Central America and Mexico will have received an enormous boost. I can't believe," he concluded, "that you want that any more than I do."

There was a thick silence. Then a prominent publisher spoke up.

"What bother some of us, Mr. President, are your assumptions. For example, plenty of people think your military advisers are wrong. What if there's no light at the end of the tunnel? What if this war drags on endlessly, like Vietnam, grinding up more and more human lives? And anyway, what makes you think that a Communist El Salvador and Nicaragua necessarily mean a Communist Guatemala or Honduras or

Mexico? And if so, so what? The peoples of those countries have every
right to decide for themselves what kind of government they want. If they
decide they want to buy some Soviet MiGs to defend themselves (and I
saw the Nicaraguan foreign minister on TV the other night, and he
*pledged* they would only be used defensively), I say let 'em. The
American people are turning against this war, and they're right.''

There were murmurs of agreement around the long table. The
President stared at the tabletop, then slowly replied.

"You may be right. But the toughest thing about this job of mine is
making the hard decisions. You know, Jimmy Carter said that all the easy
decisions get weeded out on the way to the President's desk. The only
ones that wind up here are the ones nobody else can make—or, perhaps,
wants to make. And in this case I have made my decision. Now, under
the law, Congress must ratify that decision within sixty days, by
authorizing the further deployment of our forces abroad, or, in effect,
reverse it. I don't think that law was such a hot idea, but it *is* the law, and
I respect it as such. And Congress may very well refuse authorization to
continue the operation beyond April twenty-fifth. Frankly, I think it *will*
refuse, unless you people in the media lay off. No people has ever had to
undergo the kind of psychological assault and battery you have been
subjecting the American people to in the last month or so. I seriously
question whether any people ever ought to be compelled to.''

"What about freedom of the press?'' The speaker was the controlling
stockholder of a major television network. "Are you telling us to shut up
and put our tails between our legs and start praising this cockeyed
expedition? Do you have any right to do such a thing? Anyway, even if
we did what you want us to, I doubt our news staffs would go along. I
think mine would walk right out from under me. And it'd be right.''

"After all, Mr. President,'' another voice took up the argument,
"these things that you don't like to see on TV or in the newspapers are
happening. That's not our fault. We just report what's there to be
reported.''

"I don't think it's quite that simple, Pete,'' the President replied.
"War is hell. We all know that. But one of your TV crews can go down
there and make an important achievement like the capture of Managua
look like a disaster simply by concentrating on the American casualties.''

"Suppose we do,'' someone else interjected, "—just for the sake of
argument. Don't we have that right? Doesn't the First Amendment to the
Constitution guarantee it? Even if we are in the minority as you contend,
don't we have the right to be heard?''

Again the President spoke slowly. "You have the right to speak, of course. But what I am facing here is not simply opposition but something no president has ever faced before—certainly not to anything like this extent. I am facing a situation in which the entire American media, or at any rate virtually all of them that count in the shaping of public opinion, have not only chosen to oppose this operation but are very deliberately using their control over the dissemination of news about it to turn public opinion against it. In the present state of news technology, that amounts to the power to decide the issue. The power to broadcast and to publish has become, at least in certain circumstances, the power to destroy."

The discussion continued for several hours, more or less along the lines outlined above. Tempers grew heated; voices were raised. One or two of those invited to the White House tended to side with the President, and urged their colleagues to agree to modify their coverage of the invasion to reduce the amount of "tear-jerk stuff," as one publisher put it. But the great majority were unmoved. They actually broke into applause when one magazine owner told the President bluntly, "Face it: You don't have the country behind you on this one, and you should never have launched this invasion in the first place. Now your best bet is to end it as quickly as possible."

The President's face was hard, but his voice was almost inaudible as he responded.

"Maybe so, Sam; maybe so. But I'm the guy who was elected President, and I swore to protect and defend the Constitution of this country to the best of my ability, so help me God. And I would urge you to look carefully at that Constitution. To be sure, the First Amendment says that 'Congress shall make no law' abridging freedom of speech or of the press. But neither it nor anything else in the Constitution places any limitation on the president in his capacity as commander in chief of the armed forces. We have had military censorship, to one degree or another, in every war we've ever waged. If Abraham Lincoln could suspend the writ of habeas corpus throughout the United States by executive proclamation and get away with it, I see no reason why I cannot, as commander in chief, limit far less extensively the right of journalists to brainwash the American public, by highly selective reportage, into bugging out on a military operation *in medias res*. And I might add that my attorney general agrees with me."

There was a long silence. Then somebody breathed, "You wouldn't dare."

"Wouldn't I?", the President retorted. "Want to try me?"

*   *   *   *   *   *   *   *

In considering the above scenario, it is important not to be distracted by irrelevancies. The scenario concerns a military operation against Nicaragua, and therefore risks entanglement with whatever the reader's attitude toward Nicaragua may be. But Nicaragua was chosen for the scenario merely because military intervention there, in the event of the introduction of MiG-29s to the area, has long been an acknowledged likelihood. It would be almost as easy, however, to devise a scenario involving an American military operation in the Middle East or Angola or the Philippines which would likewise pit an American president and his administration against the nation's dominant media.

Similarly, there is nothing inherently implausible, or even particularly strained, about the various journalistic tactics described. Many of them— e.g., the media's generous coverage of the accidental bombing of an orphanage, and the radio station that began each evening's news with the words "On the Nicaraguan killing-ground . . ."—are modeled carefully on actual episodes during the Vietnam War or in more recent United States military operations.

The discussion between the embattled President and the media owners is intended only to present the two sides of the argument, with somewhat greater emphasis on the President's side because it is, of course, less widely or often heard in the country today. But I certainly don't mean to suggest that the dilemma, in our wide-open and lustily democratic society, is an easy one to resolve, still less that all justice is on one side or the other.

I *do* suggest that the present distribution of forces in American politics, in which presidents are often able to amass impressive electoral majorities, only to find the major media allied with their opponents and almost unanimously opposed to administration programs and goals, presents a very serious problem when the currently available techniques of news-gathering and news presentation are used by the media to turn public opinion against an ongoing military operation.

It is certainly not enough merely to quote the First Amendment, as the President in our scenario pointed out. There is another rule of law as old as Rome: *Salus populi suprema lex*—The safety of the people is the supreme law. What shall we do, if and when those two great principles collide?

It would be far better to face the matter now, and thrash it out as far as possible before the event, or we may find ourselves confronting it some day under far more urgent and much less satisfactory circumstances.

Several years ago the Twentieth Century Fund, realizing this, commissioned a twelve-member task force of the usual distinguished types to investigate and report on the ongoing relationship between the military and the media. They had the stimulus of a fairly chewy background paper by noted journalist Peter Braestrup, which reviewed the relevant recent history and sorted out the issues. Nevertheless their final report was a thunderous disappointment, consisting largely of a series of operatic tributes to the importance of the media, interspersed with shrill demands that it be serviced hereafter less cavalierly than it was during the invasion of Grenada. The truly difficult issues raised by the above scenario were brushed aside with the dismissive comment that the media's "managers and reporters do not seek to aid the enemy in wartime."

Is that a promise?

# CHAPTER 12

# *Possible Legal Limitations on the Media*

IT IS TIME to step back from our study of the actual performance of the American media and consider from a more philosophical standpoint some of the problems involved, and some possible solutions for them.

Let us begin by noting that, critical as we have been of the media's bias, nothing in this book should be understood as leveling a general criticism at the technical competence of the American media. In this respect they are probably the equal or superior of any in the world. It is perfectly understandable, moreover, that journalists who know how hard they have worked to get a story right, and to present it effectively, should resent the cavils of relative amateurs. Every halfway competent journalist will remember occasions on which he or she reported facts that were anything but favorable to the liberal position on particular matters, and which therefore contradict, to that extent, the basic contention of this book.

But the statistics cited in the foregoing chapters speak for themselves, and they leave no doubt whatever about the basic charges of bias and imbalance. A good many journalists do not even dispute those charges, when speaking privately. But admitting them is very far from conceding that anything ought to be done about the situation—at least, anything other than relying on the media's innate good sense to rectify matters over the long haul. Can anything—should anything—else be done?

The media's claim of a special role in American society is based on the wording of the First Amendment: "Congress shall make no law . . . abridging the freedom . . . of the press." What this meant to the Framers was, of course, something very different than it means today. For one thing, the First Amendment imposed no such limitation on the legislatures of the various states. For at least the first eighty years of America's life under the Constitution and the Bill of Rights, therefore, each "sovereign state" was constitutionally at liberty to abridge freedom of the press if it wanted to. Fortunately they didn't want to; in fact, many state constitutions duplicated the prohibition in the First Amendment. But the power, nevertheless, was there. It was only after the adoption of the Fourteenth Amendment in 1868, and the subsequent rulings of the Supreme Court that this extended the prohibitions in the federal Constitution to the several states, that freedom of the press from legislative restriction became a general requirement of American law.

In the second place, the "press" whose freedom the First Amendment barred Congress from abridging was a very different thing from the media as we know them today. In his 1975 address at Yale, which summed up the view of the modern media's admirers, Justice Potter Stewart hailed the Vietnam War, the Agnew resignation, and Watergate as instances in which the press had performed "precisely the function it was intended to perform by those who wrote the First Amendment of our Constitution." The Framers, he declared, intended to promote "organized, expert scrutiny of government" by guaranteeing "the institutional autonomy of the press."

But as Stephen Bates noted in his already quoted 1986 analysis (see page 152), "The press in the Framers' time was not autonomous in any meaningful sense." Read again his analysis of the stages through which the American press has passed:

> During Stage One, prior to the Stamp Act [of 1765], the press was essentially a bulletin board for news and opinions. Thereafter, during Stage Two, the press became a partisan megaphone, with each newspaper amplifying the views of a particular faction. Stage Three, when economic strength combined with the norms of objectivity and the ideology of investigative reporting, arrived slowly and unsteadily during the twentieth century. That stage allowed the press to become, for the first time, the autonomous institution that Stewart described. To suggest that the Framers were familiar with such a press is inaccurate; to suggest that they envisioned its ultimate appearance is incredible.

Bates argues that the modern-day equivalent of the Stage Two press familiar to the Framers is "the political consulting enterprise: a small operation, often economically vulnerable, highly partisan, dependent for its survival on political sponsors, which frequently engages in related but diversified activities like filmmaking and lobbying.'' He points out that the media have "attained institutional autonomy" only in modern times.

> The major press today is a large, highly concentrated industry. To a considerable degree, its economic position insulates it from the vagaries of the marketplace and provides it with the resources for costly, long-term reporting ventures. The professional norm of objectivity . . . enhances the press's credibility with a wide audience of divergent views.
> [This] combination of economic strength, objectivity, and the investigative ideology gives the press power to help set the national agenda, power to conduct much of the dialogue between governors and governed, and power to scrutinize government closely and constantly.

Bates concludes that while "the modern press . . . does scrutinize the government," and "does so in ways that would presumably have pleased the Framers," nevertheless "by arguing that the Framers recognized the press's investigative role, and that they accordingly protected its institutional autonomy, Stewart was confusing past and present."

In other words, the institutions whose freedom the Framers, by the First Amendment, barred the federal Congress from abridging were the relatively weak journalistic megaphones possessed by every significant political party or tendency. In the ensuing two hundred years they have metastasized into the enormously powerful "autonomous" institution hailed by Justice Stewart—indeed, in Douglass Cater's phrase, into a virtual fourth branch of government, checking the actions of the other three.

Does this matter? *Ought* it to matter? If, hypothetically, the past two hundred years had, by reason of technology or other circumstances, correspondingly enhanced the power of, say, the medical profession, making it practically a "fourth branch of government," would there be any lack of critics to argue that the time had come to bring it under closer review and perhaps to limit its powers?

Much presumably would depend on how those powers were focused and deployed. And this is, of course, one of the principal arguments of the defenders of our modern media. The media's powers, they concede, are indeed formidable; but they are diffused, residing in many hands and wielded for often conflicting purposes. To the extent that they thwart the purposes of the other, older branches of government, the media simply add a fourth check, or balance, to our political system. This, they assert (echoing Bates), "would presumably have pleased the Framers."

But of course a moment's thought serves to distinguish the situation of the media. The three constitutional branches of the federal government are carefully chosen: the president and members of both Houses of Congress by direct (or, in the case of the president, virtually direct) election, and the members of the judiciary by the president, by and with the advice and consent of the Senate. But the media, and especially the effectively dominant media, are simply the product of a series of historical accidents—individual initiatives, economic successes and failures, private political schemes, dynastic ambitions, and pure luck. To grant to the heirs of this haphazard process some special authority to participate magisterially in the government of the United States, let alone to argue that the Founding Fathers had any such intention, is to stand history, law, and reason on their heads.

And the absurdity of the proposition is, of course, multiplied many times over when we observe the way in which the political power of the dominant media is deployed. There might be something to be said for protecting the political clout exercised by today's media elite if those wielding it constituted even an approximate cross-section of the political opinions now contending for influence in the American society. The media's defenders, in fact, often assert that they do; but in actuality nothing could be further from the truth. The dominant media in the United States, as the foregoing pages of this book have clearly shown, are today, with negligible exceptions, passionate allies of the liberal forces in American politics.

For practical purposes, as matters stand, this means that the media are the allies of Congress in its current battle with the executive branch. For the American people in their wisdom (and with the help of considerable artistic gerrymandering by Democratic state legislatures) have in the postwar era fallen into the habit of giving the Democratic party control of Congress most of the time, while simultaneously giving the Republican party the presidency most of the time.

This has resulted in a situation strikingly different from that envisioned and described by Justice Stewart. Instead of the media providing "organized, expert scrutiny of government" from their vantage point as an "autonomous institution," they have served diligently as the influential allies of Congress in its recurrent battles with successive presidents.

The formula has numerous variations, but its basic outlines are piercingly familiar. Citing a source who "requested not to be identified," the media give extensive publicity to some allegation of wrongdoing on the part of the president or his agents. Members of Congress (one of whom may, for all we know, be the anonymous source of the allegation) express shock and outrage, and convene a committee to investigate the charge. The media give lavish coverage to the investigation, and to the committee's ultimate conclusions—which, predictably, are highly unfavorable to the president and his men. If (as in the case of Watergate) violations of law are disclosed, they are of course zealously prosecuted. If not (as in the case of the charges against the CIA in the mid-1970s), the target agency may nevertheless be effectively crippled by "remedial" legislation.

The process has been on display most recently, of course, in the case of the Iran/contra controversy. Without getting into the merits of that large subject, let us simply note the description of the process given by Jeffrey C. Alexander, a professor of sociology at UCLA, in the June 8, 1987, issue of *The New Republic,* in an article entitled "Constructing Scandal":

> . . . The hearings present themselves as a factual investigation. They should be seen, however, as part of the scandal-generating process itself. Scandals are not discovered; they are made. . . .
> . . . Because the American opinion-making elites are primarily liberal and Democratic, only the deeds of right-wing presidents can cause political scandal. Although liberal agendas often stimulate populist resistance, they do not mobilize sustained and avenging counterforces in the metropolis where the national mood is formed.

Professor Alexander then explained how the "opinion-making elites" produce a scandal, and how he judged they were doing in the Iran/contra case as of early June 1987:

> . . . Executive incompetence, NSC intrigue, and arms profiteering are not the stuff of massive public outrage. Neither is the violation of even a raft of civil codes or, as long as only subordinates are concerned, criminal laws. Only if the public comes to believe that a great moral wrong has been done will it be aroused to a fever pitch. For this to happen, a president who has been the very embodiment of folk morality will have to be placed in a radically new light.
> Judging from the initial days of the Iranamok hearings, such a transformation seems unlikely but not impossible. A certain momentum has been successfully created. The media and intellectuals have a new framework already in place. Speaking for a large minority of Americans, they have begun to transform the extralegal *contra* aid from patriotic excess into a secret, frightening, and antidemocratic cabal.

Looking to the future, Professor Alexander concluded by assessing the prospects that the hearings would eventuate in the impeachment of the President:

> While American society has constructed a serious scandal, it has not yet produced a major political crisis. If presidential involvement begins to seem more than a possibility, this may yet occur. The stakes of the hearings will sharply rise, mortal danger to the nation's center will seem imminent, congressional questioners will become anguished, and real political drama will ensue. At this point, however, the Iranamok hearings often seem more like an IRS audit than a wrenching morality play. Only when we see contrite confessors rather than harassed functionaries will we know that we are on our way.

Despite Professor Alexander's chillingly clinical way of discussing the "construction" of a "scandal," his description is essentially accurate, and all the more persuasive because it appeared in the pages of a publication whose editors clearly longed for Mr. Reagan's impeachment.

Let me stress that I do not have any particular quarrel with the techniques Professor Alexander describes. Politics, after all, as someone has said, is a body-contact sport. There is nothing intrinsically unhealthy about this whole process except its inherent lopsidedness. Presidents and their agents do misbehave from time to time, and there is nothing in the least improper about Congress and/or the media exposing such misbehavior—quite the contrary. But where is the media's equivalent vigilance in exposing the misdeeds of the liberal leaders of Congress, or the excesses of particular committees? Or don't they ever misbehave?

Does anybody, for example, seriously suppose that the involvement of Tip O'Neill, then majority leader of the House, in the activities of South Korean lobbyist Tongsun Park in the early 1970s received the sort of media attention that a similar involvement by a high official of the Nixon or Reagan administration would have received? The number of "special prosecutors" who have pawed over the activities of Edwin Meese, Michael Deaver, and Lyn Nofziger certainly suggests otherwise. Nor is it sufficient to say that the Republican party was in control of the Justice Department and thus able to investigate and prosecute O'Neill if it saw fit to do so. Congressional probes of wrongdoing in the executive branch are invariably preceded and accompanied by a blaze of media publicity which serves to stress the importance of the issue and generate heavy public pressures for action. Without such media support, prosecutors often rightly feel that it is unwise, and may be downright unsafe, to seek indictments.

The same applies to such far more recent instances of congressional misbehavior as House Speaker Jim Wright's expensive "favors" for various savings and loan institutions in his native Texas; House Democratic whip Tony Coelho's acceptance of free airplane travel and party facilities from one such institution, on behalf of the Democratic Congressional Campaign Committee (which he chairs); and the leak of a preliminary report of the Senate Intelligence Committee on the Iran/contra affair, from Senator Patrick Leahy, its ranking Democrat, to NBC News.

As these examples suggest, the media's services to liberal causes go far beyond providing the orchestral accompaniment for Congress's operatic investigations of the executive branch. Unquestionably their greatest single service is their tendentious selection of what "news" they will report and what stress to put—or not put—on it.

Thus we saw the supposed failings of "Reaganomics" dwelt on with loving precision during the recession of the early 1980s—only to have the term virtually disappear from the public dialogue when the economy's long recovery began in 1983. We watched the NBC *Today* show's Bryant Gumbel, during the stock market's low plateau in 1982, ask a long series of not terribly notable but invariably pessimistic analysts, "What's the stock market trying to tell us?"—and then lose almost all interest in the market's supposed messages during its long climb in the ensuing five years.

We have seen the remarkably encouraging political and constitutional developments in South Africa under the Botha government misrepresented or wholly ignored, in favor of intensive coverage (until this was banned) of inflammatory incidents involving riots. We have seen the Nicaraguan contras systematically depicted as callous, cocaine-smuggling Somocistas. We have seen the supporters of Corazon Aquino "winning" their first election (narrowly) in the teeth of "massive fraud" by the backers of Ferdinand Marcos—but without, as far as American reportage was concerned, themselves stealing so much as a single vote in the entire Philippine archipelago. From "acid rain" to "hunger in America," the media have hewn wood and carried water for the liberal side of virtually every issue before the American people. If there is an exception to that statement, I would like to know what it is.

Moreover, as our "Scenario" (Chapter 11) suggested, we have by no means necessarily reached the limits of this process. How confident can we be that the major media, confronted with American involvement in a military operation of which they profoundly disapproved, would not go much further than they have hitherto gone, or been able to go, in thwarting the success of American arms? They are not required to report American victories. They are at liberty (as in the Tet offensive) to distort or misrepresent the results of enemy actions. They are free to characterize the operation in any way they wish. They can dwell, to any desired extent, on the unquestionable horrors of any military activity, and disregard altogether, if they wish, the long-range consequences of failing to undertake it. On the evidence to date, they would not hesitate to do so.

It is not, let us say again, that a reporter is not entitled to favor one viewpoint over another on a given topic. He not only may; in many cases he must, as the very first chapter of this book pointed out. But if the output of the media is to be skewed, permanently and tendentiously, in one direction—if the world is to be presented to readers and television viewers as little more than a Manichean struggle between the forces of light and darkness, represented by liberalism and conservatism respectively—then what becomes of the usefulness of this "autonomous institution" as a virtual "fourth branch of government," providing "organized, expert scrutiny" of the other three? Where is the essential *balance*?

When confronted by such questions, the media's defenders tend simply to fall back on the literal wording of their shield and buckler, the First Amendment. It is no accident that that particular amendment, and that particular segment of it, is by long odds the most famous partial sentence in the Bill of Rights and quite possibly the best-known part of the entire Constitution. We are told incessantly, by the media themselves and by the entire liberal political apparatus with which they are allied, that this is rightly and necessarily so because of the overarching importance of freedom of the press.

But, as we have seen, the importance of freedom of the press is grounded (to quote Justice Stewart again) in its supposed role as the provider of "organized, expert scrutiny of government." If the media abandon that role, to become instead participants in the political process on the side of one of the instrumentalities (i.e., Congress) created by the Constitution, isn't it reasonable to suggest that their formidable modern powers ought to be checked and balanced, like those of Congress itself, or the executive branch, or the judiciary?

The reverence accorded modern interpretations of the First Amendment is so enormous that the media and their defenders have not heretofore, so far as I am aware, often had to confront that question. But I rather imagine that, if they did, they might respond by inviting their critics, rather smugly, to try amending or even repealing the First Amendment if they don't like it. There is certainly no doubt that any attempt to do so would raise a formidable hullaballoo—and not merely from the media and those liberal institutions and individuals who benefit from its current bias, but from a great many conservatives who rightly value the general protection the amendment affords to the expression of unpopular as well as popular opinions.

And yet, if the current performance of the major American media represents, as I would argue it does, a serious abuse of the media's role in our polity, and gravely undermines the justification for the freedom granted to the press (even on such a modern theory as Justice Stewart's) by the First Amendment, then it is entirely appropriate to consider modifications of that sweeping grant. And such modifications would not necessarily have to rely on the cumbersome processes of constitutional amendment.

Thanks to the judicial statecraft of Chief Justice John Marshall, the Supreme Court has acquired the power to make definitive interpretations of the meaning of specific clauses of the Constitution. This is obviously an important power, and in many cases an absolutely crucial one. The composition of the Court, as a result, is a matter of critical significance.

May we take it as accepted that the members of the Court are in fact well aware of the political significance of their work, and are (at least in many cases) thoroughly dedicated to producing, by means of the Court's decisions, certain political, economic, and social consequences that they happen to desire? From this follows the extreme importance placed on appointments to the Court by the presidents who make them, by the senators who must "advise and consent" to those appointments, and by the public at large.

Given the present distribution of political sentiments among the justices, and their voting patterns on certain key issues, it is certainly well within the range of possibility that a Court of marginally different composition might, in the not too distant future, make some vitally important new rulings on certain subjects that defenders of our media elite have hitherto considered unchallengeable.

Just for one thing, it is only in recent decades, when liberal domination of the Court (and indeed the entire national dialogue) has been at or near its peak, that the Court has construed the First Amendment as requiring the near-total elimination of the libel laws from any impact on the political process. Under *Sullivan* and subsequent rulings, the journalistic savaging of public officials and "public figures" has become a routine aspect of our politics; but just how necessary is this to ensure "robust debate" on political topics? Britain permits such individuals to sue the media for libel almost without restriction, with the loser paying the lawyers' bills, yet there is nothing notably anemic about Britain's political or journalistic processes.

Similarly, it would not take much of a change in the Court's membership to produce a dramatic modification in its recent tendency to let the First Amendment (or rather its press clause—nobody is unduly concerned over the right of peaceable assembly) override other, apparently less important, constitutional provisions. There have already been some spectacular collisions between the supposed requirements of the First Amendment and the guarantees in the Sixth of every defendant's right "to be confronted with the witnesses against him" and "to have compulsory process for obtaining witnesses in his favor." But why, in addition, should the rights of the media under the First Amendment necessarily take precedence over the determination of a president, in his capacity as commander in chief of the armed forces under Article II, Section 2, that such familiar military considerations as morale must inform and influence the media's coverage of military developments, at least where better-balanced reportage would actually improve morale?

Or take the Fairness Doctrine, which even the present Court has upheld on the ground that broadcast wavelengths, unlike opportunities to publish a newspaper, are numerically limited and governmentally controlled, and that broadcasters can therefore constitutionally be required to offer a mixture of views and opinions. The Fairness Doctrine receives a certain amount of liberal support because it can be invoked to require the airing of extreme leftist opinions that might otherwise be ignored. A minority of conservatives endorses it for a similar reason. (Phyllis Schlafly, as already noted, credits it with being almost solely responsible for ventilating anti-ERA arguments on radio and television.) But it has become a dead letter because the chief engines of liberal opinion are perfectly content—and why not?—with the performance of the electronic media, while mainline conservative opinion is heavily influenced against the Fairness Doctrine by its libertarian component, which opposes all state controls.

But if the Fairness Doctrine were to be revived, taken seriously, and rigorously enforced, it could transform the performance of the major electronic news media overnight. Content analyses of the "news" broadcasts of the networks may be tedious, but as Chapter 3 of this book demonstrated, they are by no means impossible. (As a matter of fact, in

1986–87 Norman Tebbit, chairman of Britain's Conservative party, employed such techniques in the course of a critique of leftist bias on the BBC.) There is no intrinsic reason why egregious examples of bias on the part of the electronic media, at least, could not be demonstrated and then ordered stopped by the ordinary processes of administrative law, subject as usual to judicial review.

Of course, as Robert Whitaker has pointed out, the chronological lag caused by lifelong judicial appointments almost guarantees that the courts generally, and the Supreme Court in particular, will be "the last bastion of dying establishments"—whether the particular establishment is ante-bellum slaveowners, or reactionary businessmen in the early days of the New Deal, or liberals during and after the Reagan administration. But, as Finley Peter Dunne's shrewd Mr. Dooley drily noted, "Th' supreme coort follows th' iliction returns," and even the judiciary eventually stops trying to impose its outdated predilections on society in the guise of constitutional interpretations.

One other possible reform deserves consideration and mention here, although it is addressed in the first instance to wrongdoings by members of Congress and their staffs, rather than by the media. We have noted the fruitful symbiosis between Congress and the media, whereby an elaborate counterpoint of charge and investigation can be made to serve liberal (and exclusively liberal) political purposes. Why shouldn't the Justice Department create a special investigative and prosecutory task force, composed of blue-ribbon appointees and insulated from all other obligations, to probe instances of congressional misconduct of the type discussed on pages 204–205? And if, as would soon prove to be the case, representatives of sympathetic media were found to be involved in these activities, they too ought to be subject to prosecution by the aforesaid task force.

It was damaging news leaks in the media that recently prompted Lieutenant General William E. Odom, director of the National Security Agency, to call for the prosecution of news organizations that reveal certain intelligence details. According to the *Washington Post* for September 3, 1987, " 'Leaks have damaged the [communications intelligence] system more in the past three to four years than in a long, long time,' Odom said in a rare public forum with defense reporters yesterday."

Odom said he had urged the Justice Department to institute prosecutions under Section 798 of Chapter 37, Title 18, United States Code, which provides in relevant part:

Whoever knowingly and willfully . . . uses in any manner prejudicial to the safety or interest of the United States . . . any classified information . . . obtained by the processes of communications intelligence from the communications of any foreign government, knowing the same to have been obtained by such processes—Shall be fined not more than $10,000 or imprisoned not more than 10 years, or both.

It should be noted that this statute applies to members of Congress and other government officials just as much as to journalists.

Still other reforms aimed at current and widespread media abuses would require statutory assistance, and this will of course be difficult and probably impossible to obtain from a Congress closely allied with the media and itself involved in, or at least benefiting from, the very abuses it is being called on to correct. But here the legislatures of many of the fifty states may be willing to step in and play a part in the reform effort.

Paul Johnson, writing in *The Spectator* in July 1986, proposed two such reforms:

The first is a statutory right of reply. This works well in a number of countries. It is not the sensational change which its supporters and opponents believe it to be—in practice it is productive of much tedious copy, no bad thing. But it does make editors more careful; it does accord with most people's notion of natural justice, and it does remove one of the chief and most justified public complaints against overweening press power. Whatever editors may say, the press here could live perfectly happily with such a law. It would probably cause more difficulties for television, where in some ways it is more needed.

Secondly, I believe the overwhelming majority of people in Britain would like to see a law to protect privacy from unwarranted media intrusion. Nothing makes me more ashamed than the misuse of press power (television is less of an offender in this respect) to invade private lives. My guess is that anger at such behavior is the biggest single factor in creating hostility to the press. The right to privacy is one of the most important human rights because it protects one of the deepest human needs. . . .

A privacy law will not be easy to frame. I would favour a carefully restricted enactment, though it should certainly in my view carry a prison sentence as a last resort in the case of an editor, reporter or photographer who persistently and grievously harasses a private individual. Editors, in particular, must be made to realize that abuse of the press's freedom may involve risking their own. There is nothing more calculated to instil a few moral values into an editor than the anticipatory clang of a cell door.

There have been repeated calls for the enactment of such statutes in this country, and even a few attempts to legislate along these lines, without (thus far) necessarily running afoul of the First Amendment. A statutory right of reply would not in the least "abridge the freedom of the press"; it would merely ensure that, in proper cases, individuals and organizations were given equal access to the target audience. And the constitutional protection accorded to speech has never been held to confer on the press an absolutely unrestricted right of commentary (witness the libel laws). The Supreme Court's growing recognition, in recent decades, of a constitutionally protected right of privacy would seem to suggest that here too the claims of the media under the First Amendment must be measured against other claims of essentially equal importance.

In discussing the various possible remedies for media abuses described above, my intention has been to provoke reflection rather than endorse specific reforms. But it is important to stress that there is nothing sacrosanct about the present state of our constitutional or statutory law on the subject of the media's rights, privileges, and immunities. The media exist in the same polity as the rest of us, and they are, at least potentially, just as subject to restraint when their power becomes overweening or is grossly abused. Today, in the opinion of many serious observers, it is both.

Nor need correction of the situation necessarily require any modification of the text of the First Amendment. As we have seen, a relatively small shift in the balance of power on the Supreme Court might well result in a very different attitude toward many of the implications that have been drawn from that amendment in recent decades by Court majorities intent on serving the same liberal political interests that, during that period, have dominated the media and the Congress.

Liberals may, in fact, be in danger of making the mistake of supposing that their recent dominance of the Court and the Congress are somehow immutable, regardless of the state of public opinion that perversely insists upon electing relatively conservative presidents. They will, sooner or later, learn otherwise. The Framers vested ultimate control of the American body politic in the people—not in the president, or the Congress, or even the Supreme Court. Even today, it is well within the realm of political possibility for the people to reassert, through the processes of a constitutional convention convened without the assent of any of those three, direct control over their destiny. (As a matter of fact, at this writing a proposal to do exactly that is only 2 legislatures short of the 34 that are required to call such a convention—in this case for the limited purpose of enacting a balanced-budget amendment.)

But American society has usually been acutely responsive to perceived abuses of power from almost any quarter, and the media are already receiving a considerable share of attention in this regard. It is reasonable to hope that the contemptuous indifference with which they have, for the most part, thus far reacted to legitimate criticism may not be their final word on the subject, and that they may yet take steps to remedy a situation which, in some future military crisis of the type depicted in our "Scenario" (Chapter 11), might well get dangerously out of hand.

Fortunately the reforms needed would not be difficult to implement today. What is needed is the will, and that only the media—at least in the first instance—can provide.

# CHAPTER 13

# *The Prospects for Reform*

ALTHOUGH, AS WE have seen, the response of the media elite to charges of bias has thus far generally been, at best, halfhearted, it has tended to wax and wane in direct proportion to the amount of criticism directed at them. For all the hot denials and cries of censorship generated by Vice President Agnew's attack on bias in television news in his Des Moines speech in November 1969, the actual response of the media—and not only the television media but the print media as well—was a prompt and easily measurable increase in the quantity and balance of coverage of conservative activities, and in the presentation of conservative political commentaries. Conversely, when the media were riding high after Nixon's resignation in the wake of the Watergate scandal, even the relatively innocuous National News Council was unable to generate sufficient media support to survive as a thoughtful but sympathetic critic of media misbehavior.

The media's response to criticism, then, is likely to be greatest when the level of criticism is highest. And that, for persons interested in media reform, means keeping the level of criticism high. Such techniques as external monitoring (by *Newswatch, The AIM Report,* etc.) can unquestionably have a powerful impact over time. Even "jawboning," as we have seen, is not without its effect. It is even conceivable that at some future point, when the media are less chesty than they were in the wake of Watergate, some institution like the National News Council may yet establish a permanent foothold as a firm but friendly critic of media excesses, including political bias.

But there is no point in assuming the worst. If liberal dominance of the media arose at a time when (to quote Trilling again) "liberalism [was] not only the dominant but even the sole intellectual tradition," surely it isn't unreasonable to hope that its dominance may become considerably less absolute now that such staples of liberal doctrine as government intervention and welfare statism are under increasingly critical scrutiny. Some of the media owners, newspaper editors, and television producers who signed up with liberalism when it was the only game in town may, to be sure, have become incapable of thinking or acting in any other way; but others, equally surely, are aware that liberalism's heyday is past, that economic freedom has been shown to liberate immense human energies, and that even science seems to be approaching frontiers that are very like barriers—barriers that were wholly unsuspected by the great thinkers of the Enlightenment. There are, in other words, receptive minds in media management as well as elsewhere, and it would be a serious mistake to assume that internal impulses toward change don't exist or cannot be generated.

This may be the only real remedy in those situations—increasingly frequent, unfortunately—where a particular newspaper or television station has a de facto monopoly of national news coverage. (I say "de facto" because there are often other papers or TV stations in the area which, however, are so confined to local news coverage as to constitute little or no real competition in regard to national political issues.)

In such situations, the fact that it would theoretically be possible to launch a rival newspaper or in some cases even a rival television station is often little more than a bad joke. There may simply not be a large enough audience to support a second paper or TV station, and the established connections of the existing one (with the advertising community, for example) may be enough to stifle effective competition. But the very fact that there is a de facto monopoly imposes, at least arguably, a moral obligation to ventilate alternative views on important political questions. In addition, as already noted, the key executives just possibly may be ready to entertain fresh ideas, now that there in fact are some fresh ideas to entertain. "Let's face it," a very prominent television news executive said to me a couple of years ago, "the liberals are out of ideas. The conservatives are the ones who are coming up with all the new approaches to things."

Where no monopoly exists, one of an area's newspapers or television stations is often already marginally more hospitable to conservative opinions than its chief rival. This may be merely because the culturally dominant paper or station is controlled by liberals, while its rival reflects the more conservative views of a blue-collar constituency. Here again, however, it is sometimes possible to find executives, editors, and producers who are not determined to resist at all costs a fair representation of conservative views.

In the field of opinion journalism very considerable progress has already been made, as noted in earlier chapters of this book. A quarter of a century ago, conservative columnists and radio or television commentators, while not totally nonexistent, were certainly few and far between. Today, however, they are commoner. When it comes to offering readers and viewers a fair balance of political commentary *identified as such,* the media are at their least vulnerable.

But the situation is far otherwise in those editorial purlieus where the "news" is identified, researched, and written, and where, necessarily, some theory as to its thrust is adopted. And here the pervasive anonymity probably encourages bias. A by-line reporter for a leading newspaper may enjoy some personal prominence; certainly the principal on-camera personalities in the field of television news do—not that many individuals in either category seem greatly inhibited, by their prominence, from indulging their own political prejudices. On the contrary, many of them appear to regard their personal prominence as simply a useful means of increasing their clout. But the average writer in a television news department, or even the typical reporter without a by-line, not to mention their editorial supervisor, are largely insulated from direct public criticism of whatever bias they insinuate into the "news." These, then, are the positions by whose current holders the real damage is being done, and the latter must be successfully appealed to, or if necessary replaced, if it is to be stopped.

Fortunately, if the will exists, the means are at hand. A large number of young men and women of generally conservative inclinations are today seeking footholds in the print and electronic media. Some of them are students or graduates of regular schools of journalism, where they somehow managed to avoid or surmount the almost inevitable liberal indoctrination. Others have followed the well-worn route of undergraduate college journalism—with the significant difference that they joined or founded one of the "alternative" (i.e., conservative) college newspapers that have grown up around the country in recent years.

These conservative college papers are well known—and, of course, ordinarily very "controversial"—on their respective campuses, but are not in most cases widely publicized elsewhere. Undoubtedly the most famous, as well as one of the earliest, and one that had served as a model for many others around the country, is the *Dartmouth Review,* founded in 1980. Other well-established examples include the *California Review,* founded at La Jolla in 1982 for all the universities of the California state system, and the *Texas Review* (University of Texas, Austin), the *Illini Review* (University of Illinois, Champagne-Urbana), and the *Northwestern Review* (Northwestern University), all launched in 1983.

Talented alumni of these and other conservative alternative college newspapers have already begun to make their mark in mainstream publications. Greg Fossedal of the *Dartmouth Review* worked as an editorial writer for the *Wall Street Journal* and is now a columnist for the Copley News Service and a Media Fellow at the Hoover Institution. Terry Teachout of the *Illini Review* worked at *Harper's* before becoming an editorial writer for New York's *Daily News*. Michael Johns, an alumnus of the University of Miami's *Tribune,* is an assistant editor of *Policy Review.*

Other products of campus conservative publications are not currently employed in journalism, but seemed destined to end up there. The *Dartmouth Review*'s Dinesh D'Souza, formerly the managing editor of *Policy Review,* is currently an aide to Gary Bauer, chairman of President Reagan's Domestic Policy Council. And Michael Waller, an alumnus of George Washington University's *Sequent,* is director of publications for the Washington-based Inter-American Security Committee.

And of course a few young journalists who just happen to be personally conservative do still occasionally manage to gain a foothold in mainstream journalism, especially of the moderately conservative sort, without going the alternative-paper route. Thus David Brooks can currently be found at the *Wall Street Journal,* and John Podhoretz at *U.S. News and World Report.*

Another important source of conservative journalistic talent is the training centers that are beginning to produce young journalists of that persuasion (though rarely exclusively so). Of these, the oldest—founded in 1977—is M. Stanton Evans's National Journalism Center, a foundation-financed school for budding journalists based in Washington, D.C. The center offers its students a twelve-week course, paying them a nominal $100 per week (in effect, a $1,200 scholarship) and providing low-cost housing if desired.

The students are chosen from among hundreds of applicants from all over the country, and Evans estimates that about three quarters of them are more or less conservative. Some 450 young men and women have graduated from the National Journalism Center, and Evans says that about 300 of them are currently employed in media-related jobs. (The center maintains a job bank, and works hard to place its alumni.) Among its many prominent graduates are John Barnes, chief editorial writer for the *Boston Herald;* George Bennett, the chief investigative reporter for Evans and Novak; John Fund, deputy editor of the *Wall Street Journal;* and Richard Vigilante, articles editor of *National Review.*

Another and newer training center for young conservatives (among others) seeking to enter journalism is the Institute for Political Journalism at Georgetown University, launched by Lee Edwards in the mid-1980s. The institute offers courses (for credit) in ethics, economics, and citizenship for journalists, to students from some fifty educational institutions around the country. Financed by the Fund for American Studies, it is becoming a valuable addition to the roster of organizations interested in providing training to aspiring conservative journalists.

It is thus no longer possible, if it ever was, for journalistic employers to argue that there is simply no pool of talented young journalists of a reasonably conservative persuasion on which to draw. The question now is whether they can be persuaded to draw on it.

It is not, to repeat one final time, a question of slanting the news. Almost every story worth reporting requires the reporter to adopt some "theory" of its thrust that will enable him or her to distinguish the relevant from the irrelevant and the important from the unimportant. Quite often this process will involve value judgments as to which individuals may and do differ. There is no reason why this ought to dismay or perplex any fair editor; he will merely see to it that personal biases don't get out of control, and that the *mix* of stories (and thus "theories") ultimately presented to the reader or viewer is reasonably well balanced.

That, in any case, ought to be the ambition of any editor who purports to be purveying the "news." Unfortunately, as we have demonstrated, many fail to do this, and wind up giving their readers or viewers a steady diet of one particular viewpoint. We speculated in Chapter 1 that these editors' own prior experience as reporters, having accustomed them to adopting a "theory" concerning a given news story, lingers when they reach the editor's desk and prompts them to adopt and promote a "supertheory"—reflecting the hitherto-dominant liberal culture—about what is going on in the world, generating the events that constitute the daily grist of the news.

But the editor who does this, unconsciously or otherwise, is abandoning any pretense to be a reasonably dispassionate purveyor of the news. He has succumbed to the admittedly powerful temptation to become a participant in our political controversies rather than simply the source of the information on which they are based. In so doing he forfeits any plausible claim to some unique, constitutionally conferred special role based on his "organized, expert scrutiny of government."

There is, however, no sensible reason why the owners and editors who dominate the American media cannot acknowledge that the world has changed, and that reasonably balanced news reportage today requires a mix of stories based on both liberal and conservative "theories" of the news. If that sort of balance is simply beyond a given newspaper or newsmagazine or television network, or is rejected by it, then the impresario who dispenses biased reportage ought to be welcomed most warmly to the political arena, subjected to the heat that characterizes that famous kitchen, and brusquely told to get over the idea that the Constitution promises him anything but a precious (and limited) right to shoot off his mouth like the rest of us.

Fortunately there is reason to hope that many important and influential members of the media will respond to today's challenge in ways that deserve better of American society. If they welcome the competent young conservatives now knocking at their doors, they will find their own news product enriched by new and stimulating perspectives on events— perspectives that can complement, without replacing, those available on the left. We would all be better off as a result.

For if American journalism does not reappraise its situation and adjust its role to take fairer account of the political realities, a day may come— and not necessarily long hence—when conservative ideas will seek to crowd liberal ones out of the newsroom in much the same way that liberalism, in its heyday, muscled aside conservatism. If and when that happens, it will be distinctly in the liberal interest, as well as in the general national interest, to find room for a concept of the role of the media that calls for a reasonably balanced presentation of the "news."

# *Index*